THE MAKINGS OF MALENESS

Men, Women,
and the Flight of Daedalus

Peter H. Tatham

THE MAKINGS
OF MALENESS

Men, Women,
and the Flight of Daedalus

Peter H. Tatham

94-2213

NEW YORK UNIVERSITY PRESS
Washington Square, New York

First published in 1992 by
H. Karnac (Books) Ltd.
58 Gloucester Road
London SW7 4QY

Library of Congress Cataloging-in-Publication Data
Tatham, Peter.
The makings of maleness : men, women, and flight of Daedalus /
Peter H. Tatham.
p.   cm.
Includes bibliographical references and index.
ISBN 0-8147-8203-5—ISBN 0-8147-8204-3 (pbk.)
1. Masculinity (Psychology)   2. Archetype (Psychology)
3. Daedalus (Greek mythology)   4. Artisans—Psychology.   5. Heroes—
Psychology.   6. Men—Psychology.   7. Men—Conduct of life.
I. Title.
BF175.5.M37T38   1992
155.3'32—dc20   92-21878
                                        CIP

Manufactured in the United States of America

c 10 9 8 7 6 5 4 3 2 1
p 10 9 8 7 6 5 4 3 2 1

For Lena

CONTENTS

ACKNOWLEDGEMENTS

F irst, I must acknowledge the debt of gratitude that I owe to my wife. Without her help, her encouragement when I could see no way forward, and her insistence, the book might never have been finished; and for those reasons it is dedicated to her. I am also grateful to Fraser Boa and Jenny Donald of Windrose Films, who, by asking my wife and me to organize the Dream Film Seminar for them in Bristol, made it financially possible for me to take enough time off work, at a critical moment, to finish the first draft.

My good friend the late Arthur Cooper was indirectly responsible for my interest in the story of Daedalus, as well as for re-awakening in me a love of language and an interest in the origins of words. Over the years of our friendship I learnt a very great deal from him. Highly regarded as a translator of Chinese poetry, Arthur spent the last fifteen years of his life in a monumental and revolutionary study of the origins of the Chinese script, which was almost finished at the time of his death. Edited and completed by John Cayley, this will be published, as plan-ned, by the Oxford University Press (OUP), under the title, *Heart and Mind: Ancient Language-Making as Recorded in the Chinese Script*. I am grateful to Diana Cooper, John Cayley, and the OUP for permission to use some of Arthur's ideas from that book, and for the use of his draw-ings in Figures 1 (p. 121) and 12 (p. 215). Figures 2 and 3 (p. 128) are from Arthur's contribution to the *Oxford Com-panion to the Mind,* edited by Richard Gregory, and are reproduced by kind permission of the OUP. Part of a trans-lation of the poem, 'The Waters in the Rivers', by Liang Wu-Ti (pp. 242–243), is reproduced from the introduction to Cooper's acclaimed book, *Li Po and Tu Fu: Poems Selected and Translated with an Introduction and Notes,* by kind permission of Penguin Books. I am also indebted to Diana Cooper for permission to quote from the many and various letters that Arthur wrote to me (including personal communications, pp. 127, 196, and 203; and Figure 11, p. 204) and for allowing me to quote from his unpublished version of the *Dao de Jing*.

Anyone concerned with the story of Daedalus must be influenced by the vast quantity of writing, pictures, and sculptures on that theme by the late Michael Ayrton. Though I have made no direct reference to these works in my text, I have used some of his other writings, mostly on metallurgy. I am very grateful to his widow, Mrs Elisabeth Ayrton, who holds the copyright to all his work, for permis-sion to quote from *Rudiments of Paradise* (pp. 82–84, 149–150) and *Fabrications* (pp. 52–53). I also acknowledge per-mission from the publishers of both books, Martin Secker & Warburg in this country, while in North America thanks are due to Crown Publishing Group (*Rudiments of Paradise*) and Henry Holt & Co., Inc. (*Fabrications*).

I also acknowledge permission from Routledge and from Princeton University Press for permission to quote from the *Collected Works of C. G. Jung* (edited by R. Head, M. Fordham, G. Adler, & W. McGuire; translated mainly by R. Hull). Except where otherwise stated, references are to the *Collected Works* (*CW*), by volume and paragraph number.

The major part of this book was written before the publication of Andrew Samuels' book, *The Plural Psyche* (1989). It was therefore a delight to discover that in various ways our thinking had converged or was complementary, without any previous discussion: Andrew approaching things more from a clinical direction and I from the mythological. I am thinking especially of some of our notions on gender, on networking, as well as the 'bootstrap theory' when applied to the human psyche.

To fill out the theoretical notions about which I have written, it has seemed useful to include several vignettes from my clinical psychotherapeutic practice. To the people suitably disguised as Daphne, David, Dawn, Dennis, Derek, and Dorothy, who have agreed to allow me to include parts of their stories, I am very grateful indeed—as I am to all those who have sat in my 'other chair' over the years, and whose stories and our work together have also guided my thinking.

Finally, what was originally an ungrammatical manuscript, badly punctuated, has been turned into a readable book by the hard work of my editors, Barbara Wharton for the Library of Analytical Psychology, and Klara King for Karnac Books. I am greatly indebted to them for that, and for other help and advice. Any mistakes that remain are my own.

U ntil about thirty years ago, the nature of a man and his masculinity was little questioned. Generally speaking, it was assumed that a man would inevitably wish to be strong, powerful, and decisive, and that he would concern himself more with what went on outside the home than with domestic details. Since this ideal was assumed to arise in some way from his actual biological nature, it was therefore inescapable. Any individual who found it hard to reach this goal could be tolerated, patronized, or even pitied, provided he was seen to agree that he was failing as a man. By acknowledging his failure, he implicitly endorsed the correctness of the model. Individuals or groups, on the other hand, who appeared deliberately to flout this view of being a man were deeply disturbing. They might have included aesthetes, homosexuals, pacifists, foreigners: and their fate was to be scorned as deviant, to be criminalized, conquered, or otherwise controlled. Women were also expected to go along with this view of manliness, which inevitably made inferior persons of them also.

However, since the Second World War, the picture of an intrinsically dominant, human male has slowly changed. It is now accepted that there is a difference between a man's biological make-up and his gender role as perceived by, and acted upon within, the culture and society of which he is a member. There is also the question of his personal psychological adaptation to, or reaction from, that socio-cultural norm. The initiative for this change, and the momentum it has achieved, has been generated firstly by a woman's movement that has refused to accept being treated as part of an inferior category. Only secondarily has it become a problem for each man himself.

In the last decade of this century, the position is more confused than ever, with men less certain of what they are, how they are meant to be, or indeed what they can be. At the same time, there is an increasing interest in, and concern with, the question of what it means to be a man and in the nature of maleness as a quality. Universities are setting up courses in 'men's studies'; in the larger community, men's groups continue, exploratory workshops are held for men, and bookshops begin to have a special shelf for books about men and masculinity, next to the feminist section. One place that this book belongs is on that shelf. On the other hand, as I am an analytical psychologist and the book takes a psychological view, it is also placed on other shelves.

I make no excuses for the fact that the book approaches such a complex set of problems without any consideration of the socio-cultural perspective. In one sense, therefore, it is an incomplete study. However, because the field *is* so intricate, much of what has been written about it has been confusing and contradictory. It has therefore seemed useful to isolate one aspect of the whole—yet one that spreads right through that whole—in order to tease out and examine the assumptions to be found there. These may then be either endorsed, refreshed, or abandoned. This process, of resolving anything complex into its simple elements, is the meaning of the word 'analysis', which is a powerful tool for enlightenment in many disciplines—for example, sociology, business studies, chemistry, or psychology. There is therefore nothing wrong with an analysis, provided that the user accepts that an examination of any single element is not the answer to the whole problem. Nevertheless, the alteration of any element will necessarily affect the nature of the whole. Thus, sociological, political, and psychological analyses of the nature of maleness are all vital and important ones—for the underlying assumptions of those disciplines also suffuse the field—but each in itself is only a part-view and must be recognized as such. My book is therefore one such part-view, yet one that has something relevant to say about the whole topic.

Even if maleness were to be narrowly defined as consisting of power, control, or the ability to think logically, and to make decisions, it is clear that those properties belong as much to a woman as to a man. The same could also be said for most of the terms to be found on all those lists that set out to describe so-called masculine qualities. It is equally true for femininity, and these facts were recognized by C. G. Jung when he described the existence of contra-sexual images in women or men, *animus* and *anima,* which underlie their feminine and masculine aspects.

But the image of a woman appearing in the dreams or fantasies of a man represents not just the psychological traits of femininity, but also presents what is 'other' than he is. 'Otherness', in this sense, is a state of being that is outside of oneself, 'not-I', which, for a man, means belonging to his soul or spirit. The *anima,* as soul-guide, leads a man on to a deeper connection with an unconscious self, that contains more generally creative possibilities for himself (Jung, *CW 9,* 1 para. 111ff).

Jung's empirical observation of the archetypal nature of the *anima* has been of immense practical value since it was first formulated, in the early part of this century, being one of the base assumptions for analytical psychology. Nevertheless, the world moves on, and the ways in which any archetype *expresses* itself will also, of necessity, alter. Sometimes, however, there is a reluctance to allow fresh insights to replace familiar assumptions, although they may well have become stereotypes. What was once a vibrant new truth may have become a *cliché,* stayed with because safe, and operating in a 'knee-jerk' kind of way.

For example, maleness can be seen to exist, as a quality, in all people, whatever their sex may be. This fact is accounted for, psychologically, by the supposed existence of an archetypal 'masculine principle', which expresses itself differently in a man or a woman. There is, therefore, a 'grand narrative' that underlies the whole experience of maleness, and in calling the principle 'masculine' a closer relationship to men than to women is inevitably implied. But why should not the experience that is called 'masculine' refer instead to something different, when occurring in a man as compared with a woman, and something, moreover, that has nothing to do with the male sex? Why does it have to be an unswerving 'principle'? Perhaps the experience should be seen as a different and a shifting one for each and every individual in whom it occurs, even changing during a lifetime?

My contention will therefore be that statements beginning: 'men are . . .', 'the animus means . . .', or 'the masculine principle is . . .' have become stereotypical and therefore no longer accurately describe the empirical observations of how people actually are today. Or, rather, that such statements have come to circumscribe the events for which they account, in a way that both excludes and rejects other worthwhile aspects. They thus prevent the acquisition of fresh insight, no matter how valuable they may still, at the same time, remain.

Having been educated in the principles first set out by Jung, I accept their validity. Nonetheless, I reserve the right of trying to reexpress his discoveries in ways that may be more appropriate for the present day.

One way in which this might be done can be learned from an examination of the nature of a stereotype. This word originally referred to a printing plate of type-metal, which had been cast from a *papier maché* mould, taken from the surface of a sheet of individual type-forms (*Oxford English Dictionary* [*OED*]). It is said that when the molten metal was poured into the mould, it would make a clicking sound, the past participle of the French verb 'to click' being *cliché* (*Oxford Dictionary of English Etymology* [*ODEE*]). A stereotype thus made could continue to be used for printing long after its original type-face had been broken up and used again to make other statements. Equally, the stereotype might, in time, be melted down and its metal poured into a different mould to take up a different shape. The type and the metal remain the same throughout, but the shapes that they take up change, expressing other things.

In psychology, we are familiar with the 'click', when an insight or interpretation feels exactly right. It has also been called the 'ah-ha!' reaction. But such clicks will solidify to become accepted and familiar conscious knowledge, even reaching, in time, the status of a *cliché*, and it is this that might require fresh formulation.

This kind of word-analysis is one that will be found throughout my work, for in itself the book is about breaking down the stereotypes of meaning. Words are not just value-free communications, they are also psychic images and often invested as symbols. Each word can be organized into families with others that descend from the same original root. Consideration of those origins, as well as of the meanings given to any other words that are cognate (i.e. similarly descended) with the word in question, can refresh my understanding of it. In this way, a new light can be directed onto the very words that are used to state any working hypotheses that I use and thus to question their assumptions.

The assigned meanings of words also change over the centuries. Nevertheless, it is also my belief that a word's earlier meanings are all of them contained and implied, even when it is used in its modern sense. There can therefore be levels of meaning in a single communication, which assist the activity of the imagination. Jung himself, and Leopold Stein, have also suggested the value of this way of working with words (e.g. Jung, *CW 5,* para. 208; Stein, 1962; Lambert, 1981, pp. 54–55). From another angle, in his essay, 'Artist and Tradesman', Walter Shewring reminds us that 'sometimes we need to know the origin of a word before we can use or understand it properly . . . today', and 'sometimes again, we must learn a meaning now obsolete in order to understand texts that are still alive' (Shewring, 1984).

While on the subject of words and their usage, I would remind the reader that, in a book of this nature, it is difficult, but especially important, to write in a 'non-sexist' way that does not, unthinkingly, assign gender where none is needed or, in fact, implied. Thus, I should not write 'craftsman', when I merely mean a worker with craft, nor 'the moon . . . she' since the moon is not invariably seen as feminine. This presents textual problems, for I dislike such usages as writing 's/he', or 'her/his', or 'a therapist used his or her skills'. In what follows, I shall therefore refer to all babes and children younger than puberty as 'it', unless the actual sex is clearly stated. For adults, when a plural is possible, I write 'craftworkers . . . they'.

The way of this book is a freshening of the familiar. The known and accepted is stated and then progressively taken apart in order to make new statements that are equally true to the phenomena in question. In part one, accepted concepts of the archetypal nature of maleness are set out, together with the need for a reformulation and the ways in which this might be attempted. The discussion centres around what I see as a dominant male archetype, 'the hero', and its possible replacement by that of 'a craftsman'. As prototype for this image, I have chosen the person and story of Daedalus, the master-craftsman and metal-worker of Greek mythology. He is well known as the man who, when imprisoned with his son, Icarus, in the Cretan labyrinth, made wings of wax and feathers so that they could escape from confinement there. Icarus, glorying in flight, flew too high, so that the sun's heat melted the wax, thus leaving him to fall, featherless, to his death. But this is just one episode in the rich and varied life of the father, about whom I shall write.

By using a mythic image, I have chosen to approach the problem from the level of the world of the archetypes, which declare themselves in these stories of gods and the godlike, because it is an altered, conscious expression of those primordial images for which I am seeking. Hero and craftsman are both male images and neither more 'true' than the other; they are just different. I hope to show, however, that the craftsman, as an image, includes more within its scope and is therefore to be preferred to the heroic.

Part two is concerned with a detailed examination, and a taking apart, of the story of Daedalus, in order to reimagine its constituents, along with other mythological material whose relevance asserts itself during the process. This might seem, in advance, to present difficulties for those readers without a wide knowledge of Greek mythology, who may therefore feel intimidated by names and stories with which they are unfamiliar and which for lack of space I cannot explain in full. I have included in the Appendix a brief identification of the mythical characters who people the story. Beyond this, the whole book is, in a sense, concerned with learning to live with the unfamiliar, and so I suggest that such readers allow themselves to become immersed in the mythic material, just as they might with any other stories, and without worrying too much about knowing more about the gods and goddesses mentioned. Going with the flow of the tales in this way allows the meaning that they contain and which connects them one with another to make itself clearer. It is like following a thread that unravels the winding passages of a labyrinth, for the flight of Daedalus, the maze-maker, is not only a flying and a fleeing, but also one that flows and floats along. It is, in addition, a way to travel that includes, unlike Icarus's, a safe landing.

It is important to mention in advance that throughout this examination I distinguish between Daedalus, representing a style of ego-consciousness, and that which I have called '*daidalos*'—using the Greek spelling—to signify the archetypal field of his whole story. The distinction between the two names is clear if written upon the page, but it is less easy to demonstrate when the names are spoken aloud, because in my experience they are pronounced in many different ways. My preferred pronunciation for Daedalus, the man, is phonetically, *Dēē-dŭh-lŭss*. The story or field, *daidalos*, I say as *dȳē-dĕr-lō̄ss̄*.

But myths, however archetypal, have no value at all if they are not connected to what is happening in everyday life, which by this means they then enlighten. In part three, therefore, a discussion is found of the underlying themes that have revealed themselves. The flight of Daedalus needs to be earthed; the geography of the field must be elucidated and its relevance suggested. What emerges is a tension between order and chaos, with the craftsman as he who can best tolerate the uncertainty of its unresolved state. In this part, it also becomes clearer that despite Daedalus being male, the nature of *daidalos*, which can be translated as 'well-craftedness', is equally applicable to both men and women.

In the final part, the process of elucidation continues, leading to the suggestion that depth psychology has, up till now, possessed a *scotoma*, or blind spot, concerning any awareness of a maleness that is fundamental—in the sense of being chthonic and generative. Instead, a masculinity based upon spiritual archetypes has been preferred. Our culture has elevated the 'sky father' with his consort of 'earth mother', while forgetting the 'earth father' and 'sky mother', who are of equal value and importance. Writing of the Great Mother, Erich Neumann (1955) distinguished between what he called an 'elemental' and a 'transformative' mother image. I believe that we might adopt a similar differentiation with regard to the archetypal Great Father. In this respect, it is worth noting the Roman Catholic belief in the assumption of the Virgin Mary into heaven, as well as the increasing pressure in the Christian church for a female priesthood, as evidence of a demand for the recognition of feminine spirituality and the 'transformative feminine' in women. The earth father, or 'elemental masculinity', has not, so far, been as fortunate, since biological considerations persuasively insist upon the impossibility for a male to bring forth young. But this is a psychological text, and the absence of the generative father from our minds and souls contributes, I believe, to the distortion of maleness in our society that has been called patriarchy. What is not experienced within is projected out upon the world. The metal-worker, however, whose raw materials are from the earth, partakes, I suggest, of this divine ground, now reimagined as male.

In any confrontation, the problems of the two opponents can be resolved by focussing upon what they are arguing about and trying to minimize their differences. This approach has been the one most commonly used in any discussion of the relationship between men and women and their masculinity and femininity. However, since the notion of well-craftedness will be seen to contain many of the elements previously thought of as belonging to the masculine or feminine principle, it is therefore an attribute that is capable of rising above any battles of gender. It does so, not by solving the argument, which would be to put forward some such synthesis as *androgyny,* but by acknowledging the differences and emphasizing what both sides can share in, as *persons.* In other words, it presents a novel way of solving the problem by changing the nature of the two opponents while still allowing them to differ. This is unlikely to happen, in real-life terms, unless the images themselves that underlie maleness and femaleness change, as the women's movement has conclusively shown they can. In her powerful book, *Slow Motion,* which *does* try to take a psychological, social, and political view of the issues involved, Lynn Segal (1990) argues that the time has now come when men must indeed start to change, in order to help in forming a 'world where people are free to work and free to love and find pleasure with the maximum amount of choice and minimum amount of compulsion, constrained only by the growth of real responsibility and mutual co-operation and care' (p. 316).

The *Makings of Maleness* tries to suggest a way in which this alteration could be brought about psychologically, although the 'making' does not just refer to the process itself. For, in the plural, the word additionally implies both the ingredients that may be used in that making, as well as the potentiality they possess for being made something of, which is, in the present case, maleness. The *Flight of Daedalus* is one that, having identified difference and otherness, flies between them without demanding synthesis, bearing the inevitably uncertain consequences, and belonging to all people.

PART ONE

THE BOOK

CHAPTER ONE

Meet the hero
and say goodbye

Cultivating the hero

T he present is a time, and this is a culture, which
worships heroes. It seems as if current human
nature insists upon identifying with those cour-
ageous creatures, valuing the heroic above all else and
despising the coward or the wimp. Today, as for many centuries, the hero represents a highly prized model for male
achievement, any departure from which is deemed a
failure. Yet is that natural, or cultural? factual, or a fiction
of the human psyche?

Boys, it is said, don't cry: their quivering, though stiff,
upper lips strive always to conceal and control those weak
emotions that, if they are not male, must inevitably belong
to femininity. And so such feelings are experienced as
being 'beyond the pale'. The 'pale' was a fenced-off area of
land under one's own jurisdiction, while beyond it lay foreign, fearful, and undoubtedly barbarian chaos. To pass
over any boundary, by land or by sea, is to separate from
the familiar and so to become vulnerable to the unknown,

3

risking disaster. Over the border lies an uncharted wilderness. It has been the task of the hero to prevent this disaster from happening by staking out an ordered reality within and separating it from the structureless 'unknown' that has at all times threatened to take over, to engulf. He not only has the ability to enter the unknown and make it known, but he can also keep it intact. For if at any time he ceases to cultivate his estate, then the wild creeps in insidiously. All would soon be lost, leading to feelings of great shame. Moreover, what is so in the world out there is true also of that inner world of the soul.

David, a would-be writer turned publishing editor, dreamed that he was rebuilding a dry-stone wall, shaped like a bow, outwards and around him. In some way he knew that it was meant to be a protection. His skills were not great, so it did not seem to be very sturdy. In addition, he was aware that there was one special piece which he must find or his job would fail: and there the dream ended. David fears he cannot be the hero that he believes he is expected to be. There will always be one task that will trip him up, although now he can be aware how anxious he is about that, not—as previously—resigned to it.

Real-life heroes offer me their examples to copy. They seem to do whatever it is they do on my behalf, proving its possibility. I can believe in them and the stories of their success, even if I find it hard to believe in myself and the possibility of *my* not failing. [And the mythological hero-type is clear-cut. Born in lowly circumstances, though with at least one supernatural parent, and endangered from birth, he often only struggles into manhood, displaying no real talents, until his time is due. Then, at great physical risk (though often with divine help), he successfully slays the dragon-monster, rescues the princess, regains the treasure buried for many years, and rejuvenates the realm of the old, sick, powerless king (Raglan, 1936). That is the end of the story: or so it is hoped. But no fairy story actually ends with the bridal pair living 'happily ever after'. In the stories collected by the Brothers Grimm, the couple live just 'for a time' or 'until they died', because the tellers of such tales knew very well that the disturbance will certainly, inevitably, break out again when, in his turn, the hero has himself become an old king.)

As an image within the human psyche, heroic dragon-slaying brings about a separation from the internal mother, to deliver a welcomed freedom for each individual consciousness to be itself. Then the hero-within no longer belongs to the mother who organizes and controls, but can now exist in his own right instead and create his own world. Is it any wonder then that girls and boys, men or women, instinctively identify with or reverence pop stars, million-pound footballers, movie actors, tennis aces, as models for the roles that their male selves would wish to play? These heroes, in projection, are people who often seem to have come from nowhere but 'made good', or 'beat the system'—and a system is, of course, an organized set-ting that demands compliant behaviour, just as mother may have seemed to.(The heroic figure with his exploits seems to represent the possibility of deviating from a col-lective norm out there,)of my becoming truly an individual and accepted with praise by other more critical parts of myself. This, then, is his significance internally as a psy-chological motif.

Since Jung's exploration of this theme in his book *Symbols of Transformation (CW 5)*, the hero has been seen by depth psychologists as a most powerful image of those dynamic processes within the human psyche that seek to outgrow the care and control of the mother archetype, replacing her by *anima,* the individual soul, the princess. The hero also dethrones the father image, to become a male authority himself. I would say here that I see this process as one that belongs in each and every person, whatever her or his gender might be. There may be hero-ines, but the intrapsychic heroic figures I refer to are unchangeably masculine and occur within us all, men or women: the Jungian *animus* in one of his many guises, who would liberate *anima*; and in so doing become most truly himself. The task of the heroine is, in any case, essentially different, as will be seen later.

Initiation now

The hero's tale represents, as I have said, a description of the process of separation from parental figures. Daring to enter an unknown world alone, the hero snatches from it the values that he finds there and makes them his own. The man that he is when he returns is different from the youth who set out. He has come of age. For example, the naive and boastful Perseus swore to produce the Gorgon's head as a wedding present for his stepfather, soon regretting his impulsiveness and fearing the worst. Yet he succeeded, and the story ends at his returning not only with the severed head of the mother–monster, which then turned the bridegroom to stone, but in addition with the beautiful Andromeda, as his bride. He had slain the sea dragon that threatened her, as well as the Gorgon, Medusa. The action signifies his initiation into manhood, which, like any process, implies a before-state and an after-state, different one from the other. The second condition indicates what change has taken place, which old habit or patterns have been broken up or given away, and what new areas and styles have been entered or taken on.

Any altered social status in the outside world has always been marked by ritual events that note the new condition as well as making the passage of change safer by the presence of others who have passed this way before. These are the rites of passage and those who organize them. In Perseus's case, there were divine helpers who provided him with advice and with weapons, the craftiness and skills, that won him through eventually to his own kingship.

Initiation ceremonies, whether they take place in tribal cultures, university halls, or barrack rooms, are all good examples of these. The old is cast off and passes into oblivion, a difficult threshold is passed over, and some new state is embraced with enthusiasm. The individual both leaves the group, yet re-enters it at a different, 'higher' level. Anthropologists such as van Gennep (1960) and Victor Turner (1967) have worked out the underlying, shared structures of such ceremonies. In brief, the boys to be initiated are taken from their mothers, sometimes by force, and confined in unaccustomed situations. They are terrified by apparent spirit attacks upon them, as well as being physically maltreated, bled, circumcised, tattooed, or otherwise marked out as part, now, of the men's group. The tribal traditions and laws are passed on to them, at the same time as they learn the secrets that men keep from women. After an indefinite time they are returned to the rest of the tribe, but not to their mother's home. So what is achieved by this process, and what are its psychological meanings?

As far as the tribe is concerned, youths have been made into men by the initiating elders. They will now take their full place in society, with all the responsibilities that implies. They can now relate to women other than as children to their mother, and so may marry, have children of their own, and thus secure the future of the tribe. Since such a small social structure as a tribe must rely upon its members working together and not just for their own good, initiation makes certain that the initiates will remain bound by tribal traditions and lore as members of an extended family. They will undoubtedly have had passed on to them the nature of the punishments to be given out for transgressing the various codes of behaviour. So initiation protects the whole community from the disintegration that might follow the breaking of rules. The initiates have learnt to control or conquer fear and are now full members of society.

Although there are also female initiation rites, these are more concerned with deepening the understanding of what it means to be a woman and a mother. They confer no temporal power. Nevertheless, these rituals also follow the pattern worked out by van Gennep: a separation, a threshold or transitional phase, to be followed by re-incorporation into the social body.

It is clear from the above that, as a cultural procedure, male initiation could be seen as the tool of a patriarchal attitude that gives power to the men, frees them from the domination of women, and then protects this position, by binding the developing youths with the same ties as their fathers and forefathers. Men's societies could be seen as an understandable societal and psychological reaction to a feared supremacy of the matriarchate (Neumann, 1949, p. 141). The brotherhood of men forms a power base from which women are excluded, and yet within it some of the symbolic acts performed deliberately copy those female processes to which men have no factual access (e.g. bloodletting from the genitals or mock-birthing cere-monies). It should be noted that although there is evidence for the religious or psychological existence of matriarchy, it has seldom existed in society. Psychological reality is, however, of prime importance here.

The psychological meaning and implications of initi-ation have been well covered by Anthony Stevens (1982, p. 147ff). He points out that within the human psyche there is a resistance to change that lies at the root of the founda-tion of consciousness, with its day-to-day continuity, and which is an essential component of the sense of stability that the human ego possesses. Conversely, the anxiety that accompanies consciousness relates to a fear of the possible breakdown of that stability which would then allow unnamed powers access to the conscious world, threatening to engulf the sufferer. Stevens quotes the 'law of psychic inertia' put forward by Edward Whitmont (1969, p. 246): 'Every pattern of adaptation, outer and inner, is main-tained in essentially the same unaltered form and anxiously defended against change until an equally strong or stronger impulse is able to displace it.' This corresponds to Sir Isaac Newton's law of physical inertia, which states that bodies remain in their state of rest or motion unless compelled to alter that state because of some more power-ful force from without.

Psychologically speaking, forces for change can come from within as well as without, but what they share is in being experienced as a death threat to the ruling states of consciousness. So the initiatory process can be seen as a means that the psyche uses to overcome its own resistance to change; but it is also a means by which the psyche can change without breaking down. Any new state of mind entered upon will, in its turn, remain stable and resistant to change also, until a time may come when it too must be replaced. Quoting Bowlby's attachment theory, Stevens suggests that 'initiation can be seen as a means of facilitating the *transfer of attachment* from mother or family to the male group and tribal gods'. He also puts forward the notion that a prospective view of this process would support the idea that male initiation is an institution 'ordained by God' (or perhaps one that has developed through evolution) for the attenuation of the maternal bond when it has outlived its usefulness for survival (Whitmont, 1969, p. 168). Obviously psychic change takes place continuously and not just at puberty or at other physical and emotional milestones, but it is at these times that the ceremonies and ordeals of initiation and other rituals are most visible.

It has often been said of present-day culture that it is one in which initiation rites have tended to disappear. Becoming an adult at twenty-one years of age used to be an occasion for ritualized celebration, with the handing over of the key to the family home, the giving of significant presents, attaining the right to vote, and also becoming responsible for any future debts, as well as being free to marry without parents' permission. Nowadays, thanks to the increasing liberation of adolescents, many of whom live away from home after leaving school at sixteen, at a time when the voting age has been lowered to eighteen, and so on, the opportunities for initiation into adulthood have faded away. The only replacement often seems to be having a couple of parties, one at eighteen and another at twenty-one.

This lack of initiatory rites, which are reckoned to be such a psychic necessity, has been described as one of the great psychological failings of our culture. It leads, so it is claimed, to disaffected youth who cannot properly grow up, to vandalism, gang warfare, male homosexuality, and the breakdown of the structure of society, to name but a few of the presumed ills. There may be a point to be made here. On the other hand, adults throughout the centuries have always shaken their heads over the waywardness of today's young people, when compared with those of times past. It is a habit as old as the hills (perhaps a case of psychic inertia?) to claim that lost customs of the past were highly significant and to lament their passing. Lack of this or that is then seen as being at the root of present-day troubles. No doubt the same was, at some time, said about human sacrifice, slave-owning, or the right of the lord of the manor to sleep with all the young village virgins. Another way of looking at the situation would be to see culture as enmeshed in an unfolding process in which, like it or not, things change because they are superseded; they are then forgotten, although mourned. Our longing for a fantasized Golden Age of the past when things were done properly is merely an expression of the archetypal nature of nostalgia. Mario Jacoby (1980) has written of this as a longing for regression to a blissful stage of the mother/ infant relationship—which is, of course, unobtainable.

The nature and practice of psychotherapy can also be modelled as initiatory, fitting well into the pattern described above. The whole treatment, as well as each hour with the therapist, takes the form of a separation from one's ordinary life, a transitional period to be followed by re-entry into society as a changed person.

The very training of the psychotherapist also follows this style, and a similiarity is claimed to the initiation of the shaman of tribal society, who undergoes an ordeal during which he flies from his physical body to the land of spirits and suffers painful and frightening experiences there before returning to earthly reality with the magical powers obtained by virtue of this journey. The people who claim this similarity are, of course, the therapists themselves, just as it is often they who deplore the lack in their patients of the initiatory processes that they themselves have been forced to undergo, and which, therefore, they tell themselves that they found so useful.

If initiation as a psychological process can, in its positive aspects, make change possible and less terrifying, then what of its negative properties? The tribal initiate enters a society governed by tight rules to ensure its survival. There are few margins for individual caprice or waywardness, and this is an inescapable factor of the re-incorporative phase that is easily overlooked. In other words, although initiation into manhood holds out the hope of becoming an individual, it does not, in fact, bring freedom with it, but a strict embeddedness within the culture and adherence to its rules, just as it does with the therapists and their code of ethics. By becoming initiated into society, the young man is not liberated but constrained to do what is expected of him or be punished.

It is, of course, true that there is more to initiation than that. Joseph Henderson (1967) has written convincingly of an 'archetype of initiation', which expresses itself repeatedly throughout life, leading by stages to increasing freedom from societal demands and towards a personal spiritual experience. As he points out, this corresponds exactly with the psychological process of becoming truly one's self, which Jung called 'individuation'. But I am concerning myself here only with the progress into manhood performed in the so-called 'puberty rites' and represented mythologically by the heroic task.

There is also the implied suggestion that in order *properly* to change status, whether physically or psychically, one *must* take part in an initiatory process, administered by other initiates. That this need not be so, and in what manner, I shall explore later on.

Unseating the hero

In ancient Greece, the hero was closely associated with death, for he reflected not only 'the glory of the divine' but carried as well 'the shadow of mortality' (Kerényi, 1959,

p. 3). The cult associated with him was centred on his tomb,
where he was not worshipped as a god but remembered
with reverence. It is not quite the same today, for although
there are village war memorials and tombs of unknown
warriors, there is also hero-worship of real, live people.
Current understanding of heroes has become very partial
and two-dimensional, their divine connection having
become irrelevant, so that now it is how they make
people's maleness feel that matters. The courage of their
deeds is admired, but instead of admiration being followed
by a laying to rest, more and better is demanded of them
next time. An intolerable burden is thus placed upon
heroes of today, so that in order to live up to expectations,
they may have to cut corners or fly too high—taking ana-
bolic steroids, for instance, and faking, or ending up punch-
drunk by going on too long. And when they fail or cannot
keep up the pace, they are ruthlessly discarded. Yesterday's hero is a sadly forgotten man.

For example, the heroism that retook the Falkland
Islands for Britain in 1985 is remembered by many with
pride—but not by the young soldiers who were maimed,
fried alive in that adventure, or who suffer from post-trau-
matic shock syndrome on account of it. People do not wish
to know of the continuing tragedies of these young men,
except, occasionally, to peer at them on television to see
whether they are coping with their scarred bodies and
shattered lives equally heroically. Those who are not, or
who have broken the heroic code by complaining, or
demanding more attention, have been cold-shouldered and
demeaned. Live men who cannot continue with their heroism cause discomfort. They remind each person too much of
less palatable, more emotional bits of themselves.

If this is what is asked of today's heroes, then these are
the heroics that are active within today's psyche; and they
are the models for maleness which, archetypally induced,
will be unconsciously aimed for and desired. This shining
hero simplifies the complexities of life into easy categories,
slicing wholes into opposing entities with his sword and

banishing any darker sides of life. Discomforted by a middle ground of blurred boundaries, the hero is an extremist; and the artificial distinctions he makes between good and bad, inner and outer, upper and lower will then war against each other continuously. And to the hero, of course, fighting and might are right.

He also insists upon precision and clarity, fearing the dark uncertain corners that are more true to life as it is than is his own obsessional lucidity. A doer of deeds, he never experiences being blissfully accepted just for who he is, as he is; and he can never forget that someone once thought him of such little consequence that they abandoned him and threatened his defenceless life. Now he must do bigger and better things so as to please and regain affection, to live up to presumed expectations and never be a nobody again. Always he must be engaged in action and activity or feel at a loss. Fearing relationships, he distances himself from others. Today's hero wants no unmarked grave or divine connection to be remembered by, but carefully cultivates the records he will hand on to the future so that he may be remembered just as he was. Some will also falsify those records by exaggeration or deletion.

Of these heroes now craved for, who have taken over the collective vision of the world, Herakles is a prime example in Greek mythology. He was a killer who went in for clubbing, throttling, crushing, stabbing, as well as the cutting off of heads. In particular he captured or slew animals: the hind, the boar, birds, horses, the bull, cattle, which can all be seen as representing his own animality and body-consciousness. He even destroyed the king of that internal jungle, the Nemean Lion. Acceptance for him could only come by means of labouring, not by just being. The stable he cleared up demonstrates his passion for a sterile cleanliness in which little can grow, having been deprived of its life-promoting manure. He was revengeful, single-mindedly seeking out his adversaries and finishing them off. Not much related to women or wives, he deserted his family while carrying out his twelve tasks, even burning his own children during a fit of madness. His vanity was such that on coming across a lifelike image of himself made by Daedalus, he took it for a rival strongman and clubbed it to the ground.

Unlike other heroes whose connection with the underworld is part of their cult, Herakles was an enemy of death. He went down to Hades, not to learn from the experience, as had others such as Ulysses or Aeneas, but to put the shades to flight and to threaten and wound Hades, the god of that realm. Finally, he dragged Cerberus, its guardian hound, up into the daylight. If it is these heroics with which our culture also identifies, then it is indeed a sickness, like the poisoned shirt that Herakles could not remove and which ultimately proved to be his downfall. In agony from it, all he could do was burn himself to death.

James Hillman (e.g. 1979a, p. 110ff) has repeatedly written about the negative effects of the hero archetype, when it takes over ego-consciousness as a model for the 'strong ego'. The hero has become, he says, the only sanctioned model we know for ego development, which, by its Heraklean stance, continually distances us from the true imaginal realm of psyche, which is the underworld. Or else, by dragging its contents up into the light, it prints its upper-worldly viewpoint on psychic events, thus literalizing the imaginal, killing off the animal movements in dark corners, insisting upon cleaning up the act and setting lucidity to work. By the process of killing that many-headed watersnake, the Hydra, Heraklean consciousness suppresses the multiple view. But, as Hillman (1979a) says:

A view of reality that does not recognise other views is of course delusional. In the heroic ego's case, the delusion is self-divinisation, the perspective of the human ego as the superior, indeed the only actuality. The rest is not real. [p. 115]

His view of the heroic ego has been criticized by many people, because it is felt that he is denying any need for an individual to possess ego-strength. That way, it is said, lies a formless, boundaryless switching from one attitude to another—and, at the worst, psychosis.

I believe that Hillman is himself partly to blame here, for in many instances he fails to distinguish between strength of ego and heroic ego, as if the two were the same thing. Or, rather, he does not spell out the kind of strength that an imaginal ego (his preferred term) needs to possess, other than the heroic kind. Consequently, his opponents can justly criticize him, although they are really in the same boat as he is, by equating strength only with heroism. Yet there is, in fact, another model for strength contained within Greek mythology.

In Homer's Odyssey, Menelaus tells how he was kept from returning home after the Trojan War by the anger of the gods. Trying to discover the reason for his punishment, it was suggested to him that he try to capture Proteus, the old man of the sea, who knows everything and therefore will tell him which god he has offended and how to put it right. But Proteus is, by his fishy nature, a slippery customer who will incessantly alter his shape and nature if approached, in order to escape. The trick is to hold on tight to whatever he changes himself into, and for this feat a strength is needed that is of a different nature from one that slays dragons, or rescues princesses. Menelaus tells it thus:

> Then with a shout we rushed upon him and locked our arms about him; but the ancient god had not forgotten his craft and cunning. He became in turn a bearded lion, a snake, a monstrous boar; then running water, then a towering and lofty tree; but we kept our hold unflinched and undismayed, and in the end this master of dreaded secrets began to tire. So he broke into speech and asked outright: "Son of Atreus, which of the gods taught you this strategy to entrap and overpower me thus? What do you want of me?" [Homer, *The Odyssey* (1980, transl. Shewring), p. 45]

Similarly, Metis, the first wife of Zeus, whose name means 'wisdom', was also a shape-shifter. Trying to escape his pursuit, she passed through many of her different natures, before tiring at last of his persistence and yielding to him. As a result, she became the mother of Athene. It is this kind of steadfast, unremitting, undestructive strength, rather than the heroic kind, which the imaginal ego needs to possess. Its grip, unflinching, undismayed, will be rewarded by information, wisdom, and children. Heraklean, heroic ego-strength always implies a victim— in its negative phase. Protean strength destroys no one. It could even be said that its very nature brings about the multiplicity of different images.

Getting out from under

When any single complex, with its archetypal core, takes over consciousness, we speak of psychic inflation, or delusion. The complex becomes cut off from its own rootedness in depth, as if believing that it rules in its own right. The heroic ego today has very little of 'the glory of the divine' about him, for it is only he who lives and rules, while the gods are dead and buried. And when the gods are dead, then the complexes that represent them are acted out in the world destructively, or else we suffer them in our bodies as physical symptoms. The hero as a *single* model for maleness, as it is now experienced, has little to recommend it. In its outline and activity it reveals many of the faults described as 'the patriarchal attitude'. However valuable and necessary the hero is as a psychic process, his image has also become debased and partial in the way he is embodied. The terrorist, the lager-lout, the arbitrageur, and the rambo-esque are all aspects of a heroic style that may be longed for, envied, feared, or detested as parts of the self. Each person will feel that some of those heroic qualities should be controlled, while expecting themselves to be allowed to indulge in others. Some I can applaud in myself, while others I project into my neighbours, there to be deplored.

It is said that individuals must then learn to withdraw these projections and accept them as shadow qualities of themselves. But although this is a praiseworthy activity, it is a direct result of the single-minded approach that represents the hero himself. There may be other ways of approaching the problem.

If it is delusional not to see other ways of looking, then what is needed today is a many-headed approach in order to see the world more as it is rather than with that nostalgia for simple orderedness that those who demand more initiation and heroic ego-activity would embrace. And remember that it was a hero who killed off the many-headed serpent. In a similar vein, it was Francis Bacon who said, at the beginning of our scientific era, that Mother Nature should be put upon the rack and tortured until she gave up her secrets. Herakles would understand that approach. So would heroes everywhere, for killing the mother (imaged as a dragon-monster) in order to wrest away her treasures is a key part of their story. Perhaps it is the hero we now need to kill off, or at least to remove him from the driving seat to give others a turn. Hillman (1979a) writes:

> Ego psychology is the contemporary form of the hero cult. In the end, Hercules goes up in fire. Are the legends of the ego that we now call psychology developing into what will become tales of warlike men? Will ego psychology lead us into war and fire? [p. 111]

In 1913, Jung himself dreamed that he was on a lonely rocky slope, in the company of an unknown, brown-skinned man, when they heard the horn of Siegfried sounding through the mountains. Armed with rifles, they lay in wait, and, as he appeared with the first rays of the sun, driving his chariot, they shot him dead. 'The dream showed', Jung wrote, 'that the attitude embodied by Siegfried, the hero, no longer suited me. Therefore it had to be killed' (Jung, 1963, pp. 204–205). At the same time, Siegfried in the dream was seen, by Jung, to represent what was then being played out in Europe by the German nation, which would indeed lead to 'fire and war'.

Two world wars and a cold war later, the heroic is still being played out in our culture and needs to be replaced. But the danger of getting out from under the hero's dead weight, of letting others in, and of developing a change-able, more permeable style of maleness is, it is said, that psychosis might then be just around the corner. This would be especially likely for those whose ego is weak, so what is first required is the development of a strong ego, in order to contain the anxiety of 'letting go'. Jung was able to do this because of the presence in his dream of the 'brown-skinned man'. But the strength that can hold on to a Proteus or a Metis is one that never lets go, and yet it permits and encourages diversity.

On the other hand, once in position, does the hero ever let go of the reins? The law of psychic inertia makes it clear that he can be unseated only by a force of equal or greater power; and who is strong enough to defeat a Her-akles?

However, just as Newtonian mechanics can now be seen as a special and restricted case—not untrue, but only partial—so, too, the law of psychic inertia may not always hold when viewed from a wider perspective. Or perhaps it is used by the hero to justify his always staying in control. Yet, if he is to be unseated from the driving position, what kind of male is it who might replace him as a model?

First, he would have a different relationship towards the mother. Surely he could exist as something separate from his matrix without killing it off? That would imply also a possibility of relating to it, as and when chosen, but on equal terms. Nor would it rule out the possibility (now *per-mitted* by the mother) of his relating to his own feminine soul, as well as to the maternal.

Secondly, he need not be single-minded but would have a variety of ways of viewing his surroundings, each of equal value, and only one of which would be heroic. In fact, he would be positively against the kind of inertia that claims that changeableness is too difficult. He would remain aware of the many gods within who, by their existence, sanction this polyformity. Nor must he rely upon initiators and initiation to help him change from style to style. He has the appropriate strength to control his own protean nature.

Thirdly, he would show a capability of going to extremes and demanding certainty, while also being able to tolerate the muddled and mucky middle ground, without having to make a clean sweep of it.

Fourthly, when he journeyed to the underworld, he could look with the eyes of its rulers and inhabitants: he would receive rather than conquer. This would ensure his 'seeing through' the literalness of a concrete world to welcome and encourage an imaginal view.

Fifthly, he could exist beyond oppositionalism, embracing complexity: willing to complicate even, rather than simplify. He would have no need therefore to aim always for synthesis and integration. In fact, as I shall show, he would be for networking and diatheses.

Finally, he would not always have to be a compulsive action-man in order to gain approval, but would be capable of feeling accepted and valuable just as he is, was, or will be.

I shall explore all of those attributes in what follows, but first I should like to examine the resistance that consciousness always displays towards change.

Inertia

It is correct to see an inertial resistance to change as an important property of consciousness itself, for what is established needs to remain the same from one day to the next or from one set of circumstances to another. This continuity must have an archetypal base, like any other human activity, which is, according to Hillman, the *senex* archetype. '*Senex*' is the Latin adjective meaning 'old', and such words as 'senior', 'senator', and 'senility' are similarly derived. But, as a psychological determinant, *senex* has nothing to do with biological age. It refers to an 'oldness' within the psyche that is not concerned with chronological age, being something that is present right from the beginning. The psyche's ability to order, organize, stabilize, control, and bring to fulfilment belongs to the *senex* archetype. It is at the core of the formation of consciousness, as an expectation for things to happen as they did before.

The qualities that *senex* brings to any complex are those of ordering, structure, certainty, and the setting of boundaries. There is nothing objectionable about those qualities; they are all admirable and necessary. But in order to provide them, the *senex* must clearly be against change, which it sees as a recipe for chaos, with all the anxiety that that can bring. In a negative guise, therefore, the senex hangs on to power at all costs. It can be found at the core of *any* complex that has taken control of consciousness, thus demonstrating the inevitable outcome of its ordering potential and fulfilment. The death it brings to the psyche is that of perfectionism and accomplishment, being an image of the inescapable death through maturity, as psychological processes become familiar, habitual, and thus unconscious again (Hillman, 1979a, p. 18). This double valency of inertia—both order and disorder—is confirmed by etymology. The adjective 'inert' means unskilled or inactive. In Latin, *iners* is derived from *in-* [un-] and *ars* [art]. Art, as I shall show later, has a root meaning of order. In a negative sense, therefore, a thing that is inert or possesses inertia is de-skilled, stagnant, and disordered.

The antidote to this rule by *senex* is claimed to be *puer* or youth—the other side of the old coin; and I shall examine this now by means of a familiar mythic image: that of Icarus.

CHAPTER TWO

Must youth always follow age?

Icarus

I carus, soaring towards the sun on father-made wings and then, wax melting, with feathers adrift in the long slow fall to death by drowning, has long been taken in Jungian psychology as a prime example of the archetype of the *puer aeternus* [eternal child] and its tendencies as a human psychological determinant. Individuals gripped by this pattern have been seen as mother-bound, immature, and unrelated to outer reality: given to useless fantasy, to heady flights and (often literally) dying falls. The typical pathology of the person dominated by the *puer aeternus* has been well documented by Marie-Louise Von Franz (1971), who describes such a person as having remained too long in adolescent psychology, so that the characteristics of the teenage years are carried on into adult life. This is coupled with too great a dependence upon the mother. The typical disturbance of such a man is said to be either 'Don Juanism' or homosexuality. Later in the book the 'cure' of the *puer aeternus* is unequivocally stated as 'work'.

21

This negative view of the effect of the *puer aeternus* archetype has dominated most Jungian literature, so that *puer* has become a pejorative term describing an attitude of which the individual concerned should be ashamed and must be cured. In a similar fashion, psychiatric circles use such terms as 'attention-seeking' or 'manipulative' as derogatory labels for the behaviour of sick patients. Yet at another and deeper level it is clear that someone who is compelled to seek attention in this way does so because they need it and never got it when young. Or it suggests that the attention they received as children was of the wrong kind. In other words, the outer behaviour reflects the inner lack and desire. Attention-seeking is better described as attention-needing. Similarly, the apparently manipulative person possesses a strong sense of psychological powerlessness which they wrongly try to remedy by manipulating the environment. The acting-out is an image of what is missing within and symbolizes what must be done to retrieve it as an experience. Thus, a person in the grip of adverse, *puer aeternus*-type behaviour really needs a better connection with that archetype at an inner level.

Jung also writes in this negative vein, describing the *puer aeternus* as a 'parasite on the mother, a creature of her imagination, who only lives when rooted in the maternal body' (*CW 5,* para. 393). In his essay concerning the child archetype, writing of a 'Radiant Boy' in English ghost stories, he says:

> It almost looks as though we were dealing with the figure of a *puer aeternus* who had become inauspicious through 'metamorphosis', or in other words had shared the fate of the classical and the Germanic gods, who have all become bugbears. [*CW 9,* 1, para. 268]

In other words, the *puer aeternus* only *becomes* inauspicious but is not directly so. Jung is writing here in the context of his evaluation of the child archetype as a bringer of what is new and as hope for the future. The child, he says, appears always 'unexpectedly and in the most unlikely places' or 'in ambiguous form'. Elsewhere in the same essay, he stresses that the *puer aeternus* is one way of contacting the mother archetype, in the form of identifying with her as her son and lover. Mother–lover has a derogatory sound about it as well—and yet the *puer* represents, says Jung, a connecting link between consciousness and the unconscious ground of our existence. There can be nothing wrong with that as an image, although inevitably it brings with it a tendency towards rejection by the ruling dominant of consciousness. Jung writes:

> The 'child' is all that is abandoned and exposed and at the same time divinely powerful; the insignificant, dubious beginning, and the triumphal end. The 'eternal child' in man is an indescribable experience, an incongruity, a handicap and a divine prerogative; an imponderable that determines the ultimate worth or worthlessness of a personality. [*CW 9*, 1, para. 300]

This is quite a weight for the *puer aeternus* to carry and cannot possibly be seen only in a negative light. It describes the vast importance of that particular archetypal pattern and its more auspicious meaning for everyday life.

In attempting a revaluation, I begin by reflecting that the Latin '*puer*' actually means a young, immature child of either sex and only secondarily a boy, by which time it has become opposed to '*puella*' [a girl]. The same is true in English, where 'girl' was originally used to mean a young person of either gender (*OED*). Similarly the Greek word *kore* means a young maiden (girl, young woman, servant: *OED*). But *kore* has a secondary meaning of 'the pupil of the eye'; and this doubling-up occurs also in Latin, where '*pupillus*' refers to the eye as well as to a young person. Ultimately, that word derives from '*pupa*', meaning girl or jointed doll. The word '*pupa*' was used by Carl von Linné to describe the grub undergoing metamorphosis, within its chrysalis, into a moth or butterfly. *Pupillus,* the tiny portrait of oneself that is reflected in another's eye, *kore,* and *puer* all cluster, as images, around that stage between larva and imago when the whole body of the insect is taken apart and remodelled, while cocooned from sight. From this viewpoint, therefore, the *puer* might be said to provide a picture of the image-in-waiting, a future that will be made factual, the non-mature. Experienced within the psyche, there can therefore be nothing intrinsically wrong with the *puer aeternus* archetype; and there can be much that is highly valuable.

Looking elsewhere for origins, a description of this godlike youth can be found in Ovid's *Metamorphoses,* which chronicles various miraculous mythical changes. At the place in question, the poet is telling of a festival to Bacchus, god of wine (Gr: Dionysus).

> Then they made offerings of incense and called upon Bacchus, hailing him by different titles, as Bromius and Lyaeus, as the son of the thunderbolt, the twice born, the only child to have two mothers. He was invoked as Nisaeus, as Tyoneus of the flowing tresses, as Lenaeus and the planter of the genial vine, as Nyctelius and father Eleleus, as Iacchus and Ehuan and by all the other names that Bacchus bears among the Greeks. *For he is one whose youth never fades. He remains always a boy, the loveliest god in the heights of heaven.* When he appears among us without his horns his head is like that of a young girl. [Ovid (1955, transl. Innes) p. 94; my emphasis]

So the *puer aeternus* is none other than Dionysus himself, son of Zeus, the sky god who killed Semele, the child's human mother, when she sought to see her lover as he really was, in his glory. Rescuing the unborn baby, however, Zeus brought it to term within his own thigh. *Puer*'s mother is here imaged as one who finds herself at the mercy of the father and who is burnt up and destroyed by him for daring to try to see him as he is and not as he disguises himself. Semele tried for equality and paid the price that Zeus metes out.

Puer aeternus is described in the above as god of ecstasy, lysis, god of the night, of wine, with the shrieks, the groans, the ululations that accompany his epiphany. As Bromius and Iacchus, he is the child born to Zeus and Persephone (herself known as *the kore*) within the Eleusinian Mysteries. In Latin, the words italicized above read:

> *tibi enim inconsumpta juventus est tu puer aeternus, tu fornisi in alto conspiceris caelo....*

So his youth [*juventus*] is one that is unconsumed [*inconsumpta*]—neither eaten up nor made away with by the ravages of time, for he is that youth which is related to eternity: the age of our universe. And he is the god of this aeon as well as of the aeon to come, ever renewed and renewing. He is both a youth and, when appearing hornless, looks like a young girl. So we have confirmed for us here the image of *puer* as the non-mature of either gender. He is the loveliest god, who dissolves the old and brings in the new, who intoxicates, sending people out of their conscious minds with his enthusiasms, only to hang over them while they recover those faculties, to await their acknowledgement. The *puer aeternus* is therefore not just what is new and to come, but the very process itself by means of which the present transforms itself into something fresh— the non-mature, the chrysalis and imago itself, all within the same whole. Jung writes:

> The child motif not infrequently occurs in the field of psychopathology.... But the clearest and most significant manifestation of the child motif in the therapy of neuroses is in the maturation process of personality induced by the analysis of the unconscious, which I have termed the process of *individuation*. [*CW 9*, 1, para. 270]

It is important to reiterate that what has been called *puer* does not truly possess a gender and does not therefore need to be matched by the feminine *puella*. Similarly, *puer* is not just to do with boys but is an image of the dynamics of change itself: that giving up of the known and trusted in favour of what is unknown (because in the future) and therefore to be feared by present-time consciousness. It is the image of 'life in death'. In the same way, adolescence, as a process of change lying between childhood and being adult, has been called the time of 'no longer but not yet'. As image, rather than as a factual reality, could such a state be pathological if carried over into adult life? Is it not, rather, that adulthood would itself be abnormal—or at the least, stunted—without it? Do people always have to 'be their age'? Must they repeatedly cure themselves of youthful daydreams by unremitting work (a heroic belief indeed)? Or does that lead, on the other hand, to becoming fixed and unchanging: bound to a fantasy of historic development in which the first half of life leads inexorably to a second and even third half of increasing wisdom and seriousness? Is that the realm of a wise old man, or is it the country of the old king? Clearly it can be seen as either; but the self-important feelings of profoundness inherent to the 'wise old man' can, in their awesomeness, lead to a denial of, and defence against, the sterility of the old king's rule.

James Hillman has located the *puer aeternus* otherwise, recognizing its nature as one polarity of a split *senex/puer* archetype: youth to be paired with age, rather than as son of the Great Mother. In this reading, therefore, puer expresses an attitude of psyche that opposes the hardening tendencies towards perfection that *senex* brings. Hillman associates *senex* qualities with those of Kronos/Saturn: dryness, night, coldness, harvest, winter, as well as right-angledness, historical time, the building of cities or empires, and a pushing out of the boundaries of certainty. *Puer,* however, he equates with the antithesis to these qualities, with its sappy, formless wetness and lightning changes of direction that defy both time and space (Hillman, 1979b, pp. 3–54).

Wherever and whenever processes are coming to an end, or getting set in their structural ways, where time has run out and attitudes have become hard and fast, there *senex* rules, as I have said. Then, too, *puer* is waiting in the wings—waiting with its wings to give another revolution to the spinning wheel of circular time and thus suggest new answers for well-worn problems. *Senex* must always resist this intrusion upon its territory, for such things are never easy, or easily accepted, being associated like the birth of Dionysus with lightning bolts and fire, suffering and dissolution. These are hints of a diabolical ending to the world as *senex* knows it that is therefore rightly—if mistakenly—to be avoided.

For Hillman, then, the *puer* is not so much a mother's boy as a father's son, who must rise above the paternal world of existing order to free his own spirit, create his own world, make his own individuality. And fathers everywhere hate him for showing up their *senex*-dominated attitudes. The *puer* flies because he has to. It is, inescapably, his way of going through the world: of transcension. And yet, the dream of flight brings with it a fear of falling that easily and often prevents take-off; for, to anyone but *puer*, falling is seen only as death and extinction. But since the vertical dimension works both ways, a 'coming-down' is inevitable, whether that be seen as a fall or as safe landing. *Puer*'s nature is, in any case, one that insists on having things both ways, as opposed to *senex* journeys, which flow down one channel only. Every return trip of the *senex* is always to the station of origin, while *puer* never lands where he took off. The fall is something he is dying to risk: a risking to die, because for him there is also 'life in death'. In the same fashion, the angel Lucifer, whose name means light-bearer, fell from heaven into the underworld, which he then lit up.

Flying and falling can, of course, be presented in a negative aspect as psychological determinants. They describe those who are not well grounded, but live in their daydreams, ever soaring to frothy castles in the sky and fantasizing about what may happen to them there. They are truly riding for a fall—to be disapprovingly moralistic about it. Falling is also what might occur in middle life to the person with an unresolved *puer* complex, when they descend sharply into disappointed cynicism with a loss of ideals as well as of creative impulse. Of this state, Von Franz says that 'it is as if Icarus had fallen into the mud and life had stopped' (1971, p. 168). Mud, earthing, groundedness are, of course, images of the mother in her fundamental role as matrix of all things.

Hillman's description, on the other hand, would be to say of individuals who had fallen that now they were identified with the negative *senex* part of the archetypal pair. And, as he points out, there is no basic difference between the negative *puer* and negative *senex*, except one of biological age (Hillman, 1979b, p. 27).

These positive or negative signs are, in any case, relative, being placed there by a judgemental consciousness. At the level of the archetype, however, they have no ultimate validity. Jung insists in all his writings that opposites always contain each other and that every vice can be a virtue or virtue, vice. *Puer* and *senex* are in themselves neither good nor bad but will inevitably be experienced in life as being one or the other, the plus or minus being put there from a conscious standpoint.

Jung, Von Franz, and Hillman all agree that it is the question of ego-identification that makes the difference between the healthy functioning of any archetype and its pathological experience. It is not my possession of a *puer* or a hero or initiatory complex that is the problem. They are, after all, structural components of each and every psyche. But it is when the complex has *me* that I'm in trouble. The individual who is identified with puerile trippings and trappings will unavoidably see anything belonging to the *senex* in a negative light. And yet, as he lives out, acts out, that role in the world, his unconscious psyche is dominated by the changeless *senex* that strangles before birth or swallows its own children. Where is the *inconsumpta juventus* then? Alternatively, too great a conscious espousal of law, with a slavish promotion of order, will also indicate unbounded and immature unconscious relationships to events. Or, when I demand initiation for all as the *only* means of psychic advance, then I am stuck on the rails and can only see the countryside flashing past but am unable to wander around in it. Again, is this the land of the wise old man or the realm of an old king?

The country of the old king

If I am not so much interested in the process of initiation as a means of psychic transformation, it is because I am trying to get rid of the hero, who with his brute strength has been seen as the only way to overcome the ruling forces. Here I shall concern myself with the power of that archetypal ruler (indeed, the resistance of *any* ruling archetype) to withstand any change of status, and to prevent such from coming about. This resistance is related to the state in which the individual already stands, preferring to remain as he is, without renewal, without death or rebirth. There is nothing intrinsically wrong with what can be called 'resistance' (see Lambert, 1981, pp. 52–87). From one perspective, it can be seen as an enviable stability, although at times this very steadfast quality prevents and stagnates. Although it has been called a 'law of psychic inertia', in mythology it is imaged as the king, in his negative aspects.

Traditionally, the king of any nation or tribe represents the ruling assumptions by which that society operates. The king holds all powers in his hands in a horizontal plane over the whole land to its very boundaries, beyond which, in effect, lies nothingness. Originally, his powers extended in the vertical plane too, since his throne acted as the centre and axis of the world, which connected the mundane realm with the gods and spirits above, as well as the ancestors and their shades below. The king personified all of the accumulated customs, wisdom, sacred practices, and mythic foundations of his nation and its people. It was his duty to perform whatever actions or sacrifices might be necessary to maintain this situation intact and to put things to rights if they slipped out of balance. He carried three main roles—as judge, priest, and commander-in-chief. If, or when, his powers began to wane, then it was time for him to depart, resign, be replaced—however that might come about. Taking a psychological view, there is an obvious value in this, for it means that states of being or states of mind will persist, if they are useful and bring about results. They are not liable to continual overthrow by every new idea that just happens to come along. Nor are they forgotten. On a personal level this represents a continuity of the way in which the ego functions. I think today what I thought yesterday. I do not have to make it anew each morning. Nor did I have to be continually accounting for its validity and justifying my belief in it.

But, as I have noted before, situations in human societies, or in individuals, are never so static as this would suggest. Change is taking place all the time, if slowly. A properly functioning king, as image, is that ego-nature which can hold within its hands all polarities, or elements of change, without collapse. But, inevitably, there comes a time when this will prove too much for any particular carrier of kingship, owing to a tension between the need to change and the need to remain the same. The 'ruling dominant consciousness' of a society or an individual, of which the king is an image, may react to this situation by holding on to its known ways instead of by abdication. But such a dominant has then lost the ability creatively to take on board what is useful among the novelties with which it is now faced. Or, on the other hand, the novelty might be just too much.

Senex now operates in its negative aspect. Resistance becomes a positive stasis, preventing access as well as flow. The king has become an 'old king' who appears in myth or fairy story, as sick, penniless, without a wife, his realm suffering from crop failure or famine, in danger of invasion, or plagued by monsters and marauding dragons. Instead of welcoming a new order, the old king would hang on to power at all costs; and it is this state of affairs that calls forth the hero. But, such is the king's ambivalence to his insoluble problem that he often makes it difficult for the hero to carry out his proper tasks, and afterwards he will try to rob him of any promised reward. And the problem *is* insoluble, of course, because the king is trying to solve it in ways that are old and outmoded, however trusted or well-tried they might also be.

The hero, as I have said, is an untried or untested youth, who comes from outside the realm or, if from within, then from its unlikeliest corner. He is the youngest son, a discharged soldier, a vagrant, a peasant's child, the *Dummling* or simpleton. As Jung has often pointed out, he is 'the stone whom the builders rejected', and he is here because he is needed.

So we might look again at initiation as a psychic process and see it not just as one that all individuals must go through in order to transform themselves. Instead, the neophyte can also be seen as an image of that psychic function that is called into being and into action so that resistance to change may be overcome. The psychological situation can be restated thus: the young person does not need an initiatory process in order to become an adult. Rather, the adults need initiates to revitalize their old order. In tribal terms this would, of course, be nonsense. Initiates are not expected to transform the society of which they have now become full members, but to preserve it intact. Yet the natural history of the mythological hero/initiate is that he becomes the new king himself. With time and in his turn, he will harden into an old king, thus institutionalizing the set-up, so that it will continue unchanged:

hero . . . new king . . . old king . . . hero . . . new king . . . old king . . . etc.

To believe in processes is to know that all present situations will inevitably become one-sided, rigid, out of *Dao*, stuck, enmeshed, or whatever the favoured description may be, and that they will call out for renewal. That 'all kings will become old ones and must then be replaced' would be another way of saying the same thing. But is heroism the only possible version of the story? Does every sick realm just need to lie waiting for a hero to come along? Or are there other, equally acceptable styles of renewal for the old king?

The way of the bear

I have elsewhere tried to answer this question, using the Old English poem known as Beowulf (the 'wolf of bees', i.e. bear) as an example (Tatham, 1978, 1979).

Beowulf is an exceptionally strong warrior from the Swedish tribe of Geats. He is attracted to Denmark with fourteen companions, in order to try his hand at killing the monster called Grendel, who has terrorized the court of King Hrothgar for the last twelve years of his fifty-year reign, making his hall, the beautiful Heorot, uninhabitable. Single-handedly dispatching the beast without a weapon and putting Grendel's mother to the sword in her underground cavern, Beowulf is mightily rewarded by Hrothgar in material terms, but he does *not* receive the kingdom or the princess's hand in marriage, as you might expect in such an archetypal situation. Instead, Beowulf is fobbed off by the princess's mother with the gift of 'two armlets, a corslet and many rings and the most handsome collar in the world'. Returning to his own country, he then gives up all the battle treasures he has won to his own king.

Hrothgar is therefore an old king who manages to hang on to power, after using the hero as a tool. The symbolic nature of Grendel, I have argued, is as a 'killer of kin', itself a heavily proscribed crime in the tightly knit tribal society of the sixth-century Germanic world. So, it is interesting (but not surprising) to note that Denmark is later destroyed, as the poet tells us, in a veritable bloodbath of kin-killing. In other words, what the old king tries to exclude—and the hero aids him in it by killing Grendel—will one day make its entry, come what may.

Hrothgar presents a picture of a particularly mean and rigid old king; Beowulf himself, once he is eventually on the throne of his own tribe and having reigned a similar fifty years, faces the same sort of problem but reacts differently.

The land of the Geats is threatened by a fiery dragon that is searching for one item taken, by a runaway slave, from the golden hoard on which the beast has rested for three hundred years. Once more refusing help, Beowulf engages the creature in single combat, wounding it but being mortally bitten in return. It is only at this point that assistance comes to hand in the person of Wiglaf, the epitome of untried youth, who delivers a death blow to the monster. Beowulf is shown the treasure retrieved by this struggle, only to die; but the poet makes clear that since the Geats are now without a king, all of their neighbouring enemies will fall upon them and, despite Wiglaf, the tribe is likely to be destroyed (for good translations of Beowulf, see Alexander, 1971, and Crossley-Holland, 1969).

Conventional criticism has it that in the first half of the poem Beowulf is a great and glorious figure, but in the second half a failure as a king owing to his fatal pride in insisting upon fighting single-handedly when he knows already that he must fail. By contrast, my view has been that, in Denmark, Beowulf is a flawed hero because he fails to claim his dues and thus truly revitalize the realm, whereupon the outcome for Denmark is disastrous. But, as an old king in Sweden, by acting in the way he does, he brings about (albeit unknowingly) a dramatic change by releasing into his world the values that have lain dragon-hoarded underground for so long. From the tribal side of the fence, it could indeed by described as a disaster. That is natural enough, for that is the logic of the old king, and convention allies itself with this view. On the other hand, from the perspective of history, tribes may very well need to be destroyed, if nations are to be made, and that could be seen as progress. From the aspect of Wiglaf, the new king (whose name means battle-remnant), all is uncertain because it lies in the unknown future and therefore cannot be described.

I believe that the importance of Beowulf, as a psychic image, is that he provides a model for an old king who brings about his own death and rebirth. True, Wiglaf could be called an initiated hero, after the battle; but it is Beowulf who sets the process in motion and whose 'battle-remnant'—his own transformed self—the young man represents.

I have tried to point out that there are ways in which that which 'old kings' represent may itself assist at its own renewal. Other examples can be found. For example, the Dinka are an African tribe, studied by the anthropologist Geoffrey Leinhart. Their 'Masters of the Fishing Spear' represent the spirit of vitality of the people and fertility of the land, without being rulers as such. When a Master is old and aware that his death is near, he stage-manages his own passing, with joy and ceremony. Lying in his open grave, which has been ritually prepared and covered with an oxhide, he speaks his farewell to the people, who then bury him alive, trampling the earth down hard upon his body. The tribesmen sing and dance their rejoicing, saying: 'The Master of the Fishing Spear has been taken to Earth. It is very good.' In this way, the Master contrives that his powers do not desert the community with his death, but remain within the territory of the tribe, to be incarnated in another Master at some future date. Nothing is lost, but the future is secured (Leinhart, 1976, p. 117).

Song of the sick king

In his book, *Mysterium Conjunctionis,* Jung examines the whole problem of the old king and his renewal, using as his text the Cantilena (song) written by George Ripley (1415–

1490), a Canon of Bridlington, in England. Ripley was not only a clergyman, but an alchemist also (Jung, *CW 14*, para. 368ff). The song, originally in Latin, states the situation thus:

> Yet to my Griefe I know, unlesse I feed
> On the Specifics I so sorely need
> I cannot Generate: to my Amaze
> The End draws near for me, Ancient of Daies.
>
> Utterly perish'd is the Flower of Youth,
> Through all my Veines there courses naught but Death.
> Marvelling I heard Christ's voice, that from above
> I'le be Reborne, I know not by what Love.
>
> Else I God's Kingdom cannot enter in:
> And therefore, that I may be Borne agen,
> I'le Humbled be into my Mother's Breast,
> Dissolve to my First Matter, and there rest.
>
> Hereto the Mother Animates the King,
> Hasts his Conception, and does forthwith bring
> Him closely hidden underneath her Traine,
> Till, from herselfe, she'd made him Flesh againe.
>
> [verses 10–13]

The king is infertile and therefore close to his end. In our terms he is an old king. His chosen way forward is not by calling on a hero, but by submitting to the chaos of destruction and reconstruction under his mother's gown. The Cantilena continues by telling how she retires to her room, away from all other people, for nine months, sustaining herself on 'peacock's flesh' and drinking the 'red blood of the Greene Lyone'. She goes through agonies of pain and putrefaction as the poison of the old king's body is slowly transformed, until:

> Her time being come, the Child Conceiv'd before
> Issues re-borne out of her Wombe once more;
> And thereupon resumes a Kingly State,
> Possessing fully Heaven's Propitious Fate.
>
> [verse 26]

The king, renewed by 'descent to the mother', can order his realm again.

Jung also quotes from another alchemical treatise, the *Allegoria Merlini (CW 14*, para. 357), which tells the story of an old and dropsical king whose body was minced up and made into a paste, which was then heated in a crucible so that it melted and the liquid ran into the vessel below, there to reform. 'Whereupon the king rose up from death and cried in a loud voice, "Where are my enemies? I shall kill them all if they do not submit to me!" All the kings and princes of other countries honoured and feared him.'

So there are, indeed, ways other than initiation by which that blockage to change that we have called the old king might be shifted. One of these is concerned with the ability of the old king to bring about his own dissolution and renovation. However, as can be seen above, this does not really alter the overall situation, since it is still bound by the same dichotomy of *senex* and *puer*, young and old kings, as they alternate and revolve around each other. Other ways out of the bind must be found.

Is it always necessary, for instance, for the young and untried to enter adulthood only by means of heroism and initiation? Those who write about it as a vital psychic process often give the impression that it is an essential element of all tribal societies and therefore something that our culture has lost to its detriment. There are, however, tribal situations where this is not the case: where individuals grow at their own pace and take their full place in the society as, how, and when they are ready to do so. And there seems to be no need for organized ceremonies to help them with this transition. If, therefore, initiation is an archetypal process concerned with growth, change, transformation, and renewal, then it seems that there are also other, opposite archetypal models that will, in their own ways, bring about the same results.

In the Arctic

In the arctic and subarctic lands of northern Canada live the people we conveniently lump together and call Esquimaux. They are, essentially, hunting people, only resident in one place if, or because and for as long as, it suits them to be there. Accumulation of a surplus of food or goods is therefore considered stupid, for it has no point. In a very real sense, if you have too much, you can't take it all with you. Their children grow up rapidly, so that by the age of ten years or so they are taking part in the life of the family, which is wholly geared towards providing for its own everyday needs. They grow up in unrestrained freedom. What they ask for they are given, because if they ask, then they must need it. What is not asked for is not given. In his book *The Living Arctic*, Hugh Brody (1987) points out that a child who asks to be cuddled will be picked up, but that a child in a tantrum will be left where it is. To try to soothe it, unasked, would be looked on as an act of intrusiveness.

Learning takes place by example and without criticism. It is thought to be useless to get cross with a child for any sort of failure on its part, because all children learn differently, and so, when the time is ripe, the child will master the task in question correctly. According to Brody, such a process seems to foster a high degree of discipline, self-reliance, and psychological well-being among the people of the northern hunting societies.

Yet, despite this freedom, which includes sexual freedom, the young attain an early and disciplined maturity, and since they do so at their own pace, they take their own place in society as and when they are ready. There are no rites of passage or institutionalized initiation ceremonies. Indeed, 'taking their place in society' is a misnomer, since they have all along possessed a place, which, by gradual diffusion, is continually changing into something else (Brody, 1987, pp. 140–143).

It is also worth noting that among these northern hunting people there are no kings, chieftains, or tribal elders. Equally, there are no institutions of authority or any organization of power. The old are respected for their wisdom and listened to, but their suggestions may equally be disregarded. Shamans are likewise respected for their skills and expertise, as are specially successful hunters. But neither hunters nor shamans are necessarily obeyed. For, in any case, as Brody points out, it is considered that no individual can speak on behalf of another, neither parents for their children, nor an older person for his family group. No individual makes or enforces the law; and it is important to note that all of these people—the shamans, the hunters, the old people—' . . . possess powers but not power. They have expertise but not authority' (p. 115).

What can be taken from this example is not only the effortless and stageless progression of child into adult, but the total acceptance of personal rights, however individual. The value put upon expertise and its attainment is also obvious, while at the same time there is an absence of any accompanying control of others. The entry of the twentieth century into the Arctic has, no doubt, modified this picture.

Jean Liedloff (1975) made strikingly similar observations from her years spent among the Yequana Indians of South America of the way in which the young grow into their place in society. Of this process, she writes:

> Each age group (of children) grasps the conceptual structures appropriate to its development, following in the footsteps of the children a little older than themselves until they have a full complement of verbal thought forms able to take in adult views and the whole content which has been available to them since their infancy.

and:

> One of the most striking differences between the Yequana and any other children I have seen is that they neither fight nor argue between themselves. There is no competitiveness and leadership is established on the initiative of the followers. [pp. 92–93]

CHAPTER THREE

On and off Crete

Lord Minos

I have written of the old king as a mythic example of the negative aspect of a *senex* archetype, and of the hero as the *puer* who replaces him, following his initiation. I have also suggested that there are other ways in which change might be imaged as taking place. What can be seen of this in the story of Icarus? From whom is he flying? To what is he a reaction?

He and his father have put on wings to escape from within the Cretan labyrinth to which they had been confined by Minos, the lord of that empire. If Minos is King of Crete, is he then also an 'old king'? Have *senex* attitudes hardened his rule and his attitudes? Is it to this that Icarus, the *puer*, responds by reaching for the skies? So what of Minos's story, and what can be seen there?

Zeus chased after the maiden Europa, who took on the shape of a cow to escape his clutches. But the sky god, in the guise of a bull, mounted her. Minos, the result of this rape, became king of Crete and was responsible for the establishment of a sea-faring and trading empire that spread across the whole Mediterranean. He rid that same sea of the piracy that infested it, and was renowned for his justice as a lawgiver. The success of the empire was also due to Minos taking good care to appease Poseidon, the sea god, until greed got the better of him.

Poseidon once sent ashore a splendid bull for the king to sacrifice back to the god. Minos thought the bull so magnificent that he put it in his own herds, taking an inferior animal to the temple instead. But one cannot deceive a god in this way with impunity. Poseidon now made sure that Pasiphaé, Minos's wife, would lust after the same bull so greatly that she must couple with it. Accordingly, she asked the court craftsman, Daedalus, to make her a wooden frame covered with cow hide in which she could lie, in order to be impregnated by the bull, thus reversing the Zeus/Europa union. As a result, she gave birth to the Minotaur, whose head and torso were those of a bull, while his arms and lower parts were human. Minos, so ashamed by this evidence of his wife's unnatural infidelity, now ordered Daedalus to build a high-walled labyrinth in which the creature could be hidden from sight. Within this maze, the Minotaur began eating human flesh.

Every seven years the city of Athens, as a punishment for the death of one of Minos's sons, had to send a tribute of fourteen youths to Crete to feed the Minotaur. On one occasion Theseus, prince of Athens, came with the group, meaning to kill the beast. He was helped by Ariadne, Minos's daughter, who had fallen in love with him. She obtained from Daedalus a ball of twine, which would enable the prince to pass both into and out of the labyrinth without getting lost. At the centre, he strangled or stabbed the Minotaur, then fled from Crete, taking Ariadne with him; he later abandoned her on the island of Naxos, where she died.

Minos, now doubly annoyed with his craftsman, made sure that Daedalus was himself imprisoned in the labyrinth, along with his young son Icarus. Since there was no obvious way out of this predicament, Daedalus invented and constructed wings for them both, with the help of which they flew from the island. But all did not end happily, as is well known, for Icarus, disobeying his father's instructions, flew too close to the sun. Its blazing heat melted the soft wax that held the feathers of his wings in place and he fell to his death in the ocean. Daedalus, however, escaped to safety. Minos, now more angry still, searched the cities of the Mediterranean for the errant craftsman, finding him at last in Sicily. There it was Daedalus himself who helped the daughters of his new royal patron to bring about the death of Minos, after which the Cretan empire disintegrated.

This story makes clear that, in addition to empire-building, judgementalism, and a wish to hang on to power, Minos possesses yet another attribute of the old king image. He has become so full of his own importance and belief in his own rightness as to think that he can do whatever he likes, even to the extent of trying to fool the gods: the sweet smell of success. It is a measure of his *hubris* and departure from 'right living' that he behaves in this way; and for this reason he is punished, losing Poseidon's protection. His beloved Ariadne is stolen away and left to die by one of Poseidon's own sons, Theseus.

It is strikingly significant that, through all of this, Daedalus is intimately involved: first in the conception of the Minotaur, then in that creature's confinement, followed by its death. Finally, it is he who brings about the old king's death, which is followed by a renewal that appears in the story, however, only as the disintegration of an empire.

On Crete, at the king's court, Daedalus just does what is asked of him, without question or moralizing. He acts the servant to his patrons. But when he is confined (as old kings themselves are confined by their circumstances) then, of his own imagining, he finds a way out. Daedalus not only paints himself into a corner, but he escapes that predicament by exercising his own ability and ingenuity. The *senex* within Daedalus is, by these means, overcome. It appears that he is capable of freeing himself from his own imprisonment—for the labyrinth is of his own making—without outside help. Like Beowulf, he can dethrone his own *senex*.

Daedalus is the possessor, above all things, of expertise, though he lacks power; yet he has skills that he controls, without controlling others: he is an author who disdains authority. Is it these crafts (seen also in the Esquimaux) which Minos—who judges, and who has power, authority, and control in abundance—lacks? Is it in search of these qualities, in the person of Daedalus, that he scours the Mediterranean? Are these the attributes without which he is incomplete and yet, in finding them, must die for?

This is no hero tale. Minos does not return as a young king. His empire is not renewed. Instead, it splinters into kaleidoscopic pieces. In this dramatic end, the ever-recurring cycle of old king/young king, *senex/puer,* with their implied identity of opposites, is broken out of; and it is the crafty Daedalus who brought about that feat. Although at all times the servant of many people, yet he still remains intact, though ever moving on. He himself is neither hero nor old king: not *senex* or *puer,* although he partakes of both. In his totality, however, he stands over and above their divisions, although his actions bring about renewal of a different kind, which is expressed by disintegration.

So, by re-searching the life and nature of Daedalus himself and what it means to be a craftsman, it may be possible to discover some of the secrets of non-initiatory renewal that the old king image within the psyche cries out for, if he is not simply to be replaced by his younger clone. Nor is Daedalus just, in Hillman's term, 'senex et puer'. His is a nature and an image that goes far beyond the healing of that split, as I shall show in what follows.

The disintegration that he brings about is also a part of his nature, which must be stayed with and tolerated.

Flying without falling

Icarus can be, and has been, described as an immature and mother-bound youth, held within some maternal labyrinth, dreaming his dreams of the outside world. By escaping, he refuses to be held by the psychological ground that is mother, acting instead the high-flyer who scorns the voice of moderation. Then, transient as any male ant or drone bee whose mating flight is the supreme moment and meaning of existence, he falls back into the maternal sea and a welcomed oblivion. Nothing is known of the lad before his imprisonment with his father. He lives, it seems, but to fly and to fall, which is the sum of his whole existence. In this fantasy we could imagine his descent as the detumescence of the mother–lover who has given his all: the orgasm as 'a little death'.

But islands, mazes, and labyrinths are not necessarily always maternal symbols: nor is the ocean of the king of the sea a feminine image. The Cretan empire was a construction of Minos, whose slave Icarus's mother was, and at whose command the labyrinth was built by Daedalus. Using a different metaphor, this captivating maze expresses the power and the containing structures of the *senex,* which prevents youth from experiencing its own freedom, flexing its muscles, reaching for the sky. Lads can be castrated by their fathers.

Yet, paradoxically, it is the self-same prison that produces flight. When the horizontal path is blocked, then the vertical must take over. If there is no rational or possible way out, the impossible and non-rational make itself available. Within this image, it is the construction of the *senex* to which abandoned flight is a corrective, whether that rigidity is imagined as walls or words of caution, prison or careful navigation.

To fly or not?

When I say that flying is good or bad for you, I am caught once more within the polarity issue previously discussed, which Jung cautioned against and to which his own ambiguous and contradictory style of writing is such a powerful corrective. Flying is as bad for Icarus as it is good for him, just as I can experience falling as becoming grounded, or else as a deathly lack of spirit and airy fantasy. To put it another way, there is nothing intrinsically wrong with flying. It is a natural activity that has existed since the pterodactyls. Birds fly; and many insects live a life of flight that is quite different from the few moments of triumph experienced by flying ant or male bee.

In Greek myth there were both those who flew through the air in positive aspect (Hermes, Iris, Perseus, Pegasus) and those whose flight was negative (Harpies, Gorgons, the Furies). It often seems as if it is only young men aspiring to flight in general and approaching the overbright sun in particular who come to a fiery end (Icarus, Phaeton).

But the present story provides us with the image of another who flew and, moreover, flew on to safety. Daedalus got away with it; and so, in this context, we can say that it is only Icarian flight that falls and kills. Daedalus—father, craftsman, executive of his patron Minos—flies without falling to land westward at Cumae, where straight away he dedicates his wings upon the altar of the self-same Apollo who had just slain Icarus, the daring and impatient son. And yet, the Daedalus who lands and acts in this way is a very different person from the man who took off, for now he has lost his son in death. Later, I shall discuss the meaning of that death and how it changed his nature.

Dorothy dreamed:

I am swimming through the air, above ground, accompanied by a fish. I know it is risky, but I can't get down. The fish disappears. I try again to swim down but find myself drifting up towards some powerlines, in which I get tangled. I fear that this is dangerous, and especially so if I try to manoeuvre across on to the pylons so as to climb to earth. Next thing, I am down, but don't know how I got there. I have been injured: feel sick and know I will always feel like that till the day I die. Nonetheless, I feel pleased at having reached ground level.

Dorothy was a person who had felt, all of her life, like 'a fish out of water'. Her parents had repeatedly said to her such things as 'What makes you think *your* opinions have any value?', which she had believed. As a result, she had grown up never feeling that she knew any tricks for the trade of living and relating to others—though everyone else seemed to. She considered that she had drifted through life, though in fact she was very able at her work and very determined. Swimming in the air was, she felt, a very good image of how it felt to be her. But when the fish disappears, then the swimming is different. Now it takes her towards the power, just as Icarus felt attracted to the open sky and the power of the sun. To tangle with it is all very well, but is she able to bring that power [German: *Kraft*] back to earth, when earthing the electricity carried by the lines will burn her up? Somehow it *is* done (without knowing how the trick was performed) and she lives, though ill. That feeling reminded her of how she felt when one of her children committed suicide aged 18. I pointed out to her that this was indeed a wound she would have to carry for life, but that it seemed from the dream not to carry the finality which she had felt since it happened.

In a similar fashion, Daedalus is wounded by Icarus's death, yet he has flown and landed and will live on.

This book spins outwards from that moment above the Aegean sea when the paths of the two men diverge. Icarus, cavorting, flies as if to hit the sun, then, scorching, falls and drowns. Daedalus, having buried the youth upon the island of Ikarios, continues his forward movement towards landfall, in a path that takes him neither soaring nor skimming, nor too far North or South, but just right. I make no value judgements as to whether this was good sense or boring caution, but operate imaginatively and repeatedly, in a manner suggested by Hillman, upon the instant thus evoked. 'When . . . then', I can say, or 'Only . . . if', to find myself faced with such statements as:

When Daedalus builds, then Icarus flies.

When Icarus dies, then Daedalus flies on to safety.

When Daedalus flies with moderation, then his son cannot.

Only if Icarus dies, can Daedalus hang up his wings.

If *puer* flies and crashes, then *senex* gives thanks.

Only if *puer* catches fire, can *senex* land safely.

All these can be said and many more about the father/son flight, for all are true and none is right, or more correct than any other (correctness being a fantasy of the *senex* alone). The truth, from the father's viewpoint, is:

Only if Icarus goes his own way can Daedalus escape confinement.

Each of the two movements (horizontal caution and vertical aerobatics) is essential and inherent one to the other. We may take none of the above statements as primary or exclusive, but only as relative to the attitude of the observing consciousness, when trying to be true to a law of psychic relativity of which these statements are themselves an expression.

Modern physicists insist that statements about the position and speed of bodies in space are relative to the position of observation. Jung similarly remarks that an image is only symbolic to a consciousness that is capable of seeing it symbolically, otherwise it remains a sign (*CW 6*, para. 814). The viewer's psychological position is involved. An archetypal theory of events-in-the-world states, moreover, that the same events can be described using totally different terms, depending upon the archetypal viewpoint that the observer possesses at the time. Thus, a *senex* perspective will be different from a *puer* view of the same occurrence. *Puer* describes Daedalus in flight as a fuddy-old-duddy, whereas *senex* commends his caution. *Senex* dismisses Icarus as a wayward fool, while *puer* yells "Right on!" And both views can be held or expressed by the same human being.

Neither and both are correct and plausible; and if that were all, there would be no book, but merely another recognition of the paradoxical nature of psychic reality as expressed through the metaphors of Greek mythology. But there is more to it than that, for the instant in the air described above forms but a single episode in the life of Daedalus. He is his own peculiar person and *not* just a representative of the *senex* or any other single archetype. There is a before and an after to his tale; and labyrinth, flight, fall, and safe landing are only a few of the elements in a story that begins with his birth in Athens and ends with his settling on the island of Sardinia. Along the way there are episodes that bear no reference to his son, or to Minos. Indeed, the escape from Crete is the only moment in which Icarus figures. The boy has a relative unimportance with regard to the complete tale, though at the same time being a vital part of it.

To try to understand what Daedalus might mean for the history of the king/hero or *senex/puer* pairs, then what needs looking at is his existence as a whole, not just the single part of it that is so well known. My focus is on the man himself, as related to various and numerous others. My concern is with Daedalus as a psychic image in his own right and not just as an adjunct to the *puer,* Icarus.

The individual and the field

I should first emphasize that Daedalus is neither god, nor hero, but all human, so he cannot represent an 'archetype-per-se'. There are, however, gods, goddesses, and heroes contained within and as background to the story, who can be regarded in this way. His whole life, then, can be seen as an individual enactment of archetypal patterns in the world—that is to say, as archetypal images and their individual workings. The tale tells how mortal people, or animals, interact with other mortals, so it can also be said to be describing conscious awareness and activities, only indirectly affected by any archetypal ground.

Daedalus himself is but one element in all of this. He has a certain priority, of course, in that it is his life; but to focus only upon him would be to get stuck in one identification only. It would be to see it through *his* eyes only, as if that were the only way of doing it. The imaginal whole, with its contrasting or conflicting views, should at all times stay within sight as well, for each element is important. In what follows, I shall refer to the totality of those versions as '*DAIDALOS*', using the Greek spelling in order to differentiate the archetypal field from the individual, Daedalus, whose story it is.

I do so, using the same convention as that in which a person who appears in their own dream is named 'the dream-ego'. The dreamer will be but one of the figures who make up the psychic totality that the dream presents. The dream-ego is of importance as an image of the sleeper's consciousness, but its value is that of first among equals. I, in my dreams, represent my own attitudes when awake, as seen from the perspective of the dream itself, which is my own unconscious archetypal ground. The dream-ego is not the boss: it should not always be considered to rule the dream; and it can sometimes seem to be unbelievably wrong or deluded. The dream is-as-it-is. So, too, in the examination here, Daedalus the father, metalworker, craftsman, is only a single personification of those who go to make up *daidalos*.

Daedalus, moving through *daidalos,* I can call the 'myth-ego'—that is to say, a conscious attitude that can look at the world as mythic and see itself as embedded within story. *Daidalos* is telling us how that conscious way of being (Daedalus) looks from a mythic ground that is closer to ultimate reality.

I have pointed out that Daedalus is not identical with the total image, which is made up of other people, places, things, and happenings. But it is also important to realize that they are all totally necessary, if the story is to be just as it is. Change any item, and we have another image. The presence of an unknown red-headed man with a cigar in my dream suggests something altogether different from my father, with his balding head, appearing pipe in hand. The meaning of the dream is changed accordingly, and the minor details are just as crucial for this as are more obvious ones.

Any whole is always more than just a sum of its constituent parts, and each element inheres, articulates, and co-responds to all others, like the members of a system, a family, or a gang. Group dynamics operate, it seems, within archetypal fields, just as at home, the office, or the clinic. And yet such an articulation should not be regarded as autocratic, final, once for all, which would be to deny the kind of psychic relativity I am concerned with. Four children of the same parents will readily describe four different families, containing dissimilar webs of relationship between the family members, in different, often contradictory ways, and each description is a 'true' picture.

In this examination of *daidalos,* Ovid's telling, which focusses on the flight from Crete, is only one. There are other, sometimes conflicting, sources; but their contradictions give further insight.

For instance, there is scholarly uncertainty as to whether the name 'Daedalus' is derived from the verb '*daio*', which means to kindle, burn, cut, or from '*dao*', to teach, or to learn (Room, 1983, p. 108). Surely it matters which is correct, for kindle, burn, cut, teach, learn are very different activities? And so it may for the classical scholar, but to a mythic way of looking, the matter can remain teasingly indeterminate. For each derivation only tells us more about the man and what he represents. He is to do with the gaining as well as the giving of knowledge, while he is associated with some burning intensity that can flare up in a nature that will also slice, divide, sever, and isolate.

Further than this, as *daidalos* is retold by transposing elements, reversing the order, or looking at pieces on their own to establish similarities as well as differences, the story becomes re-mythologized and, in the process, each reader's connection to it will be remade. This is done using the same operations with which archetypal psychologists illuminate otherwise opaque material. They allow the image to work its power upon the observer by its own proper activity of imagination (see Hillman, 1977, 1978, 1979b).

In fact, I believe that any work upon a psychic image is imaginative, even though it might be presented as historical truth, observed fact, or even proven theory. On the other hand, to impose a single viewpoint upon such material is to be untrue to its richness, by constricting it to a particular conscious stance.

It is not easy to work this way: failure is always likely, or the effort can be misunderstood. Nevertheless, in what I write, the truth of statements and insights will be affirmed and as readily denied, various alternatives being held up to view as of equal value. I shall be engaged in an un-making of the tale, while keeping the ingredients; for to do so is to take up a position closer to the phenomena described and to unconscious, archetypal dynamics, where time stands still—or at least does not only run in a straight line from past to present. On earth, stories and histories unfold; they are diachronic, having a finite beginning, a middle, and an end. *Daidalos* I shall look at synchronically, where time is circular and we begin where we like, without an end in view, for the process itself is all-important. This is the once-upon-a-time land of fairy tale, the sacred time of rite and celebration: an ab-original dreamtime.

But, as words are things and not processes, and as sentences, paragraphs, and books must both start and finish, I shall move between the two realms (synchronic and diachronic), no doubt confusingly—confusion being a *puer* delight—rather than just seeking straightforward *senex* differentiation. Overall, I shall try to act mythically, thinking concretely but not concretizing thoughts.

The kaleidoscope

This way of looking could be called kaleidoscopic [Gr: *kalos* = beautiful, *eidos* = image, *skopos* = a mark for shooting at]. Staring through the kaleidoscope, I see an entrancing image in sight. With a flick of the wrist it is gone, but another, equally beautiful, takes its place; and another, and another, and again! The very same elements and shapes make up as many different images as I care to aim at; and each has a beauty, peculiar to itself, which acts upon the vision of the watcher. Those operations (those flicks of the wrist), which multiply the images immeasurably, serve to deepen a sense of the meaning in the material elements thus manipulated. The kaleidoscope provides not only a beautiful mark to aim at, but also the chance to try a beautiful marking out, or a marking down, of that image. For the skill of the operator can become as beautiful as the object sighted. And in this case I am concerned with the kaleidoscopic image of 'well-craftedness' [Gr: *daidalos*].

For Lévi-Strauss (1962), the kaleidoscope is an image of the concrete logic belonging to the thinking of pre-literate humanity. The instrument is, he says: '. . . an instrument which contains bits and pieces by means of which structural patterns are realised' (p. 36). It is a process he has called *'bricolage'*, from the verb *'bricoler'*, to make a sudden change of direction owing to a chance encounter, as in: '. . . a ball rebounding, a dog straying, a horse swerving from its direct course to avoid an obstacle' (p. 16).

Mythical thought, says Lévi-Strauss, is a kind of 'intellectual bricolage'; and a person who is involved in such activity becomes a *'bricoleur'*, who is, he says: ' . . . still someone who works with his hands and uses devious means compared with those of a craftsman' (Lévi-Strauss, 1962, p. 16). I shall argue later that deviousness is, very much a part of craftedness, but for now, I quote this statement, by the translator of *The Savage Mind,* that:

> The bricoleur has no precise equivalent in English. He is a man who undertakes odd jobs and is a jack-of-all-trades or a kind of professional do-it-yourself man, but . . . he is of a different standing from for instance, the English 'odd job man' or handyman. [Lévi-Strauss, 1962, p. 17n]

Nevertheless, in French department stores, the D.I.Y. section is labelled: *'Bricolage'*.

A person who understood the nature of this kind of activity very well was the English painter, sculptor, filmmaker, writer, critic, and poet, Michael Ayrton. In my opinion he even provided us with an English word for *bricolage,* to describe a number of essays, collected together in the book which he entitled: *Fabrications* (Ayrton, 1972). The term used by Lévi-Strauss never gets a mention within its covers, yet Ayrton's whole book is a superb act of *bricolage,* starting with a dedicatory page, which looks like this:

In history there are no reserved areas in which the ordinary laws of evidence may be suspended as documents which are exempt from the ordinary rules of source criticism. If there were such privileged areas or documents, how would we define them?

H. R. Trevor-Roper
The Spectator 21 February 1971

As fabrications

Michael Ayrton
28 February 1971

The word 'fabric' only secondarily means a woven textile. Originally, it referred to *any* product of skilled workmanship (*OED*). Its Latin root is, however, the word *'faber'* meaning a smith or worker in metal. So, to fabricate is to indulge in skilled workmanship, while a fabrication is the result of such activity. Current usage, however, also adds that a fabrication of words is a story untrue to the facts, namely a lie. At the end of his book, in 'Facts: A Postscript', Ayrton (1972) writes:

> The historian peers at his quarry by means of the shaft of light cast by his learning and powered by his research, eschewing the densities of darkness which inevitably surround his cone of verifiable vision and which lie uncharted, a *terra incognita* rearing islands of disconnected data from the bed of the past, some of which may dimly be discerned to be connected, but many of which lie among pools of inevitable incognition. The fabricator, on the other hand, gropes his way, in partial blindness and aided only by the handrail of proper scholarship and the white staff of his imagination with which he taps his lonely way, feeling for such tussocks of probability as may bear his weight. Perpetually at risk from quagmires, which could drag him down and drown him in ridicule, he explores this landscape, the duckboard of his imperfect memory squelching omminously beneath his wary feet. Upon his wayward journey he may find himself accused of manipulating the known to serve as markers in the unknown, however rebelliously he may mutter of pedantry to his accusers who practise the high calling of historiography itself. Nonetheless the fabricator's self-imposed duty is to convince sceptics of his claim that where he ventures is not *demonstrably* a mirage and that where he lies prone he at least extends experience. [pp. 220–221]

In English, Lévi-Strauss's (1962) book is called *The Savage Mind*, though the original French title was *La Pensée Sauvage* [*'pensée'* meaning 'thought' and *'sauvage'* 'wild']. But the latter word is derived from Latin *'silvaticus'* mean-

ing 'wooded' [*silva* is a wood or forest]. If the wooded is
considered to be 'wild', then where the forest has been
cleared, nature is correspondingly tamed, ordered, and controlled. What is savage or wild is therefore merely unculti-
vated, remote from settlement, outside the borders of the
known, beyond the pale. It is a '*terra incognita*' rather than
somewhere intrinsically dangerous, destructive, or primitive. *The Savage Mind* was written as a demonstration and
celebration of the fact that pre-literate man possessed a
well-articulated system of thinking that is certainly not
primitive, though it may appear as such to the cultured,
rational, western mind, which does not appreciate the sub-
tlety of its approach.

Ayrton, on the other hand, seems to be arguing that we
of the late twentieth century might, with benefit, adopt *La
Pensée Sauvage*. Such an attitude need not be looked at
with distaste, to slash and burn it into oblivion. For all its
tangled undergrowth, the forest contains a hidden order,
which is the orderliness of the ecological. That is to say, it
is an order of the mutual relationships of organisms with
their fellows and environment. The barbaric is only 'rude,
wild, and uncivilized' to the non-barbarian whose civilized
behaviour hides a blindness to and ignorance of the natural world, which is as amazing as it is shameful. In this
respect it is we who are barbarians, for we can neither read
nor write nor understand that 'wild' language which is the
language of life. The word 'barbarian' is onomatopoeic for a
stammer, as well as the sound that so-called 'civilized'
people believed that the 'wild people' made when speaking:
'bar–bar–bar = bar—'.

In this respect, Heraclitus said:

Eyes and ears are poor witnesses for men if their souls
do not understand the language. [Diels fragment 101a,
in Kahn, 1979, p. 106]

What he wrote is, in literal translation: 'If they have
barbarian souls'; and this is the first time in Western
thought, says Charles Kahn, that the word '*psyche*' [soul] is

used to denote the power of rational thought (Kahn, 1979, p. 107).

There should be no wish to throw away the ability to think logically, at which it has taken human consciousness so long to arrive. But neither should there be denial or discredit of a person's own innate ability to fabricate, to see kaleidoscopically, to speak barbarian, to have wild thoughts. However, as well as picking my way gingerly through the puddles and the mire, I must—in Ayrton's image—be prepared to fall flat on my face in the mud. Though maybe humiliating, even that will, he says, extend knowledge, by my own horizontal length.

Lévi-Strauss (1962) also points out that the bits and pieces within any kaleidoscope are the products of breaking up other objects, or offcuts from their making.

> They can no longer be considered entities in their own right in relation to the manufactured objects of whose 'discourse' they have become the indefinable debris. [p. 36]

These pieces can, within the confines of the kaleidoscope, provide patterns which are wholly new and unique, having no real relationship to the outside world, but merely to one another. And yet:

> . . . particular objective structures such as those of snow crystals or certain types of radiolaria and diatomaceae might be revealed. [pp. 36–37]

In other words, the images in view may remind the viewers of other things. They need not therefore always confine themselves to the natural boundaries of the psychic image itself, for to do so would be to deny access to insights or information that might be part of the raw material for fabrication, brought to mind by 'the duckboard of imperfect memories'. As I peer through the kaleidoscope of my mind, the thing seen may remind me of other images, or suggest other shapes, just as ink blots do. These are not contained within the original image, but come to me through its contemplation. 'Amplification' was Jung's word for it, by which he meant the bringing in of other similar archetypally induced material to increase the understanding of what is unclear. This can also be a part of working-with-images, even if it takes me far away. For example, since Daedalus is a metal-worker, then mythological motifs of mining, smelting, casting, polishing can only tell me more about what it means to relate to him as an archetypal image within me, and thus about *daidalos* as a whole. In this respect, an *'Einfall'* must be allowed for, a German word for which there is no exact English equivalent. In the *Standard Edition* of Freud's works, it is translated, in a rather pedestrian way, as 'free association'. In fact, it denotes something that 'drops into' conscious awareness unbidden, when you might be concentrating upon a subject to which the *Einfall* has a hidden, unconscious connection—which is, of course, the nature of a free association.

While concerned with *daidalos,* it will be important to allow wild thoughts and monstrous fantasies if occasioned in the magic mirror of the imagination. Their irruption into consciousness does not have to be justified by 'ordinary laws of evidence'. The very materialization of the phantasm is enough. All that *is* demanded is that, however far away another tack should lead, it must be followed by a return to, a sticking with, the image itself, which was the point of departure.

Not about the women

It is hard to think of Daedalus without being reminded of his seemingly more memorable son Icarus. Even the rest of the story concerns men only, at first glance. There certainly appears to be a relative lack of importance of the female figures. The story operates more often within a generational fantasy, rather than being about male/female conjunction. The images concerned are those of father, uncle, son, king, subjects, age, and youth, rather than those that emphasize difference of gender. There is no making of happy marriages in this story. Ariadne, the daughter of King Minos of Crete, is deserted and dies: in itself an image of the value given to the feminine. Since Jung's psychology sets great store upon the conjunction of the male and female, the so-called mystic marriage, it is possible to wonder about the 'absent feminine' in respect of Daedalus and his whole story. Without a 'her', is he a flawed and chauvinistic man?

A different view would be to say that the tale is-as-it-is: that it operates mainly within a masculine framework, because this is the gender of Daedalus himself; and so it must be ludicrous to demand larger roles for the feminine characters of the story. For if this were to happen, we would have a different image altogether, as already pointed out above. Paint a moustache upon La Gioconda, and the image is not Leonardo's. Daedalus's story is-as-it-is, his flight path passing between fixed boundaries. The pieces within a kaleidoscope are that which they are, and the 'rules' of the instrument do not allow the addition of any new fragments to the existing mix nor regret for the lack of any that are not there—though the mixture that does exist can make many different patterns, satisfying thereby the laws of psychic relativity. If the feminine plays little part in this story, I do not *have* to demand a greater part for her—or, at least, to do so is but one reading of the drama.

Indeed, although the archetypal images that arise in each person may possess a gender—are male or female— yet these are secondary sex characteristics as far as the images themselves are concerned. The relationship of female and male is itself symbolic of 'difference', imaged in the same way that the two sexes are different. 'Archetypes-per-se', if they exist as such within the deep unconscious, possess no gender, just as Yang is not masculine, nor Yin feminine. It is only when that which the archetype repre-sents appears as an image in our individual psyche that it may express its differences in this fashion, by clothing itself in a particular gender. Hence, *kore* and *puer* are different as we experience them, yet what they share is youth and non-maturity. They are both images of asexuality—but, on the other hand, images that can be seen as subtly different because they possess different genders. What that difference represents and how it can be experienced, I shall deal with later.

Another way of looking at the difference is that of the Greek historian Hesiod, who informs us that men and women are deintegrates of an original spherical, hermaphroditic creature. Thus masculine and feminine, as images, are those of a whole that has divided and separated into dissimilar parts. In this understanding, the mystic marriage, the union of opposites, or whatever we care to call it, is an image for the experience of being in tandem, for the healing of split archetypes and the coming together of what was of necessity previously divided. But that is not the only way that the essential union of opposites can be imagined. The stance which this book assumes is to accept that even when objects are widely separated, the one half is *always* implied by, 'aware of', and connected to the other. But when looking closely at one figure of the pair, it is not always possible to see the other figure so clearly, if at all.

In much the same way in physics, Heisenberg's uncertainty principle states that if the position of a subatomic particle is measured, the observer cannot, at the same time, be certain of its speed or momentum. The reverse would also be true.

And in this respect, Heraclitus said, 'Night and day they are as one' (D. 57, Kahn, 1979, p. 107), by which he meant that the hours of darkness and of light made up a unity, though each time was of a different quality to the other. Each therefore implies the existence of the other: dark requires light. At different times of the year each will last for a variable amount of time; yet the unity of the two is always twenty-four hours long. The Greek word for this overall unit of time was '*nykthemeros*'. Although English has no equivalent, other languages do: e.g. Swedish '*dygn*'.

In addition, by daylight I am aware that night is just around the corner, while knowing also, during the depths of darkness, that dawn is on the way. It would be absurd, at noon, to demand more darkness on the grounds that this is now a one-sided condition. Nor, if I study daytime on its own, should I expect to receive complaints that to do so is only a partial and unintegrated exercise. At least there is nothing amiss in my doing so, if at the same time I accept the essential unity, as well as interplay, of opposites, which was Heraclitus's profound statement 2500 years ago.

In an exactly similar way, I find it inappropriate, when examining a mainly masculine set of archetypal imagery such as *daidalos,* to be presented with a demand for 'more feminine please'. Responding to such a call would be a way of behaving that emphasized deficiencies rather than the actual existential state of Daedalus himself. It is one of my intentions to examine the field as it is, which means accepting a relative absence of the female in what is therefore a predominantly male field. At the same time I hold on to the overall unity of the two (male and female), which is at all times implied.

PART TWO

THE STORY

CHAPTER FOUR

New ways
for old tales

On introducing story

I n this part of the book, I aim to try to understand the story of Daedalus, within his own mythic field, both in general and in its own particularity; I hope to present it to the reader in a way that feels convincing. It will be a detailed map of *daidalos* so that I hope each person approaching it will take on, at times, the cloak of Daedalus as that man passes through his own story, making it and crafting it as he goes. But first, how did he get there? How did it all come into being?

Of entry and origins

Birth, as well as being a historic event, in mythologems just as in life, can act as a point of entry into the field we are studying: that is to say, *daidalos*. Unlike biological birth it has, however, no in-built priority over any other entrance. It is just different from others. An examination of this field could as well have begun with Daedalus at

Camicus, the arrival of the Poseidon bull, or the fall of Icarus. That youth's death has, in fact, acted like a stone thrown into a still pond, disturbing the surface, so that attention ripples outwards, where and how it will. I could just as well have begun elsewhere. But one thing that birth will bring with it, which other entries lack, is a sense of origins.

Births involve and imply parents, ancestors, family trees, and a sense of historical continuity. Birth is particular. It tells from whom, or from where each infant came, and when. And it does so within the psyche too, even though elapsed time may be absent from the deep unconscious, although each image, examined more closely, more deeply, can be found to have a nature that shades off into others.

For example, in fantasy, the tree may be something upon which the young son–lover hangs himself—that is to say, the mother. But the tree is also an image of the father with an erect penis, while representing, in addition, the world axis. As suggested above, it is the family tree and also the passage of time, pictured with its branches and fruit-bearing expansion. The tree is growth, just as it is also the cross and gallows of death and extinction. And there is also the tree of everlasting life, in addition to the tree of the knowledge of good and evil. There is no such thing as a single tree. The image shades off onto others. It would, indeed, be nice to have a simple one-to-one correspondence, where one image represents only one thing; but, archetypally, matters are always this and that, as well as the other. Either *and* or rule, although each particular image will be unique and different.

Taking another stance, I might say that where the edges of archetypal fields overlap and coalesce, they form fresh entities at these interfaces, which are themselves archetypes. These are not new creations, for, in a sense, all archetypes partake of each other and always have done. It is within the 'no-man's land' between the borderlines that previously unexpected configurations occur. Thus the tree as image is formed from the conjunction of other archetypal energies, which bear with them their own separate natures.

The margins of the field of *daidalos* are its parents. To examine the origins of Daedalus more closely, from whom he descends, what he inherits and takes in from various sources, and thereby to concentrate upon him (as myth ego of the larger whole) is to differentiate the field. Yet its unity remains, intact. Within this fantasy, the family tree becomes a pyramidal structure, whose apex (whether pointing up or down or to either side does not matter) becomes the individual in question. The person is the result and a resolution of those myriad influences. In our case, that unique event is *daidalos,* with its representative here on earth, that is to say in consciousness, Daedalus.

Of that man, we can say, variously, that his father was Eupalamos (good with hands) or Metion (knowledgeable), and that both were sons of Erechtheus, king of Athens. An earlier ancestor still, Erichthonios, was born of the semen of Hephaestus, the craftsman god, when that impatient lover was pushed aside by Athene. It had been the smith's mighty hammer that split open father Zeus's skull, thus allowing the goddess to be born. For this deed, it seems, he expected sexual favours in return, only to be thwarted: his seed impregnating the ground itself. The earth-born child, Erichthonios, with lower limbs of twined snake tails, was given to Athene in a covered basket to be nursed by her and the daughters of Kekrops, who was then king of Athens. Possibly, these names imply an 'earth-shaker', from the union of the verb *erecthein* [to shake] with *chthon* [earth] (Room, 1983). This suggestion allies the snake-man with Poseidon, one of whose epithets was 'Gaiochos', meaning the same [*gaia,* earth, *ochein,* to shake] (Kerényi, 1951a, p. 181). Karl Kerényi also reveals the sexual under-tones of that epithet and elsewhere tells the story of Poseidon ejaculating while asleep on the Attic earth; he also impregnated the ground, from which sprang the horse, not known until then upon mainland Greece. Perhaps the sea god was also involved in an attempted rape of Athene, for he was certainly in conflict with her over who should be patron god of the region of Attica. In that contest, judged by Kekrops, Poseidon either struck a salt spring from the ground, or else put forward the horse. Yet Athene won the prize by producing the bountiful olive tree. Harness for these horses of the sea god, and a chariot for them to pull, were later invented by Erichthonios, thereby making these strange, unbridled creatures useful.

So Daedalus's ancestor presents the image of a person who harnesses and utilizes what came from the sea, wild and untrammelled, as well as being himself a creature of the earth. Kerényi reveals that all these stories were, in reality, re-imaginings of the birth of Kekrops himself, half-man and half-serpent, who sprang fatherless from the red earth. Kekrops, he says, represents the Attic pottery, born of clay, taken from mother earth. He always possesses a two-fold nature, being part man, part god, part human and part animal, as well as being both male and female. The marriage of humans was this king's invention, though he later placed it under the patronage of his nurse Pallas Athene. In all of these attributes, Kekrops can be seen as the union, within a single image, of two widely differing aspects as well as of the ability to hold such differences together within the body of one person (Kerényi, 1959, p. 209ff).

On his father's side, then, a god-descended and goddess-nursed Erechtheid, Daedalus possessed three possible mothers: either Merope [meaning 'endowed with speech' and therefore human instead of animal], Alcippe ['mighty mare'], or Iphinöe ['great mind']. Little else is known about these conflicting matrices, for they share with the females in this story a tendency to seem peripheral to the main action. It is possible that they are all by-names for Athene herself.

It is clear from both parents, however, that as in much Greek mythology, uncertainty rules, which is, at the same time, an approach to ancestry in keeping with the archetypal fantasy of origins of fields. Uncertainty is both an ambiguousness as well as a putting together of diverse elements, which then form some fresh image. Such origins can be variously imagined.

Once born, the snake-men, Kekrops, Erichthonios, or even Daedalus are all within the realm of Athene as nurse and tutor. She herself had been born fully grown, clothed, and armed from her father's head, after he had swallowed Metis, her mother, for fear that she would produce the son who would supplant him. An alternative genealogy for Athene mentions Metion as father and a woman called Daedale as mother. In addition, as epithets, she bore the names 'Areia' and 'Hephaestia', to denote her patronage of the warlike as well as a close connection with crafts such as spinning, weaving, pottery (without which there could have been no metal-casting), and metallurgy itself. By these names she allies herself with the two sons of the goddess Hera, who were pictured on an Attic vase fighting before their mother, who sits bound to the throne her craftsman son had trickily made her. On the pot, Ares is labelled with an aggressive epithet, 'Enyalios', while Hephaestus bears the sign 'Daedalus' (Kerényi, 1974, p. 157).

But if Athene is nurse to the earth-born, if she is patroness of the city states and their flowering, if it is under her aegis that craftsmanship developed and flourished, there is also a darker side to the goddess, as indicated by her by-name 'Aglauros', which connects her with Persephone, as queen of the underworld and death. In this area belong her aggressive qualities as well as her patronage of heroes (Perseus, Diomedes, and Odysseus, for instance). And all of these conflicting attributes she carries as the supreme exemplar of her father Zeus's wisdom (possessed by him, we might guess, only as a result of his ingestion of Metis). As Kerényi (1978) says of her:

> To put it in more general terms, it is the bondedness of the feminine portion of humanity, and of the feminine part of each individual person *to the paternal origin*. [p. 44]

One of the things she represents is 'father-right': the requirement that daughters should provide their fathers with sons, but not compete with the paternal or filial creativity. Male/male inheritance is to be ensured without interference. Hence the patronage of heroes. For this purpose of handing-down, 'father's daughters' are, in a psychological sense, as necessary as the skilful orderliness that is a part of their inheritance. This is to be passed on, through their own bodies, neither changed nor elaborated upon, for the sons to work with and themselves advance. Athene is the container, the basket, the nursemaid, which ensures that this will come about. By father-birth and bondedness, imaged as Athene arising from the brow of Zeus under the insistent hammer blows of Prometheus and lame Hephaestus, the patriarchy passes on its inheritance. It will be for maleness to develop it, just as it was imaged as maleness that acted as midwife at its birth. Athene, in this sense, is not a craftsperson, but only able to provide the setting in which it may come about: a patroness.

This is the background of *daidalos*. There is godlike and human, as well as reptilian, ancestry. Mind and its knowledge are allied with capable hands, by premature ejaculation or nocturnal emission: a mode of mating that is passionate and impatient, or disconnected and unconscious, depending upon one's view. Each process is, at any rate, responsible for the production of unknown or unmentionable offspring (horse or snake-man), which will either be harnessed and made useful or humanized by undercover nursing in the basket. The products of the earth and of nature are altered by human abilities that once were only divine. There exist, in this genealogy, attributes of strangeness, of power, of skill, of knowledge and wisdom, allied with an inventiveness that will put these to work for the good of the human race—or for its ill, since not all is bright and sunny. There is also conflict, aggressivity, the underworld, and crippling. All are within the image that is Athene, for her aegis, the emblem of her shield, is said to be the flayed skin of her tutor, Pallas, and to bear upon it the petrifying head of the gorgon Medusa.

These attributes, all of them, will be found repeated, with variation and expansion of detail, throughout the field of *daidalos*. It is the ringing of their changes, their differentiation, that will serve to fill out the picture of well-craftedness. The image examined is the development of all these hints and possibilities, as performed by the imagination that is humanity's greatest craft.

But birth is not the only method by which new aspects enter our field, for there are many other people, places, or events quite unrelated to the myth ego that will appear in the story-telling. By their very appearance they become a part of that coalescence that is the whole. Sometimes what they represent has always been there but in a different guise. Take, for example, Cocalus, king of Camicus in Sicily, at whose court Daedalus shelters, having fled from Crete. Is he not something entirely new? And if so, what does his appearance herald, late on in the tale?

Yes, he is new in that he has not appeared before; but his name bears a relationship to the word for 'snail', which allies him at once with the Triton shell that Minos brings to Sicily to tempt into the open his master craftsman. The spiral shell connects us with the labyrinth below Cumae where the Apolline Sibyl lived and where Daedalus landed after his flight; as well as to the Cretan maze from which he escaped vertically, not traversing its passages. The Triton shell, which he now threads, within the confines of its walls, takes its name from the river Triton, who was another tutor of Athene. She herself sprang from the labyrinthine convolutions of her father's brain. And so perhaps there is nothing new under the sun that shines above Daedalus in flight, just different ways of experiencing or dealing with these elements: with the making human of what was once non-human and then internalizing it. This will depend upon the situation, the surroundings—and the observer.

By exit and disappearance

As they enter, so people and things also disappear from *daidalos* by death: they are also laid down or left behind. Similarly, there is an ending of the story too. All these can be imagined as a way out of the field or, alternatively, as limits to the current ways of imagining. Cocalus and the Triton shell are, in one sense, definitive images of maziness. They are 'the state of the art', though what each represents might easily be picked up and worked with at some future time. In this sense, diachrony and synchrony intertwine. But if things die or are deserted by the myth-ego as he passes through his own field, it does not mean that they no longer exist. What has been expressed can never be totally lost. The character or thing, as it was, is still latent within and implied by the field. Its developed nature inheres to *daidalos*.

For example, Naucrate, who mothers Icarus, remains implied, though hardly appearing at all and never making another entrance. I may come to terms with what she represents within me, but I never can lose it. As slave to a ruling power (Minos), she exists merely to mother sons, a debased form of father-right, which itself came before, in Athene, or with the daughters of Kekrops and is to be repeated with the princesses at Camicus, Cocalus's daughters. They, too, are father's girls (no mother is mentioned), but they display differences from Athene's or Naucrate's ways of expressing that image. These girls are unnamed and plural though sharing a father. As girls, they are non-mature and unmarried, and they play with toys and take delight in Daedalus, a doll-maker. But to keep him, when he reveals himself to Minos, they will kill that very 'sea power' who was Naucrate's master, and which is the very meaning of her name; that was something she could not do, in order to break free. In so doing, these daughters bring about a coalescence of Daedalus and Minos. They represent an ability within the maleness, now expressed as Cocalus/Daedalus, which can take on—take in—a Minos-nature. And since, by that union, all that the king 'carried' has become inherent to the myth-ego, Minos's structure, his empire, crumbles. But it disappears *only* at the surface, in the tale, its meaning remaining secretly within the whole, which is *daidalos*.

This effected, the daughters themselves pass from view, their role inherent by turn. They are replaced, when Daedalus moves to Sardinia, by the Daedalids, children fathered by the craftsman himself, when previously banished from Athens to another town in Attica. These children, of both genders within the myth-ego, will marry Herculids, or hero's children, to colonize a wild island and provide descendants. In this way, it is clear that each part-image of the field contains all that has been expressed elsewhere within it, while adding something that is singularly its own. Nothing in fact dies or is lost, for those words themselves can now be seen as images for all that is made one's own, is introjected, is internalized, or appertains.

Nevertheless, death *must* be a different image from disappearance and carry a different value. Those who die in the story are 'placed', it seems to me, exactly where they belong. They are reunited with what they had once been separated from, the Underworld, allowing a new process to 'flow'. But that will become clearer later on.

This way of looking at *daidalos,* as steadily containing more and more worked-out attributes that were once mere hints and then become implicit again, is the way of Greek tragedy, which employs a 'proleptic' approach. Anne Lebeck (quoted in Kahn, 1979) describes 'prolepsis' as a process whereby an initial elliptical or enigmatic statement increases in significance through repetition, moving by gradual development from riddle towards clarity of statement (p. 90). Alternatively, it reminds one of the individuation process as described by Jung. People grow truly to be themselves, he said, by realizing more of their unconscious potential, in the form of inner figures or internal objects and relationships. Following this, the need is to become 'decently unconscious' of them as they work their ways within. But I am not talking here of individuation as a collective process, or even as a personal and individual one. 'Individuation' is itself an archetypal process and one, I suggest, that can go on, not only in life, but within every psychic image as well.

Daidalos is unaware of itself and the complexities that go to make it up. It could not be otherwise. Only the human mind can reflect back to the image a picture of itself—a picture focused, framed, enlarged, developed by that individual consciousness. The elaboration of the image that I carry on by using my imagination is not simply for my amusement, though it would not matter if it were just that. Nor is it just done as something useful for my way through life. No: it is an act and an attitude that I owe to the images that spontaneously arise within me and which present themselves to me, whether I like them or not. It is a homage I must pay. I do not control which images seize my mind or when. But both they and I can benefit from the encounter. We are both changed as a consequence of our meeting and of the development that follows. It is an enhancement, using that word in its photographic sense of 'to raise in degree, to heighten'. This image intensification does not dissect or destroy the picture but provides instead more clarity and discrimination of detail and of its relationships within the whole.

In this respect, the Daedalids represent father-right in an essentially mundane way, rather than as godlike alone: a universal process made flesh. They are children of a father, yet able to separate from him and his views and ways, to settle elsewhere. They represent a new dimension to the myth-ego, which enables it truly to be itself, and to bear its own children, without a backward glance. What father says no longer holds, even though Daedalus is still among them. He has neither had to reject his children, nor to be rejected by them.

The value and necessity of reflecting upon all the significant elements as well as the seemingly trivial ones that enter or leave the story is clear. So, too, is the importance of the mode and timing of both entrance and exit. But *daidalos* also contains four great deaths in all of which Daedalus is closely implicated. They will be examined later, in greater detail, as will his own passing away from view.

CHAPTER FIVE

Introducing Daedalus

The man himself

I have examined the origins of Daedalus and the flowing together of attributes that are his original
inheritance; and now is the time to look at the nature
of the man himself, whose life started at Athens in this
way. The name itself was not originally a proper name.
'Every skilfully performed piece of workmanship was a
daidalon'; and although a noun, the word really refers to a
characteristic of the thing or things denoted. For example,
many wondrous buildings from an earlier era were known
as *daideleia*, or secondarily attributed to the man himself.
The great temple of Ptah at Memphis in Egypt, as well as
the conical Bronze Age towers found in Sardinia, were
daidala. Since Ptah was the Egyptian double for
Hephaestus, the temple already had connections with a
craftsman god (Kerényi, 1976, p. 44). *Daidala* were the
carved and clothed wooden dolls used in the cult of Hera on
Mount Kithairon (Kerényi, 1975, p. 162). The festival of

Great Daidala was held every sixtieth year, while the Little Daidala occurred every seventh lunar year—'*daidala*' being the name for the performance as well as the effigies that were carried within it. Two wooden models of female 'attendants' were made each year, so that by the time the little festival came around, the goddess had fourteen Tritonian nymphs, so-called, to carry her bath water. The festival represented the withdrawal of the goddess (the absent moon); later she was tempted into re-emergence by her worshippers, who carried around an effigy of her, known as 'the false Hera' or Daedale. The goddess came out of hiding because of her envy of all the attention given to the false Hera. In this way, the lost moon was also tempted into reappearing, as the goddess was tempted back into her marriage with Zeus. It is easily taken for a woman's ritual, since the bridegroom is never present in the same concrete way as the bride and her fourteen female attendants. And yet he is inherent and implied in the last action of the festival, when the Daidala and bridal chamber are all set on fire. Zeus *is* that flaring-up:

> (the) supreme God who even in a world of nature had a spiritual character of his own, a character that he had as lighting up, an ever-near invisible presence with which he stood ready to break in. [Kerényi, 1976, p. 147]

The re-kindling of the moonlight *is* the wedding with Zeus; to put it another way, a re-emergence of the goddess precedes and brings about a flaring-up, which is the only image of maleness, and which results in the moon's appearance as a swelling belly in the sky in the form of its waxing crescent. Typically, and perhaps chauvinistically, we do not complain of 'an absent masculine' in this myth. The relevance of this digression via Daedale will appear later on.

In the meantime, it is possible to recognize a progression from a thing or things well made—a Daidalon or Daidala—to those well performed—Daidalia; and the appearance of Daedalus and Daidale as authors of all these. It is the psychic process of personification, whereby inanimate objects and actions have life breathed into them, whereby gods become incarnate in humans and the previously unimaginable becomes mundane, all clothed in story. Hence the importance of the myth-ego, which we are taking as masculine, not because the ego is always masculine, and not because it is crafts*men* I am interested in, nor since well-craftedness is a 'men-only' thing; but because this is the story of Daedalus, and he is male.

It is clear from the above that well-craftedness sits on each side of the gender divide as well as of the animate/inanimate split. Well-craftedness is a property that may and does express itself in things, events, and processes, as well as persons. It could be said that it is archetypal.

Daedalus was, claims Bradford (1972), originally a carpenter or builder, but also the inventor of the saw, the axe, the plumbline, the gimlet, glue, and isinglass. He was the forerunner of all sculptors and the inventor of masts and rigging for ships; he made images of the gods that moved, and a magic knife for Peleus. Daedalus flew successfully, says Bradford severely, because he used his head, implying this to be the hallmark of a good craftsman, in addition to his skill and expertise (Bradford, 1972). Lemprière, on the other hand, presents Daedalus as the originator of the wedge, the axe, the wimble, the level, and many other mechanical instruments. He is also said to have been responsible for many buildings in Sicily and for making jointed dolls (Daidala? Pupae?) for Pasiphaë, Ariadne, and the daughters of Cocalus (Lemprière, 1788). He built a dancing floor for Ariadne, which some say was the origin of the story of the labyrinth; and the deceiving cow frame for her mother. He was said to have immeasurably improved the art of sculpture, making life-like images of people, such as Herakles. He also carved the wooden statue of Aphrodite, which Ariadne took to Naxos, and which still exists there. On Mount Eryx, within the love goddess's famous Sicilian temple, Daedalus placed a golden honeycomb as a thanks-offering, as well as a golden heifer. But his greatest invention, to which his reputation as a sculptor belongs, was the 'lost wax' method of casting metal (of which more later).

In considering the man's reputed accomplishments, it is easy to see them as representing, in general, the problem-solving and creative qualities of humankind as well as the ability to acquire knowledge and also to play: *homo sapiens, homo faber, homo ludens*. Daedalus can also be regarded as an image of the creative flowering of Greece, of the northwards and westwards diffusion of the discoveries of earlier Afro-Egyptian and Middle-Eastern cultures, of the harnessing of what was strange or foreign, and of the mastery of fresh techniques as well as the invention of new ones.

Yet again, he can be seen as a metaphorical description of the way in which sacred ways become secularized. It is certain that most, if not all, of the artefacts made over millions of years of prehistory had an original cultic nature, whether they were cave paintings, vessels, votive offerings, or figurines. It has been said, for example, that all sculpture before the time of Alexander was religious. Slowly, with time and accustomization, the nature or use of such objects has become profane and available to all. The same can be said of the usage of alcohol and of tobacco, which were, both of them, once deemed to be spiritual activities. But *daidalos* as an image is still more than all this, as will be shown.

Where metal-working is concerned, a factor in its increased popularity was the discovery (or re-discovery) of easier ways of casting pieces, which lent themselves to methods of 'mass-production' even in classical times.

Mainly of metallurgy

Handicrafts are what, in the English-speaking world, is meant by the shortened form 'craft'. In no other language is this usage of the word 'craft' found. In its original Germanic form, *Kraft* denotes 'strength', 'power', and consequently 'skill'. What we call 'craft', the Germans call *'Handwerk'*. In Swedish it is *'hantverk'* and in French *'travail manuel'*. However, it is possible to 'learn one's craft', whatever that craft might be, where the word clearly means something much more generally like what is meant by a skill. And usage is not limited by association with the hand either, for there is the craft of poetry, or even psychotherapy. Nevertheless, whatever the word is used to refer to, it is important to remember that a craft is not just any workaday activity, but one that is personally made and results in an object that is beautiful as well as useful. Strictly speaking, an artefact that is aesthetically pleasing but has no functional use is not crafted, though it may be artistic.

It has been said that activities that imply an element of waiting and transformation are typically associated with women and are therefore by nature feminine. Laying aside the fact that it is probably men who said this, we can recognize the likeness of that description to a pregnancy, where forty weeks of waiting precede the appearance of a child, newly-made apparently from nothing, or, at least, grown from a man's semen. Until only a relatively short time ago, a woman was thought merely to provide a transformative milieu for male seed. The follicle that contains the ovum had been perceived in the female ovary by R. De Graaf in the seventeenth century, but it was not recognized as the source of eggs until very much later.

Pre-literate thinking, which connects like with like, would naturally associate pregnancy with the disappearance of the moon (a missed monthly period), after which there is an increase in size till full moon (pregnancy), to be followed by a decrease (post-parturition). So it can be seen that activities such as the planting of seed, the baking of bread, brewing, and pottery all carry a likeness to pregnancy. Slang phrases, such as 'a bun in the oven' or the 'sowing of wild oats' recognize this fact.

By the same way of thinking, so-called male activities are more direct, and involve no span of time or mysterious change of form and consistency. In this category are the making of wooden or stone tools, hunting, battle, or the carving of images.

It is imortant to state that I do not claim that such crafts *are* male or female, respectively, but just that they have been commonly associated in this way. Rather, I would claim that it is possible to recognize two types of activity, which are different in the same sort of way that a man can be different from a woman.

Weaving and the making of clothes, said to be traditionally female occupations also, do not at first sight involve a waiting process. But they are two- or three-stage operations that do involve a remarkable alteration of the original material. Flax, for example, is obtained from fibres of the linseed plant. After being treated in a number of different ways, these are spun into thread, which is then made into cloth. So cloth is in one sense a finished product, after transformation; and from another point of view, it is a raw material that will again be turned into something else: tent, altar cloth, bedding, clothes. The first stage involves a changing of the nature of the material to make it more workable, a bringing to birth, while the second allows for further elaboration.

Metalwork is the same kind of craft as spinning and weaving, for a basic material is first made, which can then be put to a large number of different uses. Metalworking was as much of an epoch-making discovery as was the making of clothes, which had freed humans from dependence upon hunting for the making of body-coverings. Metal tools worked better and lasted longer, and the material itself was more versatile than wood or stone. Not only did it replace what had gone before, but its nature, especially its ability to melt and be poured, suggested in turn all sorts of uses impossible till then. Items could now be moulded and therefore made intentionally and repeatedly, rather than by simply releasing the sleeping images from within the raw material.

But before that takes place, metal has to be made from its ore, for it is seldom found in nature, except as occasional copper outcrops, gold nuggets, and the rarest meteoric iron. To obtain metal, ore must be dug, smelted by fire, and refined to a state where it is workable. It was therefore naturally assumed by early peoples that 'seeds' were present in the earth, which would slowly ripen into true metal by the passage of time (Eliade, 1962). Humans could help this process along, by taking upon themselves the role of midwife to the metallic ore. This was, on the one hand, a sacred task; but, on the other, one that was blasphemous and hubristic, if not performed correctly. The occupations of miner and metallurgist have always been hedged about with taboos and rituals, for they were both assisting the goddess in her long-drawn-out pregnancy, but also courting the wrath of the gods by raping and stealing away what does not rightfully belong to humanity.

In view of what has been said earlier about the woman as only a container for male seed, so, too, these metallic seeds must have been regarded as merely planted there and not intrinsically belonging to the earth as goddess. This makes their theft more permissible.

Smiths in tribal societies, Eliade pointed out, are often cripples, or outcasts in other ways, who are unable to perform more 'manly' jobs. The blacksmith of the Cameroonian tribe of Dowayos was also the hangman, and therefore doubly feared (Barley, 1986, p. 101). It has even been claimed that smiths were deliberately maimed to prevent them taking their skills to other tribes, but this sounds like a later rationalization. It would be more true to say that in such societies people did what they were physically suited for, and cripples make poor warriors.

Ptah and Hephaestus were dwarfed and lamed, as was Vulcan, their Roman equivalent. The Kabirioi, Telchines, Karkinoi—all metalworkers in Greek mythology—were described as small, mysterious, underground creatures; their more modern equivalents are dwarfs, trolls, and gnomes. So the association of mining and smithing with small and twisted creatures is an ancient and archetypal one.

Smiths could be feared for their magic skills, which enabled them to avoid divine punishment when doing what was not allowed to ordinary folk. At the same time, as rejects of society, they could be despised by people at large. Smiths have always been closely associated with the shamanic holy men and healers, whose costumes were often hung about with metal objects. From all these 'primitive' but sophisticated occupations evolved alchemy, whose practitioners were, at their best, the earliest psychologists of our age, as Jung's researches have shown (CW 12, 13, 14).

Hephaestus, cripple and outcast from Olympia that he was, is clearly an archetypal metalworker. Sprung from his mother without the intervention of a father, he is very well suited for working upon her body in uninterrupted fantasy. Fatherless, he does not have to leave mother alone. Hephaestus, like all smiths, is son, lover, impregnator, and obstetrician to the mother goddess, and his actions are a rape, an incest, and a theft, as well as a bringing-to-birth. The forge within which he smelts his ores and makes his metals is itself called a uterus, while the metal is his child. He completes, in actuality and outer reality, what she herself started in secret and within. But, amazingly, he knows how to escape the fate of son/lovers, which is yearly sacrifice. Partly this is because there is little separation between them. It is also due to his being such an ugly figure of fun. Yet at the same time he is feared by his mother, for he has power over her. She needs him, since without the miner, none of her metal would see the light of day.

Hephaestus trapped his mother Hera in the golden throne that he made for her in an attempt to demand her recognition of his abilities. In the same way, an image demands and requires work upon it to bring its full nature into being.

Yet the metalworker was not just a miner and a smelter, for he also fashioned the basic material into finished products. It is, indeed, a magical process to heat lumps of rock until one may pour liquid fire from the crucible, which hardens into metal. It is truly magical to mix two soft metals such as tin and copper in different proportions, thus making durable bronze. But it is a magical ability as well to take ingots of those metals and make from them a hundred kinds of useful or ornamental objects. Then the demand for such artefacts evokes a need for more craftsmen and in turn stimulates the discovery of new skills and techniques. And in the making of things, whether by forging, casting, hammering, or carving, it is the skill (craft) of the worker which, properly mastered, allows for an expansion of the imagination and gives it full play. Until a person can actually work their material, of whatever nature that may be, they cannot ever know their own capabilities, or limitations. Nor can they ever hope to go beyond those boundaries.

Greek sculptural styles are a good example of this interconnection between technique and inventiveness. Early (sixth- and seventh-century B.C.) stone figures are carved from the block in the so-called Daedalic style. There are 'kouroi', or young boys, seen frontally with one foot advanced and arms at their sides, fists clenched. This pose, repeatedly found, is dictated by the marble in which they are carved, because its nature was such as to make it difficult to carve figures down on the twist, or with raised limbs. And so the arms remain unseparated from the torso, the legs together (Boardman, 1964, pp. 65–69). The *kore* was another favourite subject, posed in the same fashion, though often with one arm flexed at the elbow in a rigid gesture. This had been carved from another piece of stone and pinned back on. Casting figures in metal, however, means that they can be made with their limbs apart, relying on the strength of the material to support the arms, say, without fracture (Boardman, 1964, pp. 103–104). The figure can break out of the squared form, the body begin to turn, and the limbs extend. By casting the finished article in pieces, to be welded together later, further refinements become possible. But all is still limited by the method of casting used, in which the model is pressed down into wet sand, which takes an impression: the original then has to be removed from the mould without spoiling the shape in the sand that the molten metal is to take up. The lost-wax method of casting, invented by Daedalus, so it is said, overcomes this problem.

I can do no better than to leave the description of this process to the words of that master craftsman, the late Michael Ayrton. Ayrton's preoccupation with the themes of Daedalus, Icarus, Minotaur, and labyrinth resulted in a flow of images and written pieces upon them all. In another of his essays, entitled 'The Unwearying Bronze', he wrote about the lost-wax method (Ayrton, 1971):

> You will see, because you are not an initiate, several mysteries. The image is first made in wax, cast and modelled and then sticks of wax are attached to it for reasons that will presently become clear. This image the craftsman coats with a mixture of wet clay and powdered terra cotta, mantling it entirely but leaving the ends of the wax sticks uncovered. Of these, one will be larger than the others and cup-shaped, for it will be the sprue through which the metal will be poured. The figure, now buried in its clay sarcophagus, he now places in a fire so that the wax melts away.
>
> There is no figure now, for he has destroyed it. That is the first mystery. All that remains is a clay husk with its vents and openings where the wax sticks have been. Now the craftsman smelts his ores, some lumps of a heavy brown-grey rock or of a bright green powdery earth and a very little black-grey material. The lumps are native copper (the green carbonate called malachite is the most conspicuous ore) which will melt at 1000 degrees centigrade. The grey substance is cassiterite, the

ore from which the tin will be extracted. It will melt at 232 degrees centigrade. The man now blows up the charcoal fire with bellows made of goat or oxhide. You will not see it, but the copper and the tin, freed from the ores, are combining and fusing into bronze—not so pure as in later times, for there are traces of lead, nickel, silver, arsenic in the mixture. These traces will affect the ultimate colour of the bronze, but not for some time.

Meanwhile a pit has been dug. In it the dry clay husk that once held the wax figure is buried, packed in damp clay so that only the openings and vents are visible. Within that husk a perfect negative exists where the wax figure has been burned out. With long tongs the smith takes from the kiln the crucible, filled with liquid fire; the substances once brown or green or black or grey are now a blazing golden red. He pours this golden fluid into the cup-shaped opening (the sprue) until it rises through another vent and gases hiss through a third.

It must now wait for many hours to cool, but when it does and when, like a nutshell, the clay crust is broken off, from that carapace a small, heavy, rough but recognizable figure will emerge glinting and dusty from its earthen womb. That is the second mystery.

You have seen a wax figure destroyed and reborn in heavy metal from liquid fire. You have watched a brown sponge or sea-green powder become a dust-coloured image which the smith with tools and abrasives proceeds to hammer and scrape and polish into a red-gold, for that is the colour of new bronze. The umbilical cords of metal which were once the wax sticks and then the empty vents, are now cut off. Lovingly chased and burnished, the image is ready to act out your gift in the shrine. That is the total mystery. [pp. 275–276]

There is so much in that piece that resonates with what I have written so far and with what will be later understood that it is quoted here in full.

The lost-wax method, as a means of casting metal, makes a different kind of modelling possible. Images on

the turn, poised on one foot, limbs aloft, become imagin-
able, since the techniques for realizing them in actuality are
now possible. Before the skill was known, such an image
could only be an idle fantasy. However, as Jung wrote,
everything that now exists in reality was once fantasy (*CW
16*, para. 98). For example, the humourist J. B. Morton
(Beachcomber) wrote a hilarious piece in the 1930s concerning the electric toothbrush. Its humour lay in the fact
that such things did not, nor could they, exist. Today, when
the fantasy has become fact and they are freely available,
the humour is gone.

Moving from the banal to the sublime, Benvenuto
Cellini's magnificent larger than life-size statue of Perseus, made in the sixteenth century in Florence for Cosimo
de Medici, was cast in one piece, using the self-same
lost-wax method. On being released from its mantling, it
was complete, save for the toes of one foot into which part
of the mould, the liquid fire, had not fully flowed (Ayrton,
1971, pp. 278–279). Another supreme example of the craft
is Ayrton's own reconstruction of the golden honeycomb
itself, which, until he succeded in making it, was thought
to be nothing but a mythological fancy. But I shall come to
that later.

What is it, then, that is strange, mysterious, special
about metallurgy as a species of handicraft? First, it is one
of those in which the raw material demands a high degree
of preparation before it may be worked. Secondly, this is a
transformation in that the material to be used must first
be dug from the earth and heated till its nature is totally
altered—unlike, say, wool as it comes from the sheep,
which is still recognizable when it is woollen thread.
Thirdly, there is a high degree of uncertainty, both in the
mantle preparation as well as pouring of the metal, as to
whether it will succeed or not. Since one cannot see inside
the clay, it is impossible to know whether the negative
image of the wax has 'taken' (but the wax has already been
'lost', so the image can never be recovered), or whether the
molten metal has reached into every recess. By the time

the mantle is broken away, it is too late to do anything about it. Fourthly, the completed article depends not only upon the beauty of its original image or on skill in handling of the mould, but also upon the way the artefact is then chased and burnished.

Daedalus's contribution, by the invention of the lost-wax method, was to increase the risk and the uncertainty of waiting; and it is therefore what has been described as a more female attitude to craft. The toleration of risk and the mystery of the unseen goings-on within depends, in this setting, upon the degree of skill possessed by the craft-worker and the ability to contain anxiety. If the image turns out to be a well-crafted one, then that is because it was made by a person with a mastery of the craft.

CHAPTER SIX

The first great death

Talus

Daedalus had a sister, Polycaste, whose name, according to Robert Graves (1955, p. 312) means 'much tin' and therefore bronze. But she was known as Perdix [partridge], as also was her son Talus, whose own name means 'the sufferer'. Other epithets of his were 'Tantalus' ['lurching', or 'hobbling'] and 'Circinnus' ['circular']. These link him with another Talus, the giant made of bronze, a gift from Hephaestus to Minos, which daily clanked its way around Crete, mimicking the passage of the sun. In times of war it could be heated up to crush and burn any invaders to death. In its neck was a pin, whose removal made the giant fall to the ground, in pieces.

But to hobble is to possess one of the characteristic signs of a metalworker, and Talus, the youth, was indeed apprenticed to his uncle, whom, by the age of twelve, he had already surpassed in skill and ingenuity. For example, seeing the backbone of a fish upon the shore, he had the idea of casting it in bronze, inventing thereby a saw that could cut both stone and metal. A crab's claw became a drawing compass to make possible the inscription of true circles, which consequently enabled the making of metal bowls that were perfectly round. The nickname Circinnus refers to this as well as to the invention of the potter's wheel, which is claimed for him also. His ability, it seems, was in improving current practice by suggesting new techniques.

Daedalus is said to have taken the boy to the top of the Acropolis, in Athens, and shown him the distant views. While Talus looked, his envious uncle tipped him over, to die upon the rocks below. Athene, however, always watchful, changed the falling boy's soul into a bird, so that it flew off as a lapwing. Another version of the tale has Daedalus commit murder because of a suspected incestuous relationship between Talus and Polycaste. Whichever it was, while disposing of the body in a sack, Daedalus was found out. He claimed to be removing a snake from the sacred area, but his crime was revealed by bloodstains on the sack. Polycaste hanged herself, and Daedalus was banished to another town. His crime was not that of killing another person, but of sacrilege by spilling blood in the sacred precinct of the Acropolis.

Here is the first of the four great deaths in *daidalos* with which the myth-ego is connected. What are its meanings? To what attitude in Daedalus is it a response? To what do Talus and Polycaste correspond that they now become inherent in the field? Why should the craftsman be a murderer?

First, there is envy. Envy by the master of his young apprentice is a well-known motif in European folk-tales (Leach, 1949, p. 546), which has to do with the inability of teachers to allow their pupils to surpass them in skill. The physician Aesculapius's death at the hands of his father Apollo, the god of healing, for the hubristic act of raising the dead, is mentioned in this context. I have already written of the way in which *senex* will not allow *puer* his freedom, which is to take an archetypal view of the folk-motif.

But envy has also been dealt with psychoanalytically, by Melanie Klein, as the relationship between two people one of whom envies the other for some good object or quality that they would like to possess but cannot get hold of. Locating it in the earliest mother/infant relationship, Klein says that 'the first object to be envied is the feeding breast, for the infant feels that it contains everything that he desires and that it has an unlimited flow of milk and love which it keeps for its own gratification' (Klein, 1975, p. 183). Describing it more generally, Hanna Segal (1978) writes:

> Envy aims at being as good as the object, but, when this is felt as impossible, it aims at spoiling the goodness of the object to remove the source of envious feelings. [p. 40]

So, Talus dies at his uncle's hands in order to dissolve Daedalus's envy, as is clearly stated in the story. The myth-ego is both envious and, following this, violently destructive.

In the second version of the story, three people are involved, which points towards jealousy instead: an emotion concerning threesomes rather than pairs. Daedalus is concerned about the over-close relationship between his sister and her son. Since the father is never mentioned, the mother's brother may stand for him in this oedipal triangle. I could say that it is the jealousy felt by Daedalus of the mother/son couple that causes him to kill. Of jealousy, Klein says, it is 'based on envy, but involves a relation to at least two people' (Klein, 1975, p. 49). And H. Segal (1978) explains that it 'aims at possession of the loved object and removal of the rival' (p. 40): Daedalus wanting Polycaste. On the other hand, he may have been jealous of the son taking his good objects back to his mother, rather than to his uncle–tutor.

A third way of describing it would be to say that Daedalus took the drastic steps he did in order to bring to an end the improper relationship that had developed between mother and son.

Through these different perspectives, therefore, the act itself can be seen as denoting envy, jealousy, moral disapproval, or all three.

The absent father and the closeness of mother and son lead to a consideration of Talus as *puer*. His early brilliance and virtuosity, the antagonism of the older man, and the suffering of his death by falling confirm this view, whether as *puer* he is related to Perdix, the mother, or to *senex*, in the shape of Daedalus.

However, in all of these readings, psychological theory has been grafted on to the story, which can then be taken as further proof of whichever theory is chosen. Such a plurality of views may very well be possible, given the fact that there is a great number of psychological theories that describe the same clinical facts. It may also point to the nature of the human psyche as being itself intrinsically a plural one.

My point would be that all of these interpretations are acceptable and point further forward. But they have given only a negative flavour to the involvement of Daedalus with the death of his nephew. I believe that it is possible, and permissible, to take another view of a killing that represents, after all, as suggested above, nothing less than the internalizing of all that is implied by the image of Talus. With such a precocious genius involved, it would be strange if Talus and his death were to have only a negative value. It should also be remembered that such values are always ego-judgements. Theories make something conscious that was not known before, but these heroic efforts may result in that which belongs more properly to the underworld being pulled into daylight, to be seen with an above-ground perspective.

Another way of approaching myth is to allow the story to be just as it is (which is exactly as it was written, in one or more forms) and allowing that story to 'inform' existing conscious views: to widen, imaginatively, those ways of looking both at outside events and at psychological functioning. To do this means using the approach I have already called 'is-as-it-is'. This assumes that what happened in the story came about that way because, when read from the point of view of psyche, that was exactly what was needed for all parties at the time. It was the only way things could turn out, however inexplicable that might seem from a practical, factual standpoint. It requires a reading of the myth that is of the underworld and does not attempt to graft a 'real-life' dimension on to the interpretation.

Using such underworldly spectacles, the story could be retold in this way: 'Daedalus both delighted in and was envious of his pupil's prowess. But he felt concerned about the possibly incestuous relationship with his mother, which might hinder the boy's development. For these reasons he took him to the holiest height in Athens, belonging to their shared tutor and nursemaid, Athene. There he turned the boy outwards to look at distant sights beyond the enclosure. He wished to encourage his outward gaze, rather than a dwelling inwards upon feelings for the mother and containment within the nursing environment of the goddess's patronage. Then the elder man pushed him from the edge, as a mother bird is said to nudge her hesitant young to fly from the nest. Talus, as partridge, cannot easily fly from such a height, and so his mortal body is crushed, but his soul now truly gains wings for, changed into the first lapwing ever known upon earth, it finds it freedom.'

Daedalus encouraging his pupil's soul to fly is the image of a good teacher whose task is to point the pupil in the direction of making the best use of innate talents and not to confine youth to ways the tutor considers best or most acceptable. In removing the body, with his story about the snake, Daedalus also spoke the truth, for the 'snake' of Kekrops and Erichthonios that is carried hidden in a basket was the emblem for a phallus, as Kerényi has pointed out, just as that of Dionysus was carried in a winnowing fan and that of the torn-apart Osiris in a box. By removing the phallus from maternal ground, Daedalus releases male generativity, which had, until then, been locked up in contemplation of the mother's navel. There will be more about male generativity later on. Here it is also worth noting that, according to her own myth, the goddess Athene, though a virgin, continually bears children, which are also mysteriously spirited away from the Acropolis, to develop in freedom. Is not this fact directly implied by Daedalus's action? Is not his behaviour, therefore, archetypally induced?

My patient Derek had been brought up under the influence of his mother's dictum: 'do or die'. To 'do' was to live up to her academic expectations of him, while failure to perform this feat was to 'die'. Fearing the shame of failure and of disappointing her, he did no school work, failing—and therefore 'dying'—in a different way. 'I want to spread my wings', he said, but in his own ways and not those of his mother's expectations. She would have deeply disapproved of the things that he longed to be allowed, deeming them 'messy'. As a result, when he tried to 'fly' as an adult, his fantasies tended to be so grandiose, that he 'flopped'. So, either way, he died the death he feared, reinforcing his views of himself as a failure.

Though Daedalus himself was punished by banishment from Athens, yet that act, taken as it is, only confirms the truth of my version and the value of the is-as-it-is approach, as well as the meaning of the inherence of Talus. For, exiled in Attica, the myth-ego reveals his own freedom to procreate, for it is in this unnamed place that his many descendants, the Daedalids, are fathered. His own pro-creativity is freed from Athene thereby. If it was just as it was, then Talus *must* die, in turning away from his mother. But, in so doing, he is taken in by, becomes an inward part of, Daedalus. The field, *daidalos,* is enlarged. And if that is so, what exactly does he represent?

Talus is immature youth, but precocious talent: a talent not just in metallurgy, but for invention also. In his own works, he copies nature, not just by a realistic imitation, but in a metaphorical, analogical way. A fish spine is *not* a saw but suggests the *possibility* of sawing. So he imitates and surpasses nature. Something is stolen from her, and a truly human, creative act occurs. This is in itself hubristic, as will be seen when Prometheus is considered; and yet hubris—whatever it is called: having wild thoughts, over-stepping the boundaries, making the jump that asks, 'what if I . . . ?'—is also the mark of creative individuals. The leap reqires a force within, which can lead to the brink, but not stop there. For that is where the energy that pushes on beyond the leading edge is required. And the leap is not only dangerous, but uncertain too. For at the moment of take-off, those who leap can never know that Athene is at hand to save their soul. They leap, as they must, into uncharted and therefore uncertain realms, risking all. It is a fearful act, for which Daedalus is also needed, as agent. His so-called murderous envy and jealousy are but trig-gers.

Yet Talus is indeed also a mother-inclined *puer* trapped by her close identification with him and from which it is once again Daedalus who must extract him. It is clear that when the boy dies, she must follow him into death, as if she had no possibility of separate existence, as Jung main-tained.

But deaths in this story are acceptable, since the dying are marked as elements worthy of inclusion into the myth-ego. The nurturing, clinging mother has—if nothing else— sparked off an artistic, creative flair in her child. She is, like Hera the mother of Hephaestus, a 'ground' that brings inventiveness to life; both goddess and woman are, as mothers, valuable necessities. With Polycaste's death, that which she represents will become inherent, just like her son.

Still more can be learnt about those things that mother and son have to tell, by studying their actual nature as partridge and lapwing; but first let me explain why it is useful to look in this way.

An interlude for natural history

Nowadays, most people live far from raw nature, and even those who do live in the countryside are certainly not embedded within it to the same extent as their ancestors had been. Nature is an 'out there' environment, to which people relate by joining Friends of the Earth or by showing ecological concern. The *logos* of the *oikos* [home] is a science, not a reality. Similarly, the wilderness of nature within is far removed from a categorizing consciousness that seeks only to tame or exploit it.

Indigenous peoples, on the other hand, those who live in or are of the wild and whom Lévi-Strauss calls a 'people without writing', have a different experience, for their attachment to and involvement with the raw chaos is much closer than for those in the civilized west. Yet their minds still order and describe, with logic. Of the pygmies of the Philippines, the anthropologist R. B. Fox wrote:

> The Negrito is an intrinsic part of his environment, and what is still more important, continually studies his surroundings. Many times I have seen a Negrito, who, when not being certain of the identification of a particular plant, will taste the fruit, smell the leaves, break and examine the stem, comment upon its habitat, and only after all this, pronounce whether he did or did not know the plant. [Quoted in Lévi-Strauss, 1962, p. 4]

There is, for such people, an intense and truly scientific curiosity in their surroundings, though for different, perhaps more practical reasons. The Negrito, says Fox, can easily distinguish and name 'at least 450 plants, 75 birds, most of the snakes, fish, insects, animals and even 20 species of ant'. Western adults do not have that kind of knowledge, although they may be able to name a hundred different motor cars, novelists, or pop stars; and this information would not be available, meaningful, or valuable to 'people without writing' living in a tropical rain forest. Lévi-Strauss (1962, p. 6) also mentions the experience of E. Smith Bowen, who admitted her shame and confusion on arriving to work with an African tribe and discovering their much greater ability to order nature. She described a community in which her own poor grasp of mathematics was at last superior to others', but where any ten-year-old child knew hundreds of different kind of plants; and where her instructor could not realize that it was not the names of the plants that baffled the anthropologist, but the plants themselves!

Why mention this kind of fact, which is already familiar to many? Because it is too easily forgotten. Pre-literate people are still branded as 'primitive', in a derogatory sense. The sophistication of their minds and of their mind-processes, as advanced as our own, is often overlooked, because it is different. It is important to remember that their curiosity is as intense and their powers of observation as accurate, or more so (and all done without instrumentation), as are those of so-called civilized humanity; while their ability to make inferences is just as acute.

Analytical psychologists, following Jung, still have a tendency to think of the savage mind as existing in 'participation mystique' with its surroundings, the implication being that the native thinker does not, cannot, know things as the sophisticated mind does. It is forgotten that the French anthropologist, Lévy-Bruhl, whose phrase that was, is as relevant to anthropology today as Anton Mesmer is to depth psychology. Yet still 'participation mystique' is bandied about as if it were the only way such people can think. Of course, under its more modern guise as 'projective identification', 'participation mystique' remains a useful and important factor in depth psychology.

Nevertheless, the abilities of people without writing can also be too easily romanticized, harking back to ideas of 'the noble savage'. Ignorance and incompetence is also found, as Nigel Barley (1986) wrote of his own field experience:

> The basic truth abut the Dowayos is that they knew less about the animals of Africa than I did. As trackers they could tell motorbike tracks from human footprints but that was about the pinnacle of their achievement. They believed, like most Africans, that chameleons were poi-

sonous. They assured me that cobras were harmless. They did not know that caterpillars turn into butterflies. They could not tell one bird from another or be relied upon to identify trees accurately. Many of the plants did not have names though they used them quite often, and reference involved lengthy explanations: 'that plant you use to get the bark you make the dye from'. [p. 95]

But there is, I believe, another reason for this failure to understand such different ways of thinking, which is that the natural language of such people is myth. Myth belongs to the 'logic of the concrete' (Lévi-Strauss) and always has done. People without writing live embedded in explanatory story, orally passed on, in which the animals, birds, insects, and natural phenomena are metaphors for their own societal patterns and cultural norms, as well as inner psychic structures.

For all these reasons, when examining myths today, it is important to take a very close look at the creatures contained within them. They are not there just by chance, but are instead highly specific carriers of meaning, related to the observational characteristics so clearly known to those for whom it was natural to speak in mythic images. Only that animal would do and not another, like my father in the dream. Going further from that, the concrete observed facts can be built upon to express quite abstract ideas, as I shall show; though today, many centuries later, much of this specificity has been lost and is not easily recovered. It is as if I am standing in an apple tree, picking ripe fruit. But since the ladder has been taken away, I am unable to tell how I got up there.

This ability to link diverse elements together through the sharing of a single theme—which we call story [Gr: *mythos*]—has been present since humankind's earliest days. Alexander Marshack (1972), in his studies of the Old Stone Age, has conclusively proved this point. Describing a '*bâton de commandement*' made of bone dating from approx. 300,000 B.C. and found on the banks of a river at Le

Placard in France, more than 100 miles from the sea, he noted all the exquisitely drawn pictures upon it. There are two seals—male and female from the comparative size; a fish, easily distinguished as an adult male salmon in the mating season by the presence of the lower jaw hook that such fish develop; two male (because they possess penises) grass snakes or eels; a mass of lines, found by microscopic examination to be a drawing of a sprouting shoot; a flower in bud; some plants, branches, or grasses; and a simplified drawing of an ibex, crossed firmly by two lines. Such *bâtons*, widely found, are clearly not weapons, although they may be tools for straightening the saplings that were destined to become arrows. Judging by the wear that is often found in the hole at one end, they were clearly carried on a thong and perhaps at the belt. Some have complex lunar calendars marked upon their edges.

How can the various images on this particular bâton be connected? Well, salmon return to that river to spawn; and when they do, the seals follow them upstream as a source of food. At the same time, the winter snows are melting, seeds are sprouting, plants flowering; and—in those days— the ibex herds migrated northwards, as the icecap receded, making easy prey. The linking story is simple enough. It is spring. From later researches, Marshack has cautiously suggested that the bâtons may also have possessed a 'ritual' or 'magical' property and were probably passed on from parent to child. After examining so many, he has also postulated that the lines across the ibex in some way represented 'killing', although he will not infer more than that.

From the other side of the world, Arthur Cooper's exhaustive study of the origins of Chinese script has revealed that far from being phonetically based, it is in fact imagistically and metaphorically derived. It rests on the kinds of direct observational facts the Negrito or Esquimau is familiar with today. Thus, the image of a short-tailed bird in the earliest script (c. 1500 B.C.) is, says Cooper, a female bird: a bird that is brooding, apart and still. Add to that picture the image of threads, and you have a character meaning 'moored', as of a boat that is isolated at the end of its rope. Put the bird with mountains, and it carries the meaning of being isolated. With a cave it denotes a hermit. In this way of combining images, abstract qualities can also be 'written'. Furthermore, although the same bird can be found in words that also mean 'to go busily to and fro', this causes no problems from the perspective of natural history. Birds on the nest are indeed isolated and quiet. Those who are building nests or feeding their young are continually on the move (Cooper, 1989, p. 144).

If I have laboured this point, it is because such observations are part of the concrete grounding of myth. Often they are the solution to mythological inconsistencies and paradoxes. For example, when Daedalus kills his nephew Talus, also known as Perdix (partridge), the boy's soul flies off as a lapwing, according to Ovid. This contradiction is totally ignored by commentators, because it is seemingly inexplicable. They often just substitute 'partridge' for 'lapwing', assuming a mistake. But such 'mistakes' are never made by the mythmakers, and the change is of vital importance and crucial significance, as will be shown later.

Trying, as far as is possible, to know mythological motifs at this level is to remain faithful to the nature of the story. To do so allows the mythological to come alive within, so that instead of my knowing it, it knows me. It is to begin to reactivate the concrete thinking to which Lévi-Strauss refers. Piaget tells us children will grow out of it by the age of seven; in fact, it is always with them—and us too—though perhaps out of operation. Myth can bring it back.

Theories about the uses of myth in human society are many and contradictory. Prof. G. S. Kirk (1974, pp. 43–68) has categorized them as follows:

1. All myths refer ultimately to natural phenomena, such as sunrise, eclipses, storms, earthquakes, etc., which are then personified as gods; the myths are the stories of their doings.

2. Myths are 'aetiological', which is to say that they describe the origins of things and the world in a kind of 'proto-scientific' way—Why does the hare have a split lip? How did the camel get its hump? and so forth.

3. Myths provide 'charters' for customs and beliefs and the behaviour of the societies to which they belong. This represents an anthropological solution to the problem.

4. Mircea Eliade claimed that the purpose of myths was to evoke and reconnect the present generation to the time of world creation and thus to re-establish or maintain that original order (Eliade, 1968).

5. Rituals, it is said, are the origin of all mythological stories.

6. The psychological theories of myths, as put forward by Freud and Jung.

Kirk insists that none of these monolithic theories alone is sufficient to account for all myths. Some belong in different categories, while others belong in several. Myths are always, he says, multifunctional.

Trained in the school of Jung, I naturally tend towards category six. But Judith Hubback has recently made clear that each of the other theories mentioned by Kirk can be 'read' psychologically as representing aspects of individual development on an archetypal base. Thus, nature myths can refer to the powerful natural forces experienced by an infant and which it fears might—like volcanic eruptions— get out of hand. In a similar manner, she relates each theory to earlier stages and more infantile parts of the human being. Those put forward by Freud and Jung, as well as Lévi-Strauss and his followers, are, she says, the most satisfactory, in that they describe how people function in their psychological wholeness (Hubback, 1990).

Thus, there can be great depths and truths carried by the birds in this tale.

The partridge and the lapwing

The partridge (*Perdix perdix*) is a small, mottled, reddish-brown and grey game-bird that is found across the Old World in several related species. They live in small family groups, known as coveys, in a closely defined territory upon open ground. They nest within tussocks of grass or at the foot of bushes or hedgerows. They are non-migratory, and at some time in the winter the covey separates, so that the birds may pair again to be ready for the spring mating. Their flight is always close to the ground (Grzimek, 1972, p. 43). For the Greeks, partridges were sacred to Aphrodite as well as being sacrificed in her temples. And they were dedicated to the love-goddess for the same reason as the common sparrow: both were seen as always lustful, promiscuous, and indiscriminate with their favours. In *The Goddess of Love*, Geoffrey Grigson (1978) writes:

> Partridges were said to tread their females on every possible occasion. Aelian calls them 'very lustful and adulterous', sneaking round after each other's females all the time. And he said that the females hid their eggs, because the cock birds destroyed them whenever they could, knowing that once the chicks were allowed to hatch, their wives would have no time for them: they weren't going to lose their fun. These insatiable birds were also accused of homosexuality: cock birds who lost their mates promptly abused each other; which wouldn't have worried Aphrodite, goddess also of love between men and between women, as in the poems or fragments of poems by Sappho. [pp. 206–207]

The maternal instinct of mother partridge is attested by Graves, quoting Jeremiah: 'The partridge gathereth young that she hath not brought forth' (Graves, 1955, p. 316). So she will mother chicks that are not her own, but come winter they all leave her. For this reason, the partridge was also a symbol of self-deception to the church fathers. St. Jerome wrote:

Just as the partridge lays eggs and hatches young birds which will never follow it, so the impious man possesses wealth to which he is not entitled, and which he must leave behind when he is least inclined. [Cirlot, 1962, p. 250]

And, in the words of St. Ambrose:

The partridge taking its name from the word *perdendo* and in Hebrew called *kore* (to call and shout) is Satan tempting the multitudes with his voice. [Cirlot, 1962, p. 250]

The saint is referring to the custom of using a male partridge in a decoy with a labyrinthine entrance to attract other birds to it by its cries. Its voice draws them on to their death. The male partridge hobbles or lurches in its mating displays, holding one leg ready to strike at an opponent with its spur. The hobbling partridge dance was copied on Crete, and this was said to be the reason for the dancing floor that Daedalus built Ariadne. However, the hobbling of the male bird relates it to metal-workers and Hephaestus, Aphrodite's husband, who lurched and waddled around Olympus, his feet turned back to front.

Talus, having been known as partridge, is changed, at his death, into a lapwing—or, rather, says Ovid, his soul flies off as this black-and-white bird. It is also a lapwing, as he states later, that appears at Icarus's graveside to chatter at Daedalus. As already suggested, mythmakers could not possibly have mistaken one small bird for another; so that this 'soul-bird' must also be examined.

The lapwing, peewit (from its call) or plover [*Vanellus vanellus*] is also a bird of the open country and the same habitat as the partridge, nesting upon the ground in shallow scrapes likewise. It takes its name, so it is said, from the 'lapping' noise that its wings make when flying. This refers especially to the display of the males at mating times, when they fly high up into the air, then plummet towards the ground, clapping their wings together as they fall. The bird saves itself from hitting the ground at the very last minute (Grzimek, 1972, p. 181). So it is a fitting image indeed for the soul of the falling Talus, saved by divine hand.

But in fact this derivation of the name is a false etymology. In Old English, the bird was called '*hleape-wince*', the first element being identical to our word 'leap', while the second comes from a verb meaning to move from side to side, or stagger. So the lapwing is a leaper, a lurcher, and a hobbler too. It is named this way from its habit of decoying predators away from its young, by limping from the nest, dragging one wing to appear more easy to catch. By so doing, it courts its own death. It does not live in any defined territory and is a bird of huge flocks, which gather together in late summer, in order to migrate towards southern Europe away from the winter cold. Being a flock bird, the mother is accustomed to losing her young to the greater whole. She can exist without them—unlike Polycaste, who dies for loss of her son.

So if the partridge is that which would hold on to its young, the lapwing is that which can let them go. If the partridge is that which sticks close to the ground to fly, the lapwing soars high, falls low, and yet survives—a bird that can take things to the brink of disaster only to recover its balance. If the partridge is one whose noisy voice decoys others to their death, the lapwing is one who risks death in order to deflect danger and save others. If the partridge is that which sticks closely to a known territory, the lapwing is that which feels free to move farther afield. If the partridge belongs to a nuclear family and yet is promiscuous, the lapwing is that which belongs to the larger group, where sexuality is less intense.

These observed facts, taken metaphorically, illustrate the change that is brought about in the overall image by Talus's death and just what it is that now inheres to the myth-ego: both partridge and lapwing. Alternatively it might be seen as an act of discrimination of the field, where one image becomes two and both are a part of the greater whole.

CHAPTER SEVEN

Back to Crete

More of Minos and his island

T he Cretan empire pre-dated the flowering of mainland Greece, and it was peopled by a sea-faring
nation of traders. More Middle Eastern, or perhaps
Egyptian, than European, their language was not the
Greek known today as 'classical'. The word 'Minos', meaning 'lord', seems to have been more of a title than a proper
name, like 'Baal', 'Pharaoh', or 'Caesar'. However, this
story deals with a supposedly real-life Minos fathered by
Zeus upon Europa, which could be seen as an image of the
union between east and west, as well as between bull and
cow, bull worship having come to Crete from Sumer. The
pregnant Europa was married off to the then king of Crete,
Asterius, who thus became stepfather to her semi-divine
son. Minos was specially favoured by Zeus, under whose
protection his empire grew in size and richness. But it was
also always dependent upon the good nature of Minos's
uncle, Poseidon, lord of the seas.

103

If for the Cretan seafarers the ocean was a highway and trade route, it is important to realize that for the later-arriving, mainland Greeks it was not. To them, it was nothing but an inhospitable and trackless waste. As Jane Harrison (1963b) points out, for the Hellenes the sea was a place that could neither be ploughed nor sown. It was always known to them therefore as 'the unharvested'. Poseidon was a god to be feared and placated, for his sea could erode the land, flood the coastal plains, destroy ships, and drown fisher-folk. From the sea, too, came earthquakes and tidal waves, so that 'earth-shaker' had a real meaning as well as a sexual one (p. 16).

On the mainland, Poseidon was always a loser, being defeated in the contest for Attica by Athene, losing Argos to Hera, Aegina to Zeus, and so on (Harrison, 1963b, p. 29). But islands are different, being pockets of land surrounded by ocean, rather than waves lapping at a continent's edge. The relative roles are thus reversed. Islanders depend upon the sea for food, transport, trade, and communication. But for these to happen reliably, the ocean needs to be a peaceable place. So Minos's control of piracy by the size and power of his navy was justly famous, making the Mediterranean a safe highway.

It is to this Crete that Daedalus fled, and to a king powerful enough to support a renegade craftsman. Having left the divine Athene, this was a time of human patronage for Daedalus: a safe setting in which to work, which would, by return, bring honour to Minos who employed him. He laid out the dancing floor, made movable serving-maids, and, having watched the gulls soaring on the wind, invented sails for the king's ships. In this latter respect it is the Talus within who acts, copying 'as if' from nature.

Daedalus obeyed orders and fulfilled demands unquestioningly, without any moral quibbles getting in the way. This is most clearly seen in relation to the Minotaur, whose story has already been told, and whose birth, imprisonment, and death Daedalus helped to bring about, as severally requested.

Hidden within her cow frame, like an image inside its mantle, Pasiphaë is mounted by the Poseidon bull and impregnated by its fiery sperm to produce a monster. Minos himself was recognized as the human representative of the bull, his father, an animal that the Cretans associated with the sun, and which appears on coins, frescoes, and vase paintings of that nation and era. But the bull from the sea is different; it is related by Joseph Campbell (1974) to the moon:

> For as in Sumer, so in Crete; whereas the lion was the animal of blazing solar light which both slays the moon and parches vegetation, the bull was the animal of the moon: the waxing and waning god by the magic of whose night dew the vegetation is restored; the lord of tides and the productive powers of the earth, the lord of women, lord of the rhythm of the womb. [p. 60]

Campbell equates the bull of Crete with 'the ever-dying, ever-living god: the Lord Poseidon of the goddess Earth', though he gets a bit carried away, because of course the Mediterranean has no tides. He also likens the image of Minotaur with that of a moon-man or moon-king (Campbell, 1974, p. 61). But, it may be objected, the moon is a feminine image; and indeed, this is often so. But in many mythologies the moon god is male: Egyptian: Thoth; Vedic: Soma; Semitic: Sin; as well as for the African Bushmen and in Greenland. Even our culture speaks of 'the man in the moon' (Leach, 1949, pp. 743–745).

In this story, Pasiphaë acts out that part of the royal couple which would ally itself with the fluctuating pull of the moon, rather than usurp that power for itself and mimic only father sun, like Minos. Who better to do this than a woman whose name means 'the widely shining', a by-name for the moon, and herself a daughter of the marriage between sun and moon (Kerényi, 1951, p. 192). In the present union, however, moon (bull) mates with moon (queen) to produce a moon-child, which is the horrifying Minotaur.

There are two ways of considering this intercourse. First, as a bad, unnatural, and perverted thing: a punishment for her husband's arrogance or her own neglect of Aphrodite, both of which are generally accepted. Or, secondly, it is a beautiful act of passion by which Pasiphaë corrects her husband's neglect of his patron god by admitting fresh, though forgotten, functions into a worn-out realm, and by which she also relates once more to the goddess of lust. Both those possibilities must be held in mind, their relevance uncertain, while the nature of the offspring of that union is examined. There may be other versions as well. It should be remembered that, since intercourse has been seen as an image for a re-coupling of the oppositional, that which is born as a result, however horrible, must also be an image of the previously undivided, or lately rejoined, state.

Dawn is a woman in her forties. Her father left his wife and young baby for military service abroad; and soon after returning, revealed that he now had a girl friend, which then led to a divorce. Quite unable to deal with the emotions this raised in her at the time, Dawn remembers deciding that the only way to cope was to behave as if it had not happened. Visiting her father during the school holidays, she acted out the good child, all of her uneasiness suppressed within. She grew to admire her father as a highly intelligent, all-knowing sort of person who could do no wrong. She erased from her mind the fact that she felt deserted by him, or that he over-used alcohol. It seems that he himself worshipped women, putting them on pedestals to be cared for, their task being to care for him by return. They were expected, however, to remain rather childish and should never question his wisdom. Dawn remembers him once holding her up to the window to see the 'harvest moon'. It was a wonderful, memorable sight, and the child somehow felt that her father was a part of that awesome beauty. It was as if he *was* the moon. Part of our work together was to take her father (and indeed all men) off the pedestals that *she* had put them on, and which then belittled her own sense of self. Like Pasiphaë in her passion, her task could be seen as learning how to lure the moon down to earth and to humanize it as Minotaur. Then she might be able to see herself, potentially, as able and powerful as her father, her teachers, or her therapist.

Minotaur and the monstrous

Having in actuality a bull's head and feet but human arms and torso would indeed be monstrous. At first glance such a thing is equally monstrous as a psychic image. Yet the Minotaur's actual name is a beautiful one: Asterion, the starry one. What can these juxtapositions of name and image and their contradictions mean?

Europa, covered by the Zeus bull, brought forth Minos, who represents the sun in its passage. The sun is a creature of habit and regularity, even though it may shine for varying lengths of time throughout the year; and at the winter solstice early man could fear, it is said, that it might vanish altogether. At times it will be covered by cloud, to reappear later; but essentially the sun can be relied upon to remain the same and to pass across the sky in a regular fashion. It has rules that are easily discovered, and it obeys them.

But the moon, whatever its gender, is a phasic creature of regular irregularities and changing patterns. It does not rise or set at the same time. Sometimes it is unconfined by night but rides aloft in the daytime sky, morning or afternoon. Neither does it stay the same size or shape. Even worse, once each month it actually vanishes, leaving the sky empty. When it goes (and where *does* it go?), who can tell—at the concrete level of the senses—whether it will ever come back? Yet each month it does return, though turned about-face, to enlarge over the next two weeks, like a pregnant womb, shining in the sky. Its monthly course is an image of death-in-life, as well as life-in-death, those three dark days being its hidden impregnation. Asterion is not himself the moon, but the moonchild. Yet by his name he is allied with the starry sky also. He is not simply the night sky as compared to the daytime heaven—which belongs to Zeus and his son Apollo. He is, instead, an image of the dark heavens, during the time of the absent moon, when the stars in that blackness shine out as the only visible indication of any 'light principle'. Asterion is that in-between time, when anything may happen. At the same time he represents the copulation that goes on in that dark space, as well as the child that is its outcome. As dark night, he carries the risk that the moon will shine out no more; and yet he is the hope for what is to come—which is himself.

The spangled stars can be regarded as pinprick holes in the black cloak of night, which reveal a hidden shining from beyond. *That* is Asterion: the same as the light spot within the dark swollen half of the *t'ai-chi-tu*, or Yin–Yang symbol of Daoism: the promise of what will come out of, and indeed can only come *because* of, that self-same darkness. From this point of view, Asterion is an image of all that is enfolded within *daidalos*. And, just as a person can never step into the same stream twice, for the water has always flowed on, so is the swelling moon never the same as that which died. Asterion is an image of fresh possibilities born out of new connections, made under cover of his own darkness.

The moon is connected with all things that go and come and go again: with all things that wax and wane or have a monthly periodicity: with all things that are predictably unpredictable or unpredictably predictable. All things that take the risk of disappearing, yet 'pull off' the vanishing trick by their return, belong to the moon: as do those that return from that absence changed, or can reproduce themselves of themselves. The she-bear, for example, who disappears each winter in hibernation but returns in the spring with her cubs, belongs to the moon.

All of these attributes the dark sky of the absent moon 'contains' and allows to happen. But there is more to it than that, for the dark nights of absent moon now take on a more powerful aspect. The 'absence' is not a deficit or a lack of something, but the necessary pre-condition for the following phase. If the moon is seen as feminine, then those dark nights are *an archetypal basis for the 'absent feminine'* and Asterion is that aspect of maleness that relates to and survives her absence.

Psychologically, we can find this starry night in the so-called '*scintillae*' that break through into consciousness. They are the flashes of inspiration, the sparks of genius, the unasked-for '*Einfälle*' that just pop into mind, there to be elaborated. Jung (*CW 14*) writes of them:

> In the unconscious are hidden those 'sparks of light' (*scintillae*), the archetypes, from which a higher meaning can be 'extracted'. [para. 700]

These *scintillae,* luminosities, islands of consciousness, or deintegrates collectively represent what Jung termed the Self, but a Self not seen as an integrated whole. They are, instead, a chaos, rather than a 'unifying pattern-making process appearing in images like those of the mandala, lotus-flower etc.' (Lambert, 1981, p. 191). They have been described as soul sparks, or fragments of God within each individual, and imaged as fishes' eyes, the light of nature, the invisible sun, the fire point, and many things else (see especially *CW 14*). So, with these aspects of Asterion's nature in mind, it is hard to imagine why the Minotaur is so horrific or shameful that it must be shut away from others' eyes.

The fact is that the monstrousness of the bull-man exists only when it is seen through the eyes of Minos, when it is he who rules the conscious realm. It is Minos who would have him walled up and hidden away. Similarly, in the fairy tale, the Beast was seen as ugly and unmarriageable because his likeness was first revealed to Beauty through the eyes of her own father. *Any* suitor for her hand would, I suggest, have been seen by him as monstrous, such was the possessive love he himself bore for his daughter.

The consciousness that rules also makes the rules as to what is acceptable and what is horrifying. It is significant therefore that the birth of Asterion was brought about by the passionate lust of his mother, which could be said to mean that passion was judged as something unacceptable by Minos. Justice cannot be clouded by emotion, or it will not be impartial. But neither can passion thrive on neutral ground. Connection, regardless of nature, time, or place—of which this conception is an image—will always be separate from the cool detachment of a Minos or Athene. And so it all depends upon the chosen standpoint when deciding which is to be called monstrous and ugly, or which will be extolled as beautiful.

What the mother thought of her child is unknown, but since it is not said that she rejected him, it is to be assumed she was, to say the least, impartial to the so-called monstrousness of her son. She responded to her passion within the darkness of the cow-frame. She conceived and brought forth, thus doing all that was required of her as an image within the story that is *daidalos*. She re-established a link with the restless, changeable ocean. She expiated her denial of the goddess of lust and love; and the images of these religious actions is Asterion. A Pasiphaë-consciousness is one that performs her task without making a judgement upon what will result from that act; and in this respect Daedalus, who helps to bring it all about, resembles her. It is as it is: it will be as it will be.

I shall have more to say of passion later. For the moment, it is important to remember that it is also an imaginative process. The passionate feeling *longs* to bring something into being—and inevitably therefore contains an image of what that something might be or become. Remember too that lust is more than mere sexual appetite, for it is that self-same longing, as well as the pleasure of, or delight in, and sensuous desire for another object or person (*OED*).

Asterion's nature can also be illuminated by reference to the birth of Hephaestus. The craftsman god, so one tale tells, was born by virgin-birth to the furious Hera, in response to the virtuosity of her husband when producing Athene from his own head. But the babe Hera bore was so hideous that she flung it away from her and out of Olympus in disgust, letting it fall into the sea. Nursed by sea goddesses, he learnt his craft of smithing and brought his treasures back to a mother who was still none too pleased to see him. A second time she threw him away, after he intervened between his quarrelling parents; and this time, when landing upon earth, his feet turned back to front, so that he could only stagger lurchingly forward. In other words, he is a god of whom Hera insists, by her hurling, that he belongs away from her side and in the world. She acts towards her son as Polycaste could not. In bringing about this separation between them, she grounds him—in a part of his existence, at any rate. However, by his returning, he insists that his place is also upon Olympus, thus reforging the connection to his mother and the divine realm.

But, for a deeper understanding of the meaning of Hephaestus's crippled ugliness, there is another story of his begetting. This has it that his parents were secretly married, living a hidden life together for three hundred years before the world could be allowed to know, Hephaestus being born to them during that hidden period (Kerényi, 1951, p. 155). If the marriage of his parents was a hidden one—something, as it were, that current consciousness could not accept—then their secret child is a part of that image too. He was thus non-legitimate, always longing to be legitimized by the acceptance of his mother into her Olympian world. His desire is for a loving matrix to mirror back his own importance; and all of his craftwork can be seen as a means towards that end.

But there is more, for he was pre-mature in the sense of being before his time, so that the world is always unready for the qualities he carries, deeming them unnatural, unseemly, ugly, and a joke. The gods would laugh at him as he waddled through their halls; and yet by laughter he healed their quarrels and bad moods. His ugliness made linkages and mended connections in ways that were humorous rather than heroic. Hephaestus brings to mind the Trickster in Amerindian legends: that primitive, ugly, undifferentiated buffoon who is also an image of earlier consciousness as well as of things to come.

Hephaestus, figure of fun and foolery, is both archaic and from the undisclosed past, as well as skilful and anticipating things to come; and it is he, it should be remembered, who is married to the goddess of love and connection herself, Aphrodite. Her love and passion recognizes that which he bears, which is, in part, a root of the archetype of well-craftedness.

So if Asterion is, like Hephaestus, something unspeakable, whose time has not yet come, is it at all surprising that he should be shut away by a ruling, judgemental consciousness that does not wish to know what this new thing might be? Such an action has the familiar feel of repression, even though this kind of protection may be, at times, a necessary recipe for survival. The Minotaur is Minos's shame, the down-side of his sunny realm, as well as the emotional qualities he cannot admit to. Small wonder that he uses all of his craftiness (Daedalus) to contain it in such a way that it cannot escape, and that no one who visits it will survive.

The Minotaur is the *Minos-bull*, and seen through the eyes of its master it turns nasty: a destroyer of youth, whose hunger must be regularly satisfied. The confined cannibal could be likened to some walled-off complex or a psychotic corner, that drains energy from consciousness, while the maze represents the obstructive defences that are there to deny access to this feared though perhaps seminal force. No wonder that Minos would keep it that way.

But a monster can be examined from another perspective. The word has a dictionary meaning of 'something marvellous' (*OED*) from the Latin '*monstrare*', which means 'to show' or 'to display'. During the Christian Benediction, the priest elevates the Host before the waiting congregation in a *monstrance,* a transparent vessel by which it is contained. Asterion is therefore like a revelation of the sacred, as well as something that must be enclosed: some marvellous fresh insight that it might be better to contain, protecting it from danger until it can take its true place in the world. The labyrinth then becomes a life-enhancing maternal embrace, while at the centre of his secure place Asterion attracts youthful qualities into his orbit. By their death they are taken in, digested, internalized. From this viewpoint it is well to remember that the name 'Minotaur' also means the 'Lord-bull'. He, too, is a god.

There is also much about his birth that is typical of a hero's. For example, he has two fathers, one a god, is threatened from birth, shut away by the ruling king, has great strength. This hero-hood is not really surprising, for, as Jung pointed out long ago, the monster and its slayer are different aspects of the same thing. 'The hero who clings to the mother is the dragon, and when he is reborn from the mother he becomes the conqueror of the dragon' (*CW 5,* para. 580). It is right, therefore, that Asterion should die at the hands of a true hero; for whatever has been said earlier of heroes, they too have a part to play in *daidalos.* The heroic must be drawn towards the centre, as acted here by Theseus, aided by the clue that is carried by Ariadne. Asked for help once more, the myth-ego gives what is required: a ball of twine (also called a 'clew'), which will not only unwind the maze's winding path to the centre but, more importantly, reveal the passage out again.

The Cretan maze is said to have been easy to enter but hard to leave. The same is expressly said to Aeneas by the Cumaean Sibyl of his wish to enter the underworld and see his father again (Virgil, *Aeneid*):

Night and day lie open the gates of death's dark kingdom: But to retrace your steps, to find the way back to
daylight—That is the task, the hard thing. [ll. 127–129]

Nevertheless, Theseus finds his way to the centre of the
labyrinth, throttles or beheads the Minotaur, and by
means of the clew rethreads the 'insoluble maze'. The hero
then returns to Athens.

It is, says Virgil, the passion of Ariadne to which
Daedalus responds when he makes over to her the clew;
and this relates her to her own mother as a being of passion. It also helps to explain why the myth-ego reacts in
the way he does. He responds to both their passions,
revealing that he too is a passionate being, whose craft is
his longing, lustful, imaginative response.

But Ariadne [she who shines out for all] is more than
just that, for she has other names. As *Aridela* [exceedingly
bright] she is queen of the sky, like her mother, the moon.
As *Arihagne* [exceedingly pure] she is a queen of the
underworld (Kerényi, 1959, p. 230). So she partakes of both
light and darkness. She is, in addition, queen of the maze,
which was her dancing floor [a *daidalon*]; and it was her
dances [*daidalia*] that threaded and rethreaded those paths
to and from the centre. In assisting Theseus, she was
assisting at a rebirth of the light from its dark and labyrinthine womb. And we have confirmation for this story in
Kerényi's consideration of the nature of the labyrinth and
his assertion that its name in the Cretan language, '*da-
pu-ri-to-jo*', means a 'way to the light' (Kerényi, 1976, p.
95). Who better than Ariadne to perform this dance, for as
Arihagne she can find her way to the dark, uncertain, and
murderous centre, remaining unharmed; while as Aridela
she is herself the light of the re-appearing moon. This
motif is confirmed by another tale, where she is buried
alive while pregnant and, in the darkness of the earth,
gives birth to her child, which could just as well have been
Asterion.

Asterion

The moment has come to summarize the nature of the Minotaur, as seen so far, given that beheading a monster is to raise what it represents to a higher consciousness, but also that death has to do with the assimilation into *daidalos* of all that the dying one shows us.

Asterion was not the product of a lasting relationship, but the child of passionate lust, conceived outside wedlock, in the coming together of two forces that could not be kept apart any longer. His mother gave him humanity, therefore awareness and the possibility for emotion. From his step-father he inherits rule, power, judgement, suppression, majesty, expansion, and other riches. He also gains the tendency to go too far, to harden and forget the services expected of him. His true father gives divine depth, power too, but a dynamism that is unpredictable and tidal, difficult to control, and therefore dangerous. From Minos he inherits a steadfast solar clearness. From both real parents he receives the changeability of the moon and its reflectiveness. As such, he is the condition for, and the moment of, conception as well as its product, moon-child, for which the world is never ready. Above all, Asterion represents the riskiness that is entailed by all of this, as well as the possibility of being able to endure such uncertainty.

I have spoken of luminosities and *scintillae* within the psyche, which would coalesce into ego-consciousness; but this is only so within a developmental, integrative fantasy that is the sun's way. Seen as he is and not as what he could be or ought to become, the Minotaur as star-child represents an *Asterion-consciousness,* which retains an ability to exist as fragments only, each with its own scintillary awareness, of which Jung (*CW 8,* para. 396) suggested:

Such visions must be understood as introspective intuitions that somehow capture the state of the unconscious. . . .

And yet

> Since consciousness has always been described in terms
> derived from the behaviour of light, it is in my view not
> too much to assume that these multiple luminosities cor-
> respond to tiny conscious phenomena. [para. 396]

Yet each fragment, with its own consciousness, will be
different from and can oppose or conflict with every other
one, as well as be in agreement with it. Asterion, the sky
without light, is the image that contains them all and can
survive their warring contradictions.

As Tom Moore has pointed out, the image of the
Minotaur is one in which his bullish head betokens a dull-
ing of consciousness (Moore et al., 1979). But for me, it is
not all of consciousness that becomes dulled, but only
Minos's solar clarity that becomes clouded in this way.
Just as the sun will break out again, this clarity, with all
its value, will never go entirely away; it can be recovered
at will. What replaces it is an 'Asterion-consciousness' that
is by its very nature unfocussed, uncertain, discontinuous,
scintillating, and *pointilliste*. And yet each point possesses
a needle-sharp clarity of its own.

Asterion's humanity is within the chest and abdomen,
seat of the emotions, which are, in their turn, the stuff of
that state which Erich Neumann (1973) has called
'matriarchal consciousness'. He wrote:

> That the seat of matriarchal consciousness is in the
> heart and not the head means—to point out only one
> implication of the symbolism—that the ego of
> patriarchal consciousness, our familiar head-ego, often
> knows nothing of what goes on in the deeper center of
> consciousness in the heart. [p. 49]

And of its nature, he said:

> It functions as a kind of total realisation in which the
> whole psyche participates, and in which the ego has the
> task of turning the libido towards a particular psychic
> event and intensifying its effect rather than using the

experience as a basis for abstract conclusion and an expansion of consciousness. The typical attitude of this observing consciousness is contemplating. [p. 53]

In other words, the *scintillae* are not *necessarily* for integration, but for intensification, each in its own right and of its own nature. A myth-ego will intensify each by concentrating upon it; and each will, by turn, intensify a certain type of consciousness, called by Neumann 'matriarchal'. Neumann saw the moon in its male aspect as the centre of the spiritual world of this type of awareness; but also as possessing a feminine aspect (she who shines out for all, who is seen from afar) as 'the highest form of the feminine spirit-self, as Sophia, as wisdom'. He goes on:

This figure of feminine wisdom accords with no abstract, unrelated code of law by which dead stars or atoms circulate in empty space; it is a wisdom that is bound to the earth, to organic growth, and to ancestral experience. It is the wisdom of the unconscious, of the instincts, of life, and of relationship. [p. 56]

It is this kind of awareness that Daedalus brings to birth on Crete: this that he walls up or protects; and which he then raises into awareness, or makes implicit, so that *daidalos* evolves. Both the bullish monster and the severing sword are necessary. Neither alone is sufficient: each requires the other.

In the same essay, Neumann claimed that:

. . . all creative cultural achievement—at least in its highest form—represents a synthesis of receptive matriarchal and formative patriarchal consciousness. . . . [p. 58]

I like what Neumann says and what he is describing. What I would disagree with is his labelling of the two styles by attaching a gender to them. A consideration of that, however, can be left till later.

At the moment of Theseus' sword-stroke, the Minotaur embodies that coming together of the two styles of being that are carried by Theseus and Asterion, so that both become inherent to the field, the one by death, the other by his sailing away. Yet the centre of the labyrinth is not left empty. How could it be, for psyche, like physics, abhors a vacuum. The monster's place is taken by Daedalus and his son Icarus, now mentioned for the first time. It is therefore possible to put forward the equation that Minotaur equals Daedalus plus Icarus; and that Theseus plus Ariadne, midwives or murderers, bring about this change.

Viewed negatively, it could be said that Daedalus, too clever by far and too detached from the moral considerations of his work, finds himself cut off in a maze of his own making. Looked at prospectively, however, something previously hinted at and now newly made has been added to the myth-ego by this substitution: Icarus, a thing not seen in quite this shape before. He is life-in-death as *puer,* but also a representative of the dark night-sky.

The amazing labyrinth

It is necessary to say something about the nature of the labyrinth, that maze of passages similar to, though more complex than, a spiral. In one type, there is merely the task of threading your way along a defined route, which sometimes approaches the central chamber, only to swing away again, though getting nearer all the time, until finally you arrive there. The floor maze in Chartres cathedral is of this type. Others, of which the Cretan one was said to be an example, have moments of choice, when it is possible to take a wrong turning and end in a blind alley, so that a retracing of steps is required. Once at the centre, getting out is as difficult.

The real purpose of any labyrith is that it has no goal other than its threading. Like a spiral, which possesses a similar goallessness, the labyrinth is an image of the *way* to be travelled, rather than the prize to be gained by doing so. Treading a maze is an image of 'process' at work, and its meaning is in the journey trod and retrod that leads to a deeper sense of self. In one of the central chambers of the Arkville maze, built by Ayrton in the Catskill Mountains, stand Daedalus, working on the maze, and his son Icarus, poised for take-off; in the other stands the Minotaur. Since both chambers are lined with bronze mirrors, the travellers also see themselves reflected (Ayrton, 1971, p. 304).

To enter a maze is to pass from the conscious world towards the unknown, while moving outwards is to leave an inner complexity in favour of outer reality with its objectivity and singleness of view. The left-handed path moves towards seeming chaos, an entropic, downward vortex; just as passing in the other direction is negentropic, moving towards structure, aspirations, and hope. Jill Purce (1974) has said of the spiral:

> It is at once the cosmos, the world, the individual life, the temple, town, man, the womb—or intestine—of mother earth, the convolutions of the brain, the consciousness, the heart, the pilgrimage, the way. [p. 29]

The function of a maze is twofold, writes Ayrton, both to arrest the intruder and to protect the centre; he mentions in this respect the enfilade of modern trench warfare and the recursive entrance walls of the Bronze Age enclosure known as Maiden Castle, in England. He also likens the maze that Theseus must tread, and from which Daedalus must escape, to the cedar forest traversed by the Sumerian hero Gilgamesh in search of 'the entrail demon', Humbaba, whom he eventually kills. The maze, he goes on, is repeated in the curled and coiled intestines, which must have been a source of wonderment to the ancients, ignorant as they were of the processes of digestion (Ayrton, 1971, pp. 298–299).

An image of the maze can also be seen in the convolutions of the human brain, from which Athene emerged, the honeycomb of a beehive, and the Cumaean caves. To these can also be added Cocalus, the triton shell, and the star called Helice (see below).

Heroes are often associated with the labyrinth: Gilgamesh, Jonah in the foregut of the whale, Theseus, prince of Athens. In *daidalos* the latter needed Ariadne to assist him in its threading: the ball of twine attached to the outside world, which will magically roll towards the centre and, more importantly, act as a marker on the way out.

Shamans must keep a hold on the outside world so as not to be lost in a spirit maze. It was, said Jung, his patients, his family, and his play with stones upon the lake shore that kept him from psychic disaster during his own great encounter with the contents of the deep unconscious (Jung, 1963, p. 214).

The twine unravels the coiled pathways of the maze, and, even without its prefix *un-*, the word 'ravel' expresses this precisely; the word means both to wind and unwind, to tangle and untangle. Cooper has shown that the Chinese word *luan* has exactly the same paradoxical meanings. It can be translated as both 'chaos' or 'order', according to context. The oracle bone drawing of this character (FIGURE 1) shows that it is made up of two hands, a spool, and some thread. It is possible for the hands either to wind or to unwind the thread, though the two motions are in different directions when viewed from the side. The same image is therefore used to represent both directions of the ravelling, for the *thread* is the same, whether wound or unwound. In the maze, it lies crooked, but could be laid straight. It represents the thread of each individual life, which runs through all byways, no matter how twisted or seemingly disconnected.

From a psychological view it could be said that a maze can represent the process whereby a person can banish what is distasteful to consciousness (repression) and may nurture that which is fragile and new, and, in addition, feel able to protect it from external attack. Nevertheless, there will come a time when that which has gone in must reenter the outside world.

FIGURE 1

During the course of his therapy, David brought me two kinds of dreams: one sort, which he described as 'ordinary', was filled with anxiety; the other sort he called 'archaeological'. I might have called them archetypal. Many of this second kind concerned ancient cities of winding streets, Venice with its canals, or places with underground passageways, and always containing churches, crypts, or cellars. One of them he told as follows:

I'm in a bazaar—like at Istanbul—full of labyrinthine passages, subterranean, with arches above. There are lots of stalls filled with valuable and interesting things. I'm going with the flow of people, which, in a real-life place like this, inevitably takes you out into the open through one of the many exits. In the dream, all such exits are blocked up with foul-smelling latrines, on which dark men are squatting with their trousers down. We come to the centre, which is open to the sky and contains a restaurant, all painted white and blue, as such places often are, in the Mediterranean. There's me, Sue [his wife] and John [a neighbour], and we sit down to eat. The hors d'oeuvre is a whole sea-bass, laid out on a plate, although it's pink and more like a mullet. It's very beautiful in shape, colour, and texture, it costs £10.00. I think that this is too much for just an hors d'oeuvre, because what will the main course cost? I get up to leave by the way we came, feeling ashamed because of my lack of adventurousness. John is probably willing to stay. He may do so.

The dreamer is drawn to the centre of this labyrinth, going against the flow, because the exits are blocked by shifty men who, he thinks, might be parts of himself. The Mediterranean area he associates with a hedonistic time spent there after leaving university and remembered with nostalgia. Sue does not like this kind of trip. John is rather an abrasive person who has recently shown evidence of a much softer side. In real life it would have been John who complained at the price of the fish, and David would have stayed because he could not have said 'no'. The bass is a fish of the base, the bottom, from the deep, or maybe a *sea-boss,* which would be Poseidon. It felt very much as if this numinous creature, at the centre of a dark labyrinth but in a blue and white setting open to the sky, was a communion meal. But it is one of which he does not partake, because he will not pay the price.

This interpretation could be seen as an expression of feelings he still had in real life, namely that therapy was all very well, but what did it actually achieve? But it seemed to us both, on the other hand, that leaving the maze by retracing his exact way in (and there was no other possibility) was also highly significant, as if he had completed a task. In this reading of the dream, seeing the fish, just as it is, was enough. It was a monstrance, or similar to the holding up of an ear of wheat in the Eleusinian mysteries, which would then tell the initiates everything that they needed to know. David has threaded the labyrinth, but not as a hero, and he takes back with him an enlightenment. There are of course other meanings for this dream, which I will not share, but which would include his transference projections onto me, for John, like his therapist, is a doctor.

CHAPTER EIGHT

Falling to death

Of Icarus again

I began with Icarus, his youth and his pyrotechnics. Now is the time to learn more about his nature as image, starting with the earlier statement, that when the Minotaur dies he is replaced by Daedalus and Icarus. I could go on to say:

If Asterion dies, Daedalus is imprisoned.

Only when Daedalus is stuck does Icarus appear.

Icarus begins to function when Daedalus cannot.

Using an integrative fantasy, the youth can be seen as a new content that needs to be incorporated within the myth-ego; or, working from an Asterion viewpoint, hailed as another luminosity asking to be both noticed and acknowledged. And, as must be said again, both views have to be looked on as demanded by the field that is *daidalos*. But what is Icarus now, when grounded and en-mazed? Ovid says of him there:

> . . . not knowing that the materials he was handling were to endanger his life, (he) laughingly captured the feathers which blew away in the wind, or softened the yellow wax with his thumb, and by his pranks hindered the marvellous work on which his father was engaged. [Innes, 1955, lines 194–198]

Leaving that prison by air—the only realm that was not under Minos's control—had been the father's idea. His was the serious business of escape, while the son's, it seems, was one of hindrance. Icarus does not present as a picture of imaginative inventiveness—that was the nature of Talus. Instead, he is someone who responds to serious business by laughing, with pranks and unawareness. I could say that, when earthed, no *puer* can be himself, because his true realm is the sky. But, on the other hand, seen here in the labyrinth, his attitude shows a genuine flightiness, which hinders work: the very thing that has been called his ultimate cure. This lack of seriousness could certainly be seen as a flaw in his nature; but another way of looking at it might be to say that the precise task of every grounded Icarus is to get in the way. He is there to impede work, to stop Daedalus from taking himself so seriously, and to inject a note of play, with enjoyment. This lack of purpose could be a dangerous naivety, for flying on man-made wings is a risky business. But, on the other hand, a person who does not recognize the danger has nothing to fear. Icarus possesses the so-called 'beginner's mind', which attempts and succeeds at the impossible, for the very reason that he does not know it *is* impossible.

What is known defines the unknown: it is a distraction, a small island of awareness in a sea of unknowing. This piece of knowledge, whatever it may be, can easily turn into what is 'true', so that anything else must therefore be untrue, impossible, to be rejected. By this process I become stuck in a high-walled passage that may indeed be going somewhere but denies the existence of any other possible paths towards the same goal. This is the labyrinth in its negative, concretizing aspect. The beginner's mind succeeds, however, because it does not acknowledge the containing walls as having any relevance; it does not even see them, and so is free to wander.

This is, of course, only one view of the labyrinth, for that structure also exists to protect what goes on at the centre, as I have pointed out before. In the present case, what goes on in there, at the turning point between dark and light, is a joint action between—as it were—at least four principles, already recognized. Talus is there, constructing and out-crafting Daedalus. Asterion is there, replacing the mono-lithic with the multiplex. Daedalus is there, copying nature as it is as well as using his head. And Icarus light-ens the project with his airy vapourings, by melting any tendency to leaden seriousness, which can also hinder actions, while at the same time pointing it to the skies. As that ferment works unseen, remember one who is not there in person, yet who got them there—namely, Minos. He hinders in his own way, by containing and constricting, so that he actually brings about that which he would prevent: that is to say, escape.

But there are others present too, as yet unnamed: each essence inherent. There is Pasiphaë, passionate and deter-mined queen; Naucrate, the slave, of boundless power; Ariadne, a father's daughter, who dares to go in as well as turn towards the light; and Perdix, the sorrowing mother. It is Daedalus's passionate longing for freedom that makes him consider flight and light. His power is craft and skill; and he too dares the unknown. In addition, as he strapped on his son's wings, 'the old man's cheeks were wet with tears, and his fatherly affection made his hands tremble' (Ovid, lines 210–211, in Innes, 1955). For the first time, Daedalus displays emotion and for this the presence of Ica-rus seems to be responsible: for a person needs an object on which to bestow feelings. *This* child is his own, unlike Talus, or Asterion, or Ariadne.

Launching

At take-off, the father's instructions for the coming flight
are clear:

1. Do not fly so high that the sun will melt the beeswax.
2. Do not fly so low that the water will wet the feathers.
3. Do not veer towards Helice or Boötes.
4. Do not let your course wander towards Orion.
5. Follow me.

These are words of caution and moderation, for in any
new venture it is sensible to take care. Daedalus gives
good advice, on the practical level as well: beeswax melts
at finger heat, while sea-birds must repeatedly waterproof
their feathers by preening, so as to prevent themselves
from sinking and so drowning.

His next warnings concern a north/south axis, for Helice
and Boötes circle the Pole Star, while Orion stands in the
southern skies. Helice is the final star in the tail of the
constellation known as the Plough, or Great Bear [Gr:
arktos]. It points towards Polaris, also known as Cynosura:
the cynosure or centre of attraction, which is the skywards
extension of the world axis and the pivot of the heavens
around which Arktos and Boötes spiral (a helix). Boötes is
the figure who stands behind the plough, driving it, and it
was into this constellation that Erichthonios was placed at
death, presumably for his skill in harnessing. He became
Arcturus, brightest of the stars, whose name means
'the watcher of the bear' and who was assumed to let
all the other stars out at dusk as well as shut them up
by dawn (Leach, 1949, p. 464). Of this star, Heraclitus
wrote:

The limits of Dawn and Evening [is]
the Bear; and opposite the Bear, the Warder of
luminous Zeus. [D. 120]

Polaris, says Kahn, 'is that point around which the sun turns in its daily course'; and the bear warder is the sky god's representative by night (Kahn, 1979, p. 162).

Bears are strange animals. Treated as sacred over hundreds of thousands of years, they are strong, aggressive, and dangerous, as well as being, at times, harmless and friendly; but above all else they are unpredictable and not to be trusted. Yet the bear is also an image of nurturing and good motherhood. As I have mentioned above, it is associated with the moon from its tendency to disappear in hibernation and to emerge with new-born young. The earliest Chinese pictograph appears to be a crudely drawn picture of the animal itself (FIGURE 2). Since, however, the Chinese have never drawn anything crudely, the presence of a long tail on an animal makes one doubt if this is indeed a bear. Cooper's researches have shown that this picture is in fact an amalgamation of three drawings: that for a 'deer or large animal', which would possess an obvious tail; secondly that of 'flesh'; and thirdly the profile of a 'carrying hand', which is known from other contexts to mean 'bearing' (see FIGURE 3). The combination therefore implies a large, meaty animal, able to bear things.

In Chinese, the three meanings of the word 'bearing'—as in pregnancy, carrying, or demeanour—as well as the animal itself, are all written using this pictograph. In English, too, the same family of meanings is recognized in the spoken language—though not by etymologists! The bear in the heavens is therefore well able (another word from the same root image, as in German: *trinkbar*, drinkable) to carry the weight of the heavens and turn the skies around Polaris (Cooper, personal communication). Nevertheless, the bear is a changeable animal who must be watched by Boötes. So the two constellations are trapped in opposition, circling around each other. On the one hand, then, Daedalus is telling his son, factually, not to fly north, while on the other he suggests that Icarus should not take too much upon his shoulders, nor follow the example of his

A Bear

FIGURE 2

ancestor harnessed to an eternal task that provides no freedom of movement.

As far as the south is concerned, the constellation we call Orion has been associated, from the earliest days of astronomy and astrology, with a hunting giant put into the sky for his impiety. In Greek mythology, this giant was a son of Poseidon. Blinded for sleeping with a mother-figure, Orion regained his eyesight by exposure to the rising sun. As a hunter he was so successful that he threatened to denude the whole world of creatures, and he boasted that there was no living thing he could not vanquish. But the earth sent a scorpion, which stung him to death. Artemis, who loved him (and another story says she actually and mistakenly caused his death), placed him in the southern sky. In Egypt, the same constellation was thought to be the hero-king Osiris on his nightly journey backwards from

Deer   Flesh Physique·   Carrying Hand

FIGURE 3

the west, towards sunrise. Being blinded and then regaining his sight by dawn's early light is the same image as the heroic night-sea journey of Osiris.

If the bear and its warden represent the daily east–west passage of the sun, as well as being law-keeper of the cosmos by night, then Orion by night represents, on the one hand, the law-abiding return journey of the solar orb, but on the other shows the impiety of the wild hunter who goes too far. Even in the skies he roams, with his dog at his heel, chasing the hare and the doves, who flee in front of him. In this he represents a different kind of strength from the watched-over, harnessed, muzzled bear: one that is free to roam and kill as it pleases. Orion's actions are very predictable. He lives out hubris, that capacity to act on impulse without ethical consideration: to break the laws of the cosmos or its ruling deity. He carries the polar opposite of the ordered principles that shine so brightly through Arcturus, representative of Zeus and of his first wife Themis, 'right-living' herself. Orion *is* dis-order.

Daedalus's instructions to his son can be seen in many contradictory ways. This should not be surprising, any more than that a dream might be found to carry many conflicting meanings. But if I were to take an 'is as it is' view of what Daedalus is saying, I would see the father as telling his son: 'Do not follow your harnessed, obedient ancestor, nor go to the other extreme; but follow me.' So just who is the 'me' whom he is supposed to follow?

A flight for Daedalus

Daedalus has travelled a long way from the old snake-man ancestor, specialist in harness and harnessing, as an image for maleness. Much is now contained within the myth-ego and his field as he launches himself from Crete. He is both cautious and moderate, following Themis at all times, though he is hubristic in his invasion of the upper air, realm of the gods. Harnessing is certainly useful, for he must strap on his wings, but in other respects it may be too controlling, if it prevents *bricolage*. And there is an in-built paradox to all he says and does that is worthy of Heraclitus himself. It is as if Daedalus is saying: 'Copy me, for I know that all the ambivalences are there all right, but I just fly through the middle of them.'

It would be useless, however, to expect obedience from Icarus, who has just been advised to harness himself to the known while being provided with a means for exploring the unknown. To this youth belongs the possibility of learning a new technique and then exploiting it to the full, for its own sake, rather than just to bring about a successful outcome. Ovid tells us that the two men were mistaken for gods as they passed over Crete, heading north-east for Asia Minor; it is then that the younger one begins his adventures, not because he wishes to reach the sun, but 'from eagerness for the open sky'. It is an urge that draws him up and on and into limitless, unconfining space: a very different image from labyrinth or harness.

Daedalus used his invention for a purpose—namely: escape. The means are hubristic, though allowable, it seems, because of the moderateness of his demands. Icarus is concerned with the total experience and a freedom to explore, which forgets purpose: the means being an end in themselves. Icarine flight both soars and plummets: it invades the gods' realm, paying them no heed; it goes where the whim takes it and heads for Zeus (the open sky). Icarus both flies towards the north *and* emulates Orion in his self-inflation. By pushing the adventure as far as it can go, he discovers the limits of the equipment and technique in a way that moderation never could. He tests it to destruction and, in plummeting, brings that knowledge back to earth.

The moderation of Daedalus, however, belongs to and comes from Minos in Crete. In this respect it is an outlook that performs only what is seemly or possible, a judgemental nature that wins through by taking pains. And if flight is only like this, then it lacks panache: a commuter shuttle rather than a flying circus. And of course it is certainly easy to be moralistic over the parts of any person that act like an Icarus; but it should be remembered that:

It is only when Icarus goes too far that Daedalus flies on to landfall.

Each man solves the problem of the opposites within him in his own style. Daedalus's way is contained within his speech, ending with 'follow me'; while the answer that Icarus provides is to seek the open sky, and to transcend the problem in that way.

For a time in flight they separate, as opposites must, not knowing each other's whereabouts, just as neither understands the other's nature. It is death that reunites them, and the dying fall has already been recognized as an example of the inherence of all that he-who-dies can mean within the person of he-who-lives. Everything that the son represents has now merged into the myth-ego; whereupon the lapwing makes his reappearance, to crow its joy. It might be Talus, delighted that the sorrowing Daedalus has himself suffered a bereavement like his sister Perdix— which is certainly Ovid's intention. Could it, instead, be the soul of Icarus, likewise saved from his broken body? Or should it be read as the joy of the falling, soaring soul when two of its conflicting tendencies (here imaged as Daedalus and Icarus) have been separated and explored, but can now be contained in one person. They do so, moreover, without at the same time losing their identities or natures. Outside the maze, Icarus represents the wild flight, while Daedalus carries the ability to survive falling, which was once just a lapwing image. And the epiphany of the lapwing at this moment signals its inclusion within *daidalos* as the trick of flying-without-falling.

Westering

From his son's graveside on the island of Ikarios, Daedalus's flight takes him in a westerly direction, copying the daytime sun. He lands in safety while the sun falls into the ocean to return eastwards by its 'night-sea journey', a province of the hero's task. Daedalus, landing in one piece, has decribed a path with no known wanderings, just like the sun, or as a carriage horse when blinkered for reliability. The journey is like that sure path that can thread and unthread the winding labyrinth to its goal, without deviation. Or, as the actual waters of the Maeander, despite the river's twists and turns, can still be relied upon to reach the sea. Yet there is more to Daedalus's flight and its direction than that.

Since to face east and the dawning sun is to 'orient' oneself to that flaring up which is the innate spirituality of nature, it follows that to move westwards is an action of dis-orientation, even if it should also be the sun's regular path towards apparent death. Western Apollo is the dying god, dying to be reborn in the east at dawn, whose returning light can only be preceded by a darkness and a deliberate move towards that obscurity. Westering implies that sinking feeling. It acknowledges the unavoidable ravages of time, as well as being the sinister process of the left-hand path that spirals down and inwards (unlike Icarus in flight). Not only does it mimic the trusty sun, but it images as well the way of introversion and re-entry. For Cumae, where the myth-ego comes to earth, is not only sacred to solar Apollo, but it also possesses an entrance to the underworld of Hades.

When mother Gaia clutched the earth in her birth pangs, keeping silence in order not to betray the birth of Zeus to his infant-eating father Kronos, there sprang from her finger-marks the Kabirioi, dwarfish people of the earth. Those born of the right hand were metalworkers; from the left came healers and magicians. Left-handed, downwards westering travel can be seen as a one-off, shamanic journey to the spirit world and back again. It is 'widdershins', or 'widersinnes' in Middle High German, meaning contrary to the sun. But 'going west' also invites the traveller to depart on voyages of discovery, to dare chancy opportunities, to take to the wild, to make it or break. But at this point in *daidalos,* the two, right and left, have come together. Westering represents not only that wild, heroic, Icarine flight, but a journey that is reliable, as well as uncertain, and which can take in loss, sorrow, and death. Over all it is 'lift-off', 'flying fit to bust', 'flying without falling', and then 'happy landing'. And it will be followed by a laying down of wings.

Landfall at Cumae

Cumae stands at the northern end of the Bay of Naples, a massive acropolis, jutting into the sea. On its summit is a temple of Apollo, and it was here that Daedalus landed and laid up his wings as a thanksgiving to the god; and here that he made carefully chased golden doors for the temple itself. They told the story of what had gone before, except that his grief repeatedly prevented him from sculpting the death of his son.

Verticality was deadly for Talus (from another acropolis), and for Icarus too, but Daedalus lands gently. To him belongs not only the mastery of flight, but that of take-off and landing as well. He can go down as well as up, like the lapwing—something indeed to give thanks for upon the altar of the god whose passage through the sky he had just copied. It is natural to be grateful for favours received, as it is natural to make offerings to gods or goddesses to avoid their anger. The dedication of his wings and the making of the golden doors can be seen as an 'apotropaism', like carrying iron to drive away the thunderbolts, or calling the grizzly bear 'Old Grandad'. But it might be thought that Daedalus seems too easily to have forgotten that in effect it was the self-same Apollo who had just killed Icarus. Should he not fear the god himself, hate him even, or wish for revenge? But whatever I, as a psychologist, might think of a person who acts reasonably in order to avoid and repress their aggressive feelings, in the context of *daidalos* it can only be said:

'When Daedalus lands, he gives up flying.'

'The death of Icarus is a cause for thankfulness.'

I believe that such phrases open up the field in an unexpected and ultimately creative fashion. Wings have got him this far. They were a concrete response to his strong desire for freedom and a means to an end, which, once he had reached it, he needs no longer. Wings, though abandoned, must inhere too; and the ability to fly without falling, or to copy Apollo in his westering, is not lost to the field. If such skills—and the image that Icarus provides can be seen to represent a skill—were now an intrinsic part of Daedalus, it would be natural and sensible for him to give thanks.

And Cumae was, as has been noticed, a very special place to land. Had Daedalus just wished to worship Apollo, it would have been quicker and closer to stop off at the god's sacred birthplace on the island of Delos. What is unique about Cumae is that at the base of the rocky outcrop lived the Cumaean Sybil, in the deepest passages of a labyrinth of caves, which were the entrance to Hades.

Sybils were originally wandering women who had been inspired by Apollo to speak prophecies. The most famous, who lived at Cumae, had been a nymph to whom the sun god promised fulfilment of any wish if she accepted his lovemaking. She asked for everlasting life, but forgot to ask for everlasting beauty too; so that by the time she had reached the age of seven hundred years, she was a wizened and dried-up creature who hid herself away in these caves. As an immortal being, and therefore suggestive of an archetypal ability, she lived and spoke at the junction of the worldly with its underworldly counterpart, with access to both.

The Sybils uttered Apollinine prophecies, with shrieks and riddling words. It may seem ironic that the god of clarity, of light, youth, music, archery, and healing should also have a babbling, un-rational hag as his mouthpiece, from a darkened cave. But such facts imply that clarity alone is not enough. For completeness, a person must remain in contact with that other world, where meanings are hidden or uncertain, and of ambiguous or plural interpretation. Today there are still riddles to be solved, and too often people will still look for only such skills as help to banish the irrational in a clear-headed Apollinine way. Present-day riddles may have changed in nature from palaeolithic and pre-literate times, or even from those of classical Greece; yet the process remains the same, for the setting and solving of riddles have an archetypal nature. Apollo needed to remind and be reminded of the equal though opposite power of uncertainty and confusion, by means of his Sybils. There is a similar need in our culture to learn to accept that many possible meanings intertwine within seemingly straightforward answers; and that clarity is only a part of the picture of how things really are.

The noise and babble of the entranced Sybil recalls the sun god's half brother Dionysus with his accompanying maenadic women, and the *ecstasis* and *enthousiasmos* that were the hallmarks of his arrival. Heraclitus says:

A man when drunk is led by a beardless boy, stumbling, not perceiving where he is going, having his soul moist. [D. 117, in Kahn, 1979, p. 244]

Moistness of the soul is a property of the *puer,* here presented as the beardless boy who is also Dionysus. Among other things, the master of riddling, multi-levelled remarks is warning against the loss of *logos* caused by passing into the watery element of Dionysian drunkenness. This statement could be reversed to claim that the possession of a watery soul requires intoxication, for only by this means is it possible to get away from the Apollinine control of superego-consciousness that is often mistaken for selfhood. Of course, it is not by alcohol as such that this should be achieved, but by trying to allow a Dionysian frenzy to come alive within. And 'frenzy' is derived from the Greek word *'phrenes'*, which denoted the mind as felt in the region of the heart and lungs (Onians, 1951, p. 28).

Promethean fire

Apollo's rays are dry, hot, and fiery ones, scorching down out of the sky. His nature as fire can also be compared with that of Hephaestus, whose fire is from within the earth. The sun's heat is steady, and the time span that it represents is linear as well as cumulative. It is the steady heat of the smith's forge, when the ores are smelting. The fire of the earth, however, which flares through volcanic eruption, or as forest fire, has no such regular qualities. It is unpredictable, destructive, and irregularly occurring. It is fire that must be tamed, harnessed, and contained if it is to be useful. This variable fire, with its flaring up and dying down, is also needed at the forge, control of both types being demanded of the smith.

But fire is not just sacred or godlike, for we cook our food and heat our homes with it. Its arrival on earth was described in Greek mythology as a theft from Olympus by Prometheus, another metallurgist, and therefore amplificatory of the theme of *daidalos*.

Prometheus was one of the Titans who ruled Creation before the Olympian gods came upon the scene. Titans were gigantic creatures, often clumsy, with a tendency to go too far and over-reach themselves; for they were said to know no *themis*. Realizing that the inevitable battle with the Olympian gods would soon be lost, the wily Prometheus persuaded his brother Epimetheus that they should side with Zeus. The two Titans represent separate aspects of a single nature. Prometheus, of the crooked thoughts, can see how things will turn out in advance. He is the forward thinker who can and will take avoiding action. Epimetheus, his brother, can, on the other hand, only learn after the event, so that he naively enters into actions and events that just as often finish with his coming to grief.

Prometheus helped Hephaestus at Athene's birth, for which the goddess rewarded him by teaching him architecture, astronomy, mathematics, navigation, medicine, metallurgy, and other crafts. When Prometheus made humans out of clay, Athene then breathed souls into them. But Zeus soon was bored with these simple humans and wished to destroy them, being persuaded not to by Prometheus himself. To the Titan was then given the task of finishing his own creation, by teaching these humans all of the skills he had learnt from the goddess, as her father's daughter. Zeus, seeing the ingenuity and inventiveness of humankind that resulted, was furious and insisted that they should now be made to sacrifice to him as their master. But Prometheus so arranged the sacrifice that the Olympians received only the worst part of the ox and had to be content with that. Even more enraged, Zeus then withheld the gift of fire, so that human beings had to eat their meat both raw and cold. Nothing daunted, Prometheus stole the fire from the gods' own hearth, for which he was punished by being sent the beautiful Pandora, an artificial woman fashioned by Hephaestus.

On the assumption that it is unwise to accept a gift from a god as it is always likely to be a trick, Prometheus rejected Pandora and advised his brother to do the same. But the heedless Epimetheus did not listen, and as a result the box that Pandora brought with her was opened, so that all sorts of problematic qualities escaped into the world. Prometheus was punished once again—this time for his craftiness in seeing through Zeus's trick—by being chained to the Caucasus mountains, with an eagle to chew at his liver by day. Each night the bird left him alone, and the liver regenerated, so that there was another meal for the gigantic creature by morning. This sentence was to continue, without reprieve or parole, for thirty thousand years.

Prometheus is a tricksterish figure with craftsmanlike talent in many spheres. He separates the human world

from that of the gods, cutting the umbilical cord that joined
them, so that now the people relate to the gods only by
worship and sacrifice—or not, as the case may be. For the
first time what is theirs by divine right can be withheld,
and humankind is free to invent or to do godlike things
and to get away with it. Prometheus always operates outside the boundaries of what is right and proper: outside
themis. Indeed, *themis* is itself an Olympian possession, for
it is said of the Titans that they did not know it. Stolen
from the gods, however, just like fire, the world can live by
it—or not.

But knowing nothing of *themis*, or what it represents,
means that it is impossible for Prometheus to act
hubristically, since the one quality can only be defined by
knowledge of its opposite. It is the beginner's mind again,
the innocent eye, acting simply, within its nature, to take
whatever it desires; although this nature also includes
making a mess of things, as Epimetheus does. However,
such action will bring in its train the suffering of chronic
woundedness, as well.

The Caucasus, to which Prometheus is chained, can be
seen as an image of the world axis around which all turns,
just as the eagle is the bird of Zeus, king of the gods; and
the liver was once thought to be the seat of life (Onians,
1951, p. 85). This punishment is an attempt to hold him in
the centre, so as to disempower his crafty tendencies, for
Prometheus's skills are peripheral and borderline ones.
Yet it could also be said that because he *is* in the centre,
those marginal tendencies are pulled right to the mid-point
where they can work most powerfully, without their true
nature ever being completely destroyed. For just as he separates the two realms, Prometheus holds the two together
in connection as well: he is the means by which the archetypal can be embodied in mundane living. Once stolen and
made real, such things can never be taken away. What was
once an unknown potential, now exists. In archetypal
terms, the borderline has been centralized, but without losing its own liminal nature, or being disempowered.

Moreover, although Promethean consciousness is not hubristic, seen from within its own nature, it *is* a crime against themis, when looked at with Olympian detachment. It is therefore Zeus who punishes, while it is Prometheus who accepts the punishment on humanity's behalf. Every new skill consciously acquired, or fresh technique, whatever their field, brings more with it than was bargained for. Each time, another Pandora's box will be opened, letting fresh strife and disorder loose upon the world—although each of these is archetypal also and therefore *must* exist. Thus people have to learn to suffer, for their craft and for their cleverness, just as Prometheus did. Indeed, he represents the very ability to do so.

Daedalus is clearly Promethean, able to create images *de novo,* stealing flight, and harnessing fire. In fact, it is by the management of heat, as I have said, that the master metalworker reveals himself: controlling it at all times. He knows whether it needs to be steady and unchanging or when the work requires its intermittent and variable nature. The whole of *daidalos* is shot through with images of metalwork. There is lost wax casting, magic weapons, golden doors, a gilded calf, as well as the many human metaphors for the craft, which have already been studied. It is by his creative urge and imaginative powers that Daedalus 'steals' things from the gods and makes them factually real. Yet he stores up trouble for himself by the Pandora's boxes that he lets loose upon the earth. And the Prometheus in him, lacking *themis,* will find those contents difficult to control. Yet Daedalus is prepared, like Epimetheus, after-thinker that he is, to act naively too and then work with the consequences. As Ayrton pointed out, it is valuable to be prepared to fall flat upon one's face, for even that implies new understanding.

CHAPTER NINE

Sicilian times

At Camicus

W hat does it signify that Daedalus, the master craftsman, now settles in an unheard-of Sicilian town at the court of a king of whom nothing is known, just to make playthings for young royal girls? These questions need to be answered, for it is clear by now that all of his actions, however trivial they may seem, can also be deeply significant.

Sicily was said to be a gigantic rock thrown by Zeus in order to crush the dragon Typhoeus, who was then threatening to renew the Titanic war; and the eruptions of Mount Etna are the trapped beast's furious belchings. They also announce the fiery forges of Hephaestus's Roman double, Vulcan, who worked here, assisted by the Cyclops, those simple one-eyed giants who, just as the Titans, possessed no *themis*. Homer writes of them:

> The Cyclops have no assemblies for the making of laws
> nor any settled customs, but live in hollow caverns in

the mountain heights, where each man is lawgiver to his
children and his wives and nobody cares a jot for his
neighbour. [*The Odyssey, IX,* l. 103, in Shewring, 1980]

They sound like hunter–gatherers, such as the
Esquimaux, whose derisive name means 'raw-flesh eaters',
or all those peoples who live by the laws of the wild world
that is pre-Olympian, perhaps lacking fire.

It was on Sicily, also, that Herakles fought and killed
Eryx the royal son of Aphrodite and Poseidon, thus proving, it is said, that immortals may die. Eryx then gave his
name to the mountain sacred to his mother. But the part of
the island to which Daedalus came, Camicus, was
renowned for nothing: it was associated only with its king,
Cocalus, whose name probably comes from the Greek word
'*cochlias*', meaning a snail shell or screw [English: cockle].
So much for the island, but what happened there?

On the one hand, I could describe it as that of a man who
is past his prime, his creative muse spent, and who moves
into a second childhood, where all he is fit for is the making of jointed dolls for young girls. This version would fit in
with a view that sees the death of Icarus as a serious loss
of inspiration, following which all is, for Daedalus, down-
hill. And it would fit with taking his future move to Sardinia as that of an old man, put out to grass, transported to
the colonies, and living a rustic life similar to that of
Kronos (god of the *senex*) upon the Isles of the Blest, still
further to the west.

But this would be to ignore the making of the golden
heifer, or golden honeycomb, and the threading of the Triton shell, all of which belong to this period. Genius has not
been abandoned, and indeed provides evidence of its own
pinnacle. In addition, since Sicily is Vulcan's home, it
could be said that Daedalus has come now, more than ever,
closest to the archetypal core that is his own nature,
namely the underground fire that metalworkers obtain
from their maternal origins (Typhoeus was half-brother to
Hephaestus). Yet since they have inherited the fire, the

craftworkers will now chance their arm and harness the unknown to make it useful, transformative, creative. But neither of those versions can be the whole story, so another approach is also necessary.

At Camicus, Daedalus is again near young people. Talus was the apprentice who surpassed his master; Icarus the son who knew no bounds; and the girls demand the ordinary—dolls and hot bath water. And who is whose apprentice now? Although I have noted above that a girl can be a young person of either gender, yet the change that is demonstrated here from *puer* to *kore* must be significant. There has been a shift of concern from identity with, and competition between, the generations (parent/child) to one that also introduces 'difference' and 'the other', as imaged by the opposite gender. *Puer* has not been abandoned or outlived, nor is it even that all he represents is now inherent. It can only be said that at this moment, in this situation, in this region of the field, the myth-ego is relating as father to daughters. Any advance for *daidalos* will now be through a father/daughters perspective. Note the plural, for there is no one-to-oneness as with Zeus/Athene or Minos/Ariadne. It is open to the line of Cocalus to descend, in various female directions, through each of his un-numbered daughters; and, since this is the nature of this area of *daidalos*, Daedalus moves on as well. Within the context of Camicus, he is concerned with the girls, their play, the hot water, Minos and his Triton shell, and all that these will be seen to represent. While over and above soars Mount Eryx and the temple of the love goddess.

The name of that summit suggests the heather that covers it [Latin: *erica*], along with the nectar-gathering bees who signify a less evolved nature of the goddess of love and relationship: Aphrodite Melissa. Originally the temple was a Phoenician one, dedicated to Astarte, famous for her doves and for temple prostitution. Astarte is the aspect of Aphrodite previously seen as imaged by partridge or by sparrow. But in Greece the love goddess is more, for she had become not just a patron of sexual attraction. As

Aphrodite, she is also a wife (to Hephaestus), a mother (of Eros), and a lover (of Ares). As a result of the affair with Ares, she gave birth to Harmonia; for such a goddess, this is an unexpected parentage, of love *and* war. The word *harmonia* originally meant no more than the *fitting together*, snugly side by side, of two separate things, like planks of a ship's deck (it was a carpenter's term)—or two lovers in a bed, perhaps. Later it came to be used of the reconciliation of opponents (such as love and war), while only thirdly was it a pattern of musical notes (Kahn, 1979, p. 197).

Caught in the act of infidelity by her husband with his golden net, and laughed at by the other gods, Aphrodite, when released, returned to her birthplace in Cyprus, so as to bathe and restore her virginity. For not only is she a mother, but she is also goddess of the virginal in the sense of all that is to come. And, being a goddess, she can easily contain both contradictory elements, the touched and the untouched, within her image. It is to this virginal aspect of her nature that young girls dedicated their dolls, on Mount Eryx, when they reached maturity and set them aside; and it is in this role that her emblem is the heifer. On Eryx, where Daedalus placed its golden effigy, the bulls of Zeus and Poseidon have given away to another image: that of the non-mature, unmounted, un-impregnated cow that is Aphrodite. The possibilities are all unknown—contained and yet to come. Beginnings stir within and not without, for it is nature itself that is now concerned, not some pale copy.

Although neither virgin nor prostitute can be 'wrong' archetypally, just different from each other, the nature of the process emphasized at Camicus is one that is more uncertain and incubatory.

It is these skills that the myth-ego can learn from the maidens who are his very different patrons at Camicus. He has moved on from Athene, the divine tutor, to the demigod Minos, and then to the all-too-human Cocalus with his daughters. They do not ask him for dancing floors, cow-frames, or labyrinths, but merely toys. In Sicily he has become a craftsman of the ordinary for his patrons, though genius remains to be used when, and especially where, appropriate. By separation, it has been freed from the mundane.

Minos returning

But Minos, it seems, can never be far behind. He has been seen as an empire builder, a gatherer of all things into his own hands, a maker of law, and a judge of souls. He finds it difficult to allow anyone or anything to escape his grasp. Minos-consciousness is inclusive and enclosing, for its monolithic nature sees flight from the centre as 'getting away with something' and so as a loss of its own control. Whatever or whoever it might be must be brought back. In this view of him, he is quite different from the starry nature of Asterion, or from a father with daughters. Minos demands simple and single answers to the problems set, answers with which Daedalus himself once complied, just as he cannot resist complying now.

It is important not to become judgemental of the king, for that would be to take on his own role. He is not all bad, someone to be booed off the stage whenever he appears. The qualities of Minos are *valuable* and by their containing or making of boundaries they set the problems, as well as providing a secure setting for their solution. His reappearance now is as it is and recalls the fact that *daidalos* can never, must never, lose those qualities that become those of the negative *senex* at *end-phase*. What *senex* needs in order to remain out of that dried-up state is craft; just as, vice versa, what Daedalus must embrace now is his Minos nature. So it is appropriate that Minos draws *his* craftsman back into the open with a task that is worthy of him alone. At this moment, the myth-ego needs to relate to a Minos within.

The Triton shell the king carries is a spiral, screw-like seashell, which he asks to be threaded along the line of its passages. The shell is like a labyrinth but in three dimensions, spiralling into or away from the centre, when viewed in plan, and from above down (or vice versa), if seen from the side. Horizontal and vertical axes are combined within its nature. Daedalus achieved this task by drilling a hole in its apex and dripping honey through the shell. Then, attaching a thread to an ant, he persuaded the creature to traverse the spirals by following the sticky, sweet trail. Minos, threaded shell in hand, demanded his renegade, but Cocalus demurred, made no decisions, and asked the mighty sea lord ashore to dinner.

The shadowy nature of the Sicilian king as psychological determinant now begins to make itself plain. Like any snail, he is vulnerable within his easily crushed shell, and more so when extended. He is slow to move, but quick to retract and draw in his horns, blowing out a froth to put off foes. The snail is not a hero or a creature of bravado or attack. His defences are to withdraw and sit tight, still, waiting, hoping. Cocalus cannot possibly overpower Minos and his troops, but neither will he give up the dollmaker, it seems. Instead he prevaricates and plays for time, without provoking aggression. He associates with the marauder on his own Sicilian ground, without looking for any hero from across the seas. Within that territory, it is not he himself, but his daughters who now become active. Being unwilling to give up their connection with the myth-ego, they draw Minos into inherence instead. Their play now serious, with Daedalus's assistance they construct a system of pipes through which to pour boiling water upon the bathing king, so that he scalds to death. In the same way, shellfish are boiled, while still alive, before being eaten.

Cocalus is an image of someone who withdraws, not through panic, but craftily and for effect. He plays with time, in order that time may provide an answer, which it does; for the playful daughters use their own innovative skills, which belong more to Daedalus and his 'means to an end' than to the king as patron. Indeed, the father hands over effective action to his young. These daughters can do what he could not. This trust in the skill of others and in 'allowing it to happen' is the antithesis of the father that is Minos, who, in this realm of Cocalus, has moved outside his own known kingdom, into trouble. It is not surprising if he gets himself into hot water.

It is a strange and secret death, his own sailors being told that he tripped over a carpet and fell into a cauldron of water. His body was buried in Aphrodite's temple, and his leaderless troops moved on to colonize another part of the island. His death is like the death of the 'old king' studied earlier. The heat, the water, and the vessel may recall the dropsical king who was minced in pieces so as to be renewed. And yet the positive and important role that Minos plays once he has arrived on the Sicilian scene, must be noted and held on to.

What he has provided for his craftsman, and what his nature still provides, is patronage—that is to say, an attitude that protects the craftsman, lending him influential support so that he is free to advance his art. What he expects in return is performance. Daedalus can perform the useful task with ease, even to the making of wings. On Sicily, however, he has flown with Icarus and can now attempt the *bravura* exhibitionism that was that young man's gift to his father. But he needs a Minos to tempt it out of him, for genius lies not only in the craftsman who makes great artefacts, but in that part of him—the Minos part—which can also pose great questions.

Yet the threading of the shell is not only this. Daedalus escaped from the Cretan maze by ignoring its boundaries, by going up rather than along. The labyrinth presented to him now incorporates both directions, as it is a three-dimensional helix. This is the differentiation of *daidalos*. Any solution to a problem becomes a part of the next task to be fulfilled: the exception becomes the rule, and loopholes are progressively stopped up, demanding fresh escape routes. Yet the threading of the shell shows that for the well-crafted there will always be answers, just as a myth-ego can always tell more stories.

Minos is laid to rest, surprisingly, on Mount Eryx. Why should this be so? Earlier I have suggested that death in this story can represent the placing of images exactly where they belong; and the death of Minos has also been likened to a renewal of the old king. Thus power, single-mindedness, judgement, questioning, and his other attributes belong with Aphrodite. Stripped from any negative coating provided by Minos as man, these are now transformed by his burial in the temple into love and relatedness. He has joined up with the passion that was previously only experienced by Pasiphaë, as a bull is with its heifers. As far as Daedalus is concerned, the posing of questions has now become inherent, so that he can do it for himself, releasing his own virtuosity, available as or when required: the unity that was Minos is replaced by leaderless troops who colonize the island: and these two (Minos plus troops) represent the renewal of the old Cretan king.

Here is another of David's dreams:

Tom has died. It is our responsibility to take the coffin to his house, or workplace, which looks like a factory. It's the centre of his business empire, and the important thing is that his body should lie there, where it belongs. Only I have the key to the door and only I know the code of the complicated burglar alarm that protects the building. As I unlock the door and prepare to turn off the alarm, two scruffily dressed men leave the building further up the road and make off. They are burglars, and I know that they have got all of Tom's treasure: everything that he worked to amass. Maybe they are apprehended. It's uncertain.

Tom, who was David's closest friend at school, excelled academically, so that David gave up competing and took to sport. 'I can never excel, or compete', he says. Nowadays, Tom is very ordered, very single-minded, and very ambitious, and he has a high-ranking position. He has also had therapy himself. Everything about him is very well turned out and 'hi-tech'. 'There's a big part of me like that: the doer', David said. There is also a burglar part who would like to make off with the treasure he has not earned. As we spoke about the dream, David realized that he did not have to be any one of those parts exclusively, but could be either or both. Nor does either part have to compete or excel. He has the key and can get into the empire, but the act of his doing so also releases the men with the treasure, which David saw as representing his creativeness. The important thing was to do *something* and thereby to get each aspect of himself into its proper place, like putting Tom's body where it belonged, or releasing the 'robbers'.

Another quality of *daidalos* has first been implied, then mapped out, and finally put in its rightful place. For this Daedalus gives thanks with his offering of a golden honeycomb in the temple of Aphrodite, the bee goddess, where also lies the body of the king. Both are in a harmonious relationship side by side: king and comb, the question and the ultimate brilliance of execution. The golden honeycomb is an example of art for art's sake, a slavish copying of nature that has now been laid up by the master craftsman, as his wings were before. Of what use is a golden honeycomb, other than to be filled by bees? They would have done this even if given a more workaday structure. But this honeycomb, existing as a fact and not just in imagination, is a fantastic amalgam. It is a coming together of top-flight skill with precious material, so that on looking at their harmonious interlay one can only marvel that such things are possible. It is sheer virtuosity: the most grandiose fantasies fleshed out. In his book, *The Maze-Maker,* Michael Ayrton described how such a piece could be made and was challenged to do just that. Using an ordinary beeswax comb as a model and mantling it with liquid clay before pouring it full of molten gold, he succeeded. This golden comb, put in a hive, was actually filled by the bees with honey (Ayrton, 1967, p. 304).

But any honeycomb, whatever its materials and however brilliant its execution, is, in one sense, nothing more than a container: like a mantle, like Minos, and like Cocalus. Honey would run away and be lost, if not held in something, just as a person might not find the pathway through a labyrinth without its surrounding walls, and as the Triton shell contains the stream of honey that the ant follows. And yet, a comb is a different kind of container from a bowl or honey pot. Each hexagonal cell within the comb is separate and individual, so that, taken together as comb, they provide a single object made up of many different parts.

Curiously, the gift of the comb to the bee goddess is in response to the actions performed by the ant, which is itself an image of Daedalus as a problem-solver, or the treader of his own mazes. What, therefore, is the nature of these two creatures, and their relationship to *daidalos*?

Ant and bee

Both the ant and the bee are industrious insects, living in communal groups, and like humanity in that respect. Or is it the other way around? Since insects are evolutionarily much more ancient than mammals, might *we* have inherited *their* social ways instead?

The cutting insect

Ants live mostly under or on the ground. Their nests, if opened up, present a maze of wandering, irregular passages, with no very clear pattern to their meanders. What goes on inside the nest looks just as chaotic as the architecture, but closer inspection shows that the seemingly random comings and goings are ordered and purposive. Each ant is about its own business, which is the business of the colony, however much it zigzags along its way. Their devotion to this task is amazing, even surviving the curiosity of some scientists who have progressively amputated, section by section, the bodies of ants that were carrying an object. Even a truncated ant-head will, it seems, try to continue with its task, legless and bodiless.

Ants make their nests in the earth by digging out the passages and by using organic matter (leaves, twigs, grasses), which they chop up with their jaws to fashion the walls, leaving the material still fairly recognizable. They do this with their usual thrifty (nothing wasted), patient (taking all day if necessary), and tenacious (not asking for help) ways, till the task is completed. Some species enslave other ants who live in the captors' nests and do much of the labouring. Others extract a milky substance from various kinds of aphid insect, which they visit in their own habitat, on bushes or trees—even the tops of tall pines. These are the so-called ant-cows.

All this would have been known to the Greeks and so to the hearers of these stories, although they would not have known that ants communicate with one another by secreting subtle chemicals called 'pheromones', which are so specific and so sensitive that a single molecule can be effective. This discovery makes sense of the apparently miraculous ability of ants to co-operate, or to know instantly what is happening elsewhere in the nest, or in the neighbourhood. For example, on a suitably fine day in summer, the mating flight takes place. Winged virgins and the slightly smaller males, also with wings, congregate excitedly outside the nest. The same thing is happening, at the same moment, outside many other nests in the neighbourhood. It might look as if a communal decision had been taken that this was the one day in the year for mating; in reality, however, the phenomenon is due to pheromone excretion. For this same reason, all the ants will take off together, which ensures that the resulting fertilization will foster a sharing of genetic material from various nests. After mating, each new queen lands and sheds her wings, for which she has no further use, with a single shrug. She then buries herself in the earth, to begin the task of laying eggs and building up a new colony, which may or may not survive, for it is a risky business. The males, meanwhile, have landed, and shortly they die, their task completed. The likeness to the flights of Daedalus and Icarus is clear, though Daedalus as queen ant is a new and startling image.

The Greeks would probably have regarded the creature at the centre of the nest as a king, as they did with bees. However, ants have always been associated with the mother goddess in her role as queen of the earth. The teeming ants are similar to the Kabirioi, as attendants upon Gaia and her daughters. Some Ethiopian ants were reputed to bring up droplets of gold from deep within the earth, which confirms the image of them as miners and smelters (Von Franz, 1980, p. 82). The sting of their bite is due to formic acid, which itches and burns, so that ants have also always been regarded as fiery creatures as well as cutters and chewers. In his book *The Visions Seminars,* Jung (1976) refers explicitly to the ant as an image of multitude. He says:

> The figure in the vision was very great, a universal God, and these ants are exceedingly small but many; so there is one big one against many small ones. The fact that the devil is said to be lord of all such creatures—of fleas, rats, vermin of every description—indicates that when God is not one, then he is all over the place. [p. 331]

He also remarks that ants are images of the vegetative nervous system and symbolize unconscious activity at body level. From another view they represent the hidden order of unconscious material, which, when viewed by the conscious mind, may indeed seem a chaos. But since like cures like, only this kind of unconscious orderedness can overcome that which is externally chaotic.

The one that quivers

Honey bees, on the other hand, the 'quivering insect'
(*OED*), are far from being earth-bound. They make their
homes in hollow trees or rocky cavities and even hanging
free from branches. They do not dig or delve. As has been
said before, the Greeks thought of the creature at a hive's
centre as a king bee, an idea derived from Egypt. All the
other inhabitants they assumed to be his wives. Bees,
unlike ants, have an extremely ordered and regular nest
structure, which they are constantly building onto, repair-
ing, sweeping, and clearing of marauders or debris. In the
wild, their nests are made of natural material too, but it
has been chewed to a pulp and mixed with a cement (propolis) that makes it look more like a leathery paper. Mice,
another of Aphrodite's creatures, will sometimes enter a
beehive during winter for the warmth, their nests being
tolerated by the bees. The whole beehive is filled with hexagonal cells that are perfectly regular and in which are
found eggs, larvae, and, of course, the queen. The honeycomb, made of wax secreted by the bees, is composed of
similar cells. Of this comb, Maurice Maeterlinck (1958)
wrote:

> No living creature, not even man, has achieved in the
> centre of his sphere what the bee has achieved in her
> own; and were someone from another world to descend
> and ask of the earth the most perfect creation of life, we
> should needs have to offer the humble comb of honey. [p.
> 172]

If the ant resembles a miner, then the bee is more like a
craftworker, who takes his material and transforms it into
things that are totally different: paper, propolis, wax, and
above all else, honey. Maeterlinck makes the point that
the making of honey involves more than just the collection
of nectar from flowers, for it is then mixed with digestive
juices and lies in the comb cells, incubating and transform-
ing. The whole process of its making is, says Maeterlinck,
an example of the creature's industriousness as well as its

altruism; for in all probability, the honey that each bee makes so fanatically she will not eat herself. It is there to sustain a future generation of bees, who will feed off it during winter, thus ensuring the survival of the hive for the coming year. Another sign of their altruism, he says, is their sting, for if they use it, they die. Thus aggression is only for the common good.

It is, however, possible to argue that these activities are not at all altruistic, but happen only in order to foster the survival of each bee's own genetic material (see Dawkins, 1976). Since all the bees in a hive are children of the same queen, they are genetically identical, so that the work of each bee for itself only *appears* to be a labour on behalf of all.

Bees co-operate in the collection of nectar, and a bee that has found a good supply will pass on the news of its whereabouts to others by dancing. Nowadays it is known that these messages are received by the 'listening' bees being highly sensitive to the movements of the air caused by the vibrating wings of the dancers.

Humans have kept bees in hives for centuries of centuries, for the sake of the honey stores they produce. Honey, being semi-fluid, would be useless if it were not for the containing wax of the comb, as I have pointed out earlier. It is with the beeswax of which the comb is made that I am now concerned, a humble and inert substance that is one of the few naturally occurring waxes. Beeswax is commonly found and easily collected, sought out by sculptors and modellers, who have valued the fine texture that makes it suitable for expressing subtle details. But its low melting point requires careful handling, or else the image will vanish. That it will melt is the reason for its being used for lost wax casting, when the original model is deliberately destroyed by heat. Beeswax tablets were also used as early writing material by the Babylonians, since the characters could be stamped into its surface (Greek: *tupos* as in typing, or archetype).

The mating flight is something that the bees share with ants, but following her fertilization, the queen bee is escorted back to the original hive, rather than always making a fresh nest. She also keeps her wings, though the drone bees die, like ants. In conditions of plenty or of over-crowding, however, a second queen will be produced, who then migrates from the hive, taking some of the inhabitants with her to form a daughter colony.

Both

At Camicus, the qualities belonging to these two insects intertwine. They are miners and smelters, cutters and collectors, takers of what others produce, transformers of material, creatures of relationship. They are chaotic and yet orderly, purposive, hard-working, persistent, communicative, wide-ranging by land and air, aggressive and destructive as well as nutrient and nurturing, self-serving and altruistic. All of these they bring to *daidalos* as typical activities of the well-crafted: the master craftsman. The association of ant and bee together could be seen as that of mother earth with sky father—or perhaps just earth and sky, leaving out any question of gender. They represent both an inner turmoil and outer order: in-cubation as well as an elaborative ex-ploration. In addition, quite apart from the concrete activity of Daedalus in the story which expressed the similarity of the insects' behaviour to that of humans, there is, in respect of the bee, a likeness at another level. Just as bees can transform nature in order to make honey, so does humanity; but what it makes is culture. Maeterlinck (1958) puts it well:

> And just as it is written in the tongue, the stomach and mouth of the bee that it must make honey, so it is written in our eyes, our ears, our nerves, our marrow, in every lobe of our head, in the whole nervous system of our body, that we have been created in order to transform all that we absorb of the things of the earth into a

particular energy, of a quality unique on this globe. I know of no other creature that has been thus fashioned to produce this strange fluid, which we call thought, intelligence, understanding, reason, soul, spirit, cerebral power, virtue, goodness, justice, knowledge; for it has a thousand names, though only one essence. [p. 182]

It could also be called 'imagination', and the likeness to honey is greater if it is accepted that most human mental activity will sustain and inspire the generations to come.

All of these characteristics, whether of honey or culture, demand containment; and of this the unfilled golden honeycomb is a supreme image. If the human equivalent to honey is inspiration or imagination, then it is not enough for that to exist without expression, for that would be to let it drip away and be lost. It asks for a vessel worthy of its nature, the expressive medium, which will perform this task. Filled by bees in the temple sanctuary, the golden honeycomb is a token of that. Only by this means can the precious fluid be passed onwards into the future and not dissipate or be lost forever. Fantasy unexpressed is a useless vapour. Imagination is, in its several ways, fixed by all works of art and craft in wood, stone, metal, paint, on paper, by music, or through dance. It is also contained by language—in some respects the most subtle container of them all. And all those vehicles are themselves, in *daidalos*, merely images for the putting forth and passing on of what we call information.

Nor is the honeycomb a container in the same sense as are bottles or jars, since each cell is unique and separate from all its neighbours. In the hive, its natural environment, honey is not stored in mass, but in small, discrete, individual amounts. The cells are also, therefore, images for the starry sky, which has previously been seen as belonging to the Minotaur.

But the golden honeycomb, while being an image of this necessary boundedness, is also an image for a laying down of the use of skills for skills' sake only. It may also be a sign for the recognition of tasks completed.

It has been said of Prospero, in Shakespeare's 'The Tempest', when, in the final scene, he broke his staff and drowned his books of magic, that he stood for Shakespeare's decision to write no more—and therefore of his retirement from the stage. Yet it is difficult to believe that such a person would ever retire from his own world's stage. Possibly other explorations were now felt to be more appropriate. Perhaps Shakespeare put himself out to grass in Warwickshire in order to explore himself, just as Daedalus, his archetypal forbear as craftsman, left Camicus when that phase was ended, to settle in Sardinia.

Honey and its comb

But before trekking further westwards with him, there are other matters to consider, the first being something else about the nature of honey, that miraculous substance which Maeterlinck compared with imaginative activity.

Honey has been used as food since the earliest times, as neolithic rock paintings show. It seems always to have been regarded with awe, being something that occurs in nature yet is also unnatural. On Crete, honey was associated with the births of both Zeus and Dionysus, being regarded as divine amniotic fluid: the water that surrounds and supports the foetus, and which was originally thought to nourish it as well, a maternal image. Minos's sea-green son Glaukos was found drowned in a vat of honey: possibly some memory of a cult of the dead, on Crete. So honey can be death-dealing and preservative as well as food and life-enhancing.

The nectar of the gods was thought to be honey and water mixed. When such a mixture is exposed to heat in a closed vessel, it changes into mead, the first intoxicating drink known to the Mediterranean area, preceding wine. In the Greek language, to get drunk [*methyein*] comes from the same root as the word 'mead', while Dionysus was a god of mead before he was a wine god. The making of mead took place at certain times of the year only and was hedged about with cult and mystery, as is any craft of transformation. The brewing took place in a leather sack, so the change was one that happened unseen and unexamined, its outcome, too, was uncertain.

As well as this similarity to a pregnancy, with the amniotic sac and its contents, mead and its container provide an image of 'life in death', according to Kerényi; it is an image of the awakening of the spirit by means of decay and fermentation within the oxhide, just as bees themselves were thought to arise spontaneously in the rotting carcases of bulls.

Mead brought euphoria, which meant 'well-bearing' before it meant 'well-being'; and this would replace any state of mind that was present *before* its bearer became drunk. Drunkenness implies a loss of control and *logos*, as has been suggested. In one's cups, it is difficult to disguise folly, though what is deemed foolish may be so only to sobersides and rational minds. The dissolution of that order, by mead, may allow for breakthroughs of a different kind. New life can arise in the death of the old order that intoxication may bring about.

But alcohol is also depotentiating in a sexual sense. It was when well plied with mead that Kronos slept deeply enough to be castrated by his youngest son Zeus, says an Orphic tale. But this story seemingly muddles up the action of un-manning with that performed by Kronos himself upon his own father Ouranos. Whatever the mix-up, the image is still that of removing the old order and its replacement by a new style (Kerényi, 1976, pp. 29–41).

Of Aphrodite

Camicus is the place of a father with daughters. Earlier, I have traced a progression, or established a likeness-with-difference between Athene, Ariadne, and the young girls of King Cocalus. Now it is time to look at Aphrodite as another example of a father's daughter, but one of a different type.

She arose, it was said, from within the unnamed yet feminine ocean into which the cut-off genitals of Ouranos had been flung by his castrating son, Kronos. The false etymology tells us she was 'born of foam' [Greek: *aphros*], which was both the foaming billows of the sea and her father's foaming semen. In this account of her birth she rides ashore upon a shell, naked but fully formed in her matchless beauty. There is no childhood mentioned, no nursing or protection, no tutors to teach her. In that respect she differs greatly from Athene, who also sprang, fully formed, into existence. But Athene was cared for and tutored to gain her full knowledge. Aphrodite's wisdom is of another kind, for she is fathered by the phallus rather than the head. She is, it seems, another example of life-in-death: the life that follows orgasm. To be fathered by nothing more than a floating penis could truly be said to be the child of cut-off sexuality and a detached masculinity. Yet if it is-as-it-is, then what follows is the notion that nothing is of relevance to the archetype of relating that is Aphrodite herself, except the phallus. Connection at that level is all, but if that kind of connection sounds offensively patriarchal, a fresh meaning will be explored in a later chapter. If Athene is the father's daughter who knows and discerns, passing on his knowledge intact, Aphrodite gives us another kind of attachment to father—that of sexual attraction. It brings with it, inevitably, the fear of incest and of a connection that can go too far.

Aphrodite's predecessor on Eryx, the Phoenician goddess Astarte, presents us with many styles of woman in one person, being wild, wise, warlike, and erotic. But in Greece these qualities were given to various goddesses: Athene (wisdom and war), Artemis (hunting and wildness), and Aphrodite (erotic love); and all three are virgins. Athene is untouched and untouchable. Artemis is untamed, untameable. But Aphrodite, who loves, marries, and bears children, can remake her virginity anew. She is virgin in the sense that each connection is complete in itself yet evokes, in turn, another similar encounter: it is virginity seen as fulfilment, yet ever calling for more. In this way, as image rather than nymphomaniac, she represents relationship that is never satisfied, yet without which humans cannot survive, for they are creatures who thrive on the making of community.

Through her lust for connection, she is the goddess of love, whether sexual or otherwise. To her belongs the love that joins man to man or woman to woman (identity of archetype), and as such she is therefore contained within my exploration of the male archetype. But she is as concerned also with the union of man with woman (conjunction). She watches over the love of persons of the same generation as much as that of parent and child. Hers is the love that is permitted and that which is frowned upon, both incest and perversity. Faithfulness, adultery, and promiscuity are also under her protection (Grigson, 1978). Naturally, it was Aphrodite who inflamed Pasiphaë with that unnatural passion, one of her own epithets being Pasiphaëissa.

Nobody asks to be invaded by the goddess, or struck by her son's arrow, which is every bit as aggressive or inflammatory as Athene's lance or the sting of both ant and bee. Encounters with passion are chance affairs to be realized—or not. Something can be made of desire, or it can be put aside: for people are not as bulls and cows, creatures of compulsive instinct alone. Aphrodite presents them with passion as well as the possibility of holding back, in which case passion, unrequited, becomes suffering. At the same time, she speaks of patience and the ability to hold on to suffering—to suffer it—unprotected. Seeing her from this view is to rise above the merely sexual and to realize one of the meanings of Aphrodite as an image of passionate connection that always contains an image of what *might* be, in the future.

Thus she signifies the force that can bring about a coming together of the separate pieces of an individual imaged as partners. There is no fusion or synthesis implied, but instead a harmony—a lying beside one another, like spoons. The relationship might be one of mutual attraction, of chance encounter, of lasting union, or even of abstinence. All are relationships brought about by lust, in its fullest sense as desire for pleasure, appetite, relish, delight—which transcend the purely sexual meaning that we usually give that word. Jung emphasized that the numinous encounters with archetypes (gods, goddesses) were passionate affairs and not just an intellectual exercise, and Aphrodite is the archetype of that passion. It is these things that the goddess now brings to *daidalos* and to the myth-ego itself by means of her human representatives, the royal girls of Camicus.

Fathers and their daughters

Still in bud, playing with their dolls, they represent the non-mature parts of an individual who has not yet given up playing with toys, and might never do so, refusing ever to see the world as un-playful. By the same stroke, they *will* grow up, become lovers, marry, and bear children. So they are also those parts of the same person that long for all that is yet to come, but who can await the unknown future, uncertain and unknowing. And while in waiting, they always play.

But their play is more than just a time-passing activity of little value. It is both a learning and an education into life itself. It is a making of consciousness, in the same kind of way that a kitten makes its instinctive behaviour patterns real by performance. The stalking, crouching, leaping, pouncing with which it and its siblings play will one day be the real thing. It has its own innate repertoire of patterns awaiting fulfilment in the world.

Michael Fordham (1969) has described much the same activity in the human infant, at a psychological level. Archetypal de-integrates in the child's psyche await their objective realization in the outside world. The reintegration which follows this meeting will result in the formation of ego-consciousness. In this sense all the new characters that appear in *daidalos* could be dubbed de-integrates, which are, in any case, also likened to *scintillae*. The style of ego I am describing may, however, be different from Fordham's.

In his book *Magical Child,* Joseph Chilton Pierce (1977) describes this same development as following a 'cycle of competence', taking much of his schema from Jean Piaget. Pierce divides it into four phases: (1) a roughing in of some new skill or piece of knowledge, followed by (2) a filling in of details; next comes (3) a period of practising of the possibilities that result, and finally (4) an exploration of the variables that this new skill affords (pp. 76ff). Educationalists know this very well, acting their part in the process as safe containers within which it might all occur: they are different from those teachers who stuff their pupils' heads with facts until they are as deformed as the livers of Strasbourg geese. *'Educare'* in Latin means 'to lead outwards' *(ODEE)*, and good teachers do just that, turning their pupils' eyes to distant, indistinct horizons, encouraging them to find their own mazy path through the undergrowth, thereby developing what is peculiar to each pupil by means of copying, practising, discovering. This is true play; and play is, for the child, its work—work on what is to come, taking place in that intermediate space described by Donald Winnicott (1971, p. 41ff) as being neither inner nor outer; this space has been likened by Samuels to the *mundus imaginalis,* or imaginal world (Samuels, 1989, p. 167).

If the child is an image of what is to come, then the father as allowing tutor (Cocalus, Daedalus) is that which already exists, as well as one who encourages without giving the answers that he himself has come to. Those things that he allows the child to discover are not necessarily those that belong to the teacher's own bias, but are instead the real, personal originality of the child itself. The child is made, then, in its own image and fashions its own mantle, rather than being poured into somebody else's ready-made mould. In this respect, it is interesting to know that many mythological tutors were deformed, primitive, or unearthly beings: monstrous to a ruling mind that feared the innovation that they promised the child. The tutor's is a mind that does not seek to rule, but to extend: it has powers but no power, skills but no authority. Or, rather, the power and authority that any teacher possesses by nature of his role should not be used to preform or deform. Neither is the tutor a master envious of his apprentice.

But under the protection of Aphrodite there exists, in addition, also the erotic connection between father and daughters, which Andrew Samuels has termed 'erotic play-back' and which, when truly and positively experienced without passing over into actual incest, can act as the source of true, feminine individuality (Samuels, 1989, p. 66).

At Camicus, therefore, father-with-daughters becomes an image of what is to be: of letting it become; and also of the ability to accept, not knowing in which direction it will travel. Since there are more girls than one, Camicus also suggests a plurality of ways in which the parental spirit may descend and differentiate. The father is now part of that image, as a force that does not insist on knowing best; while the child is a fitting image of whatever will be.

In his essay on the *kore*, Kerényi (1951b) has remarked that there is a unity of image in the apparent triad of maiden/mother/child, describing three aspects of a being that dies, gives birth, and comes to life again. As the maiden aspect, she cannot know if there will ever be a child, or, if there is, who will be its father, whom the baby will resemble, what it will be like, or even to what gender it will belong. That is nature and what nature intends. She may have hopes, wishes, dreams, but she can never *know*; and, in any case, they may all be dashed. 'Not knowing' fosters for any mother-to-be an openness to the future that does not stamp the child-to-be in advance with any of her own preconceived notions. No possibilities (even monstrous or deformed ones) are ruled out, as they would have been by a Minos-consciousness. It is both the ability to accept an uncertain future, as well as being able to bear the anxiety towards those unknown things to come, of which the budding maiden is an image.

It is important, at this point, to repeat what has been said before concerning the gender of images. Although I speak in terms of 'fathers' and 'daughters', they are not real persons: they are neither male nor female. The psyche borrows and uses their gender in order to make statements about itself and to be more precise about the differences concerned and the style of any possible relationship between them. There is a 'daughter' operating within each person's psyche, whether man or woman, be they nineteen or ninety years of age, just as the 'father' expresses itself in everyone as well, even in a new-born babe.

CHAPTER TEN

The Sardinian experience

Fade-out

'**O**ld soldiers never die', goes the song, 'they only fade away'. Perhaps old craftsmen just go on and on too, working until they drop or are dropped. At any rate, nothing more is heard of Daedalus after he moved on to Sardinia. There, it is said, he put up many buildings that lasted into late antiquity, but nothing is known for certain. No dying or being killed; no translation to the stars; nothing but the silence. It is, however, expressly said of his move from Camicus that he *settled* in Sardinia with the Daedalids. To understand this region of *daidalos*, therefore, a view is needed that takes the nature of the place, of those who accompanied or joined him there, and of what is meant by settlement or colonization.

Sardinia, after Sicily the largest island in the Mediterranean, was originally called Sandaliotis, from its resemblance to a foot. It was said to have an unhealthy atmosphere but was free of wolves and poisonous snakes, while the ground was so fertile that it became, in time, a granary for Rome. There was only one poisonous and bitter plant there, eating which was claimed to have caused death, the mouth set in a twisted smile: the 'risus sar-donicus', which was also seen upon the faces of those crushed to death in the embrace of the bronze giant Talus. Nowadays the sardonic smile is a sign of the illness called tetanus.

Several other people were said to have joined the crafts-man on the island. Iolaus, Herakles' charioteer, the son of his mortal brother Iphicles, arrived leading the fifty Her-culid sons fathered by the hero upon the fifty daughters of Thespius, in as many nights. The insignificant Norax came from Libya, and Aristaius also. The latter was a son of Apollo and the wood-nymph Cyrene, with a name meaning 'the best one', which refers presumably to his father, or to his grandfather Zeus. He was a minor rustic god, but important here for his invention of beekeeping.

It seems there is nothing very special about the people who settle in Sardinia, nor about the things they do. Instead, it seems to be a place for agricultural pursuits, for retirement, and for the descendants of gods or heroes. It is a place of toil and human fruitfulness. For Daedalus, it could be an image of doing nothing special, of being ordin-ary instead of exceptional, as well as of a colonization of the new and a cultivation of the wild and untamed.

To colonize is derived from the Latin word 'colere' to cultivate the land, for agriculture was a prime task of any colony. That word is secondarily shortened into culture— the cultivation of the mind. The Roman 'colonia' was, basically, a civilized spot among barbarian surroundings. Often old soldiers were paid off and encouraged to retire and farm locally, thus providing a basic population in the area on whom the Empire could rely. Originally they would exist in scattered farms or settlements, but in time these might coalesce, until barbarity itself vanished or was transmuted. As a psychological image within *daidalos*, it is back to Asterion-consciousness and the scintillae. A colony is a lone and unique star shining in a dark wilderness: a defined spot among unknowing, flux, and uncertainty.

The word 'settle', stems from the verb 'to sit', but it has six classes of meaning that are worth considering (*OED*).

First, it means to seat or cause to be seated; second, to come to rest after flight or wandering; third, it is used of something that sinks down gradually to its proper level; and fourth, to come to rest after agitation, so that a sediment settles out. The fifth class of meaning suggests a rendering of things stable, fixed, and permanent; and the last implies a solution to things that have been in dispute.

In this one word can be recognized many of the themes that have concerned me in the delineation of *daidalos,* associated with the myth ego and other characteristics. There is much that suggests *senex,* while the final class recalls to mind the actions of Aphrodite or Harmonia. What is significant by its absence is any suggestion of *puer,* except as an earlier state: flight and wandering, being above ground level, agitation, instability, and ambivalence or disunion.

Viewed negatively, settlement might be remarked upon as a state where nothing much happens, where there is little tension, all problems stand solved, and *senex* rules. But it is not possible always to live in a state of agitation and flight, however valuable they may be. Sediment and stagnation are necessary contrasts, and it is also in the stillness that *Einfälle* can occur.

But this settlement is not one such as the Isles of the Blest, where a Golden Age mimics the bliss of infancy. In Sardinia there is a colony, which therefore implies a state of tension between settlers and native inhabitants—barbarians, so to say. Civilization lies within the stockade, scalpings or poisoned blowpipes outside, the cooked and the raw. And, if it is-as-it-is, then settlement here suggests a sense of freedom from that anxiety of the unknown which will enable those who settle to do so freely and cultivate their patch. All of this can be seen to have been gained by *daidalos* as a result of what went on at Camicus.

In such a situation it is good to have Aristaius there, for he can control the wild creatures and extract their honey. Iolaus is also present, and it was he who tipped the scales towards victory in Herakles's battle with the many-headed Hydra by cauterizing the severed necks with fire, before the serpent grew more heads. He is not just concerned with harness and driving in harness—though he can do that too—but in dealing with the one and the many. The Daedalids, who are also there, will marry Herculids to provide a child-full future for the settlement.

Fade-out is not burn-out. It does not denote a failure any longer to cope. Rather, it seems to signify a renewed, though different ability to face an uncertain future in unknown surroundings with an equable spirit, confident in skills and tools to hand. Settlement, here envisioned, demands excellence of the colonizers (the best ones), but it does not continually put upon them the requirement to compete with and excel above each other. Nor is there a ruler to exercise power and authority.

Though it comes at the end of the tale and might be taken as some kind of blissful retirement, it has already been noted that no one lives happily ever after. The tension between any settlement and its 'savage' surroundings has also been remarked. As such, it also represents a rest-point from which the myth-ego could take off again in any direction, should he so please—marsh gas bubbling up to ripple the stagnant pool. An action of unsettlement is always possible.

The Sardinian experience is also a way out of the field that I have been crafting, while at the same time repeating what has been said on so many previous occasions—that it is Daedalus's ability as a craftsman, with all it entails, that carries him through. The myth-ego, on his journey, has made himself and his own story. Some of his skills, which in one sense were present all along, now cluster visibly around Daedalus himself, as well as others that inhere. The colonization of Sardinia is (like any other scene in the story) an epitome of the entirety of *daidalos,* as well as being merely a piece of the same whole.

Fade-out itself, as an image, also evokes the unknown, unknowable future that might at any time come into being.

PART THREE

THE NUTS AND THE BOLTS

CHAPTER ELEVEN

Earthing it

Begin again

P laying with myths is fun and games. I can get carried away, just like Icarus, marvelling at my own
virtuosity and hoping to carry the reader with me.
But is there no more to it than that, then?

His flight, remember, was undertaken in order to avoid
entrapment in too rigid a belief in ordering and groundedness. So levity is important; but no one can, in the end,
escape gravity. For a craftsman there must always be a
return to earth from inspiration, just as there was a vital
part of him that never left. Nothing of what has been said
in the previous chapters will, therefore, have any relevance at all unless it is drawn back, or fed, into life as it is
lived. Any message it bears must be earthed and secularized, put to work. Landing safely, by choice and not out
of control, is a metaphor for doing just that. But life may
take off too as a result of that earthing.

It has been a demanding and chaotic flight: a tangled
skein of clews, with some connections seen and made, some

knots unravelled. But this un-doing has also resulted in the making of as many other twists and ravellings. The labyrinth seems as much a maze as it ever was, with no straight paths or gateways to enlightenment. It may seem that order has been jettisoned merely for the sake of disorder, which was then called a 'different' kind of order.

Under orders

Ordering: the organization of a field is, of course, no unreasonable demand. It is a biological activity, undertaken by all animals so as to know and feel safe in their surroundings. Marshack (1972) has shown that in Palaeolithic times there already existed sophisticated techniques for making lunar notations. Many of the seemingly random scratch marks seen on ancient pieces of bone are just that; and their extreme accuracy must represent long-established practice. The earlier material on which these calendars were marked was probably perishable, and so no records remain. It is not known why such ordering was required, but the evidence that it was possible and that it was done persists.

Early languages confirm the importance of ordering. Vedic Sanskrit contains the word *ṛta,* which 'designates order as a harmonious arrangement of the parts as a whole'. This description sounds very much like the English word system: meaning 'a whole composed of parts in orderly arrangement according to some scheme or plan' (*OED*). Emile Bennveniste (1973), whose definition I have quoted, emphasizes that *ṛta* governed the orderliness of the universe as well as society: macrocosm as well as microcosm. It ruled the connections between human beings and the gods, as well as the way that people related among themselves. 'Without this principle everything would revert to chaos' (pp. 379–380).

Derivatives of *ṛta* are found throughout the Indo-European family of languages. In Greek there is *'ararisko'* [to fit, adapt, harmonize], and 'arithmos' [to order by numeration). Latin has artus [a joint] and hence articulate as well as arthritic. In English we have 'art', 'ritual', and 'rhyme', each in their own way related to the making of order. And no individual can escape order, for the growth of ego-consciousness from infancy onwards is itself an ordering process, making sense of the environment so that it becomes predictable: the giving of meaning.

If in part two of this book I have not made myself clear, it could be assumed that I am not clear myself and so have no sense of order to communicate. Or, on the other hand, I do know what I mean but cannot set it out coherently. Thirdly, it could be a deliberate effort on my part, setting the whole book under the sign of Asterion, the spangled sky. Each star, imaged as scintilla and therefore possessing its own small consciousness, is unique and separate from all others. But even the starry sky, though scattered at random across the heavens, has been ordered—as the earliest written records can reveal—into higher images, the constellations. And if we accept the evidence of megalithic stone circles, humans have studied the stars from before that time (Thom, 1967). I have already mentioned Boötes and Arktos as examples of 'constellations'—'a number of fixed stars grouped together with the outline of an imaginary figure traced between them' (OED). The stars themselves are fixed, and their positions relative to one another do not alter. Their groupings, imaged as pictures, bear little factual resemblance to what they are said to represent. They are, in fact, constellated by the human mind. What goes on in the spaces between the stars is the activity of human imagination, which links them in a certain way, as well as being one that may vary from time to time or place to place.

For example, the seven stars that point towards Polaris have been called variously the plough, the great bear, the dipper, the saucepan, Odin's, or Charlemagne's, wain (wagon), the seven wise men, seven pigs, etc. In the same fashion, Boötes is a bear warder, a ploughman, or charioteer (Leach, 1949). The fragmentation of heavenly light, which Asterion suggests contains its own order—chaotic like an ants' nest—is an order that does not order the viewers around, telling them what they should always see. There is, it suggests, no ultimately true, single image to be found in the deepest recesses. Instead, the night sky of the darkened moon, lacking any stronger, more demanding lights, gives free play to the imagination and indeed requires it, if any sense is to be made of those myriad points. It is this 'order in chaos' and how to stay with it while, at the same time, making something of it that is the nature and strength of the craftsman. It is that which the third part of this book examines.

Chaos and order

Daidalos has been much concerned with the twin concepts of chaos and order. They have been expressed in the field by such contrary images as Athene/Poseidon, Minos/piracy, entrapment/freedom, moderate flight/aerobatics, cast article/molten metal, the cultured and the wild, knowing/uncertainty, beehive or anthill. This is hardly surprising, since we live, it has been said, not in a universe but a 'duoverse', which is antinomial, dualistic, and oppositional—or, at least, it can be experienced in that way. These notions of duality are as old and as widespread as the human psyche, in which, according to Jung, consciousness stands in an antithetical relationship to the unconscious mind. But it is also important to remember that the two are part of a greater whole, just as night and day are. Plato gave us the image of two horses harnessed to the same chariot, but straining away from each other. It is the task of the charioteer to control their tendency to veer apart, converting it to forward movement.

All of the words we use to describe this condition enshrine a state of disagreement. *Anti*-nomy means two parts against one another. *Contra*-dict is to speak against. An *op*-posite is a thing placed against another on the further side of an intervening line. To *com*-pensate means to counter-balance, make amends for. Even to *com*-plement means that the two must join together as a greater whole. Each of these terms implies that any single factor is insufficient and incomplete until or unless compensated for or complemented by its contradictory opposite. All of this therefore tends to devalue the singleton. It is back to the cry of 'what about the feminine?' which puts down any attempt to study maleness on its own.

Perhaps a better view of the duoverse would be to see it as binomial, 'divided into two parts' (*OED*), with nothing said or implied of the ways in which the parts might relate. Only one of these would be a way of relating as contraries. Guggenbühl-Craig (1971) has suggested as much, when he wrote of a 'split archetype'. He points out that such images are always experienced with reference to another term: indeed, they can only be defined by the presence of the other. They are, in effect, bipolar, though often experienced as separate (p. 81). This bipolarity is never a once-for-all-time thing, but variable, for example:

father/mother

father/son

father/daughter

father/childless man

father/grandfather

What is seen depends upon the conscious viewpoint, rather than some unchangeable law of nature; and this is rather more like Hillman's (1975b) suggestion that we look at things archetypally, rather than examine archetypes (p. 138). The adjective describes a mode of looking rather than a thing to be looked at, or for. *Senex* and *puer* are good examples of this, for they have very different visions yet can be seen as parts of a split archetype. Hillman would prefer to speak of pairings, tandems, juxtaposition—all words that avoid any sense of an inevitable antagonism. Chaos and order will therefore be regarded in what follows as parts of a tandem, both being examined singly or paired with each other; in accord, or by contradiction; as an existential statement, or in need of compensation.

To order, to impose pattern on the formless, is, as I have already said, an age-old biological process. *Senex* has been described as that which promotes order; and it orders by ordering. The pair to this is chaos, regarded as disorderly, confused, irregular, deranged, lawless, tumultuous, and riotous. It is not surprising that such a state should be seen negatively and cause enough anxiety to bring about a need to establish an ordered state of being. People always do what they can to convert the foreign and unfamiliar into that which is commonplace.

But Chaos was, according to Hesiod, the original goddess of the Greek cosmogony, though it is striking that the *-os* ending to her name is masculine. The family tree that 'she' originates is an ordering process, but, despite her name, she is not herself disordered or seen as confusion, except when seen from outside her own perspective. Her nature reflects a more archaic meaning of the word chaos— namely, a 'yawning void', which gapes wide open. Words such as 'chaos', 'chasm', 'gap', 'gape', 'yawn' are ultimately cognates, the root image being that of the open mouth. But the kind of gap implied by the void is not one that exists between two solid objects as boundaries, as with a ravine. Kerényi (1951a) describes it as 'that which remains of an empty egg when the shell is taken away' (p. 19). It is vacant but unbounded, as well as being a familiar description of the original state before creation. Compare:

> And the earth was without form and void [*tohu-bohu*]; and darkness was upon the face of the deep. [*Genesis*, 1, verse 2]

The Norse creation myth agrees:

> In ancient Days
> existed nothing
> neither sand nor seas
> nor swelling billows
> there was no earth
> there was no heaven
> not a blade of grass
> but a yawning gulf [*ginnungagap*]
>
> [Snorri Sturrlasson,
> quoted in Branston, 1955, p. 52]

The chaos, void, gap, gulf imagined by all three myths is not a disorderly state of many things confused, but a condition of emptiness, lack of structure, of nothingness—chaos not as disorder but un-structure: something that has not yet been made-to-be.

With regard to no-thing-ness, in Scandinavian countries, the '*Thing*' was an assembly of people meeting for discussion of important matters (*OED*). The Thing debated and decided upon various matters (things) that were brought before it, and this is the derivation of our more general use of the word. The Icelandic and Norwegian parliaments are still called '*Allting*' and '*Stortting*', respectively, while the name for a Swedish district council is '*Landstinget*' [the countryside thing]. No-thing therefore implies a no-meeting of people as well as their having no things to talk about. This notion is confirmed by the origin of our word 'empty', which comes from the negative, 'a', plus 'mot' [a meeting or moot]. When no people are at the moot, it is empty, no-thing happens, and no-thing is decided. If people do come together, there exists an interaction, a discourse, a dialectic (possibly conflictual), and from this meeting, some-thing results—perhaps some-thing new.

There is a difference, however, in the no-thing-ness that is chaos, for within that state all things are present in embryonic, unformed, not-met form. It only seems empty because no meeting has taken place. Yet, when they are mooted, then the self-same things will, as a result, be born. Thus, from empty chaos, structure results, order appears; but still the original state of empty chaos remains intact. It is a creative substratum of unimaginable, and therefore indescribable, nature.

The tandem of Chaos was, for the Greeks, Cosmos, an harmonious system; and it is only from that ordered viewpoint that chaos can be described as disorderly. It is shown diagrammatically in FIGURE 4. Movement from Chaos towards Cosmos is under the sway of *senex*. It is the means by which fresh ordering comes about by building on what has gone before, while staying within the boundaries of that order. The old is freshened by adding more of the same. The reverse movement belongs to *puer*.

I am not just speaking of things as they are in the world, let it be remembered, but as imagined within the human psyche. Since this is an open system, it represents a dynamic state of affairs, which appears stationary only as an abstraction. Sometimes it is in equilibrium, sometimes not; but most often it is on the move. Equally, it is when things get stuck or repeat themselves needlessly that a potential for change builds up and violent shifts occur. This is neither good nor bad, true nor false, selfish nor altruistic, for a definition depends upon the viewpoint. Minos's behaviour is in fact no more nor less monstrous than that of the Minotaur: each appears as or when required. If the seas are lawless and beset by pirates, then establishing a rule of law is indicated. When that becomes

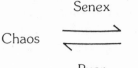

FIGURE 4

stifling, revolution or rebellion will become the order of the day.

Only if the constructive harnessing of energies becomes rigid and of 'the Establishment' is flight or melt-down required. And, however it might be in the outside world, nothing is ever lost. Death and destruction, as psychic images, are those actions that allow a rearrangement of old material and for a new order to be made, as in the *pupa*. Submission to chaos, which may seem and will feel like disaster, is therefore another way of ordering.

The kind of model I have in mind is similar to Fordham's suggestions for infant development. As described above, there is a rhythmical process by which archetypal deintegrates of the primary self are available and meet with a situation in the outside world to which they are predisposed. They then re-integrate. Yet all is not as it was before, for now there are beginnings of a true internal world and the kernel of ego formation. These processes recur repeatedly, presenting a circular model, strung out across time. The activity is one of self-organization, controlled and brought about by the self whose source and goal is its own self. Fordham's concept of the original self, in which all possibilities are contained, is very much what I have in mind when describing the latent possibilities of chaos (Fordham, 1985).

Life in chaos

But what *is* chaos? What does it look like? Where will I meet it? Well, chaos is beyond me. It is all the things I am not, which are other to the person I feel myself to be. Chaos, as non-structure, is unfamiliar ground, where I feel uncertain and insecure and therefore full of fear. Chaos is unimaginable otherness, under the sign of the god Pan and the emotion that he brings—namely, panic. Pan's name means 'everything' in Greek—in this case everything I am not—while panic is the alarm felt at being without known, safe boundaries. It is the fear of an infinite regression.

For the person of intellectual defences, chaos is deep emotional contact with another person. For the hysteric, it might be intellectual rigour. To a person who is habitually under tight control, a sense of freedom, though perhaps longed for, is chaotic. To the irresponsible, self-discipline seems to be a terrifying and a yawning void. To those who live in a shambles, on the other hand, with every object scattered across the floor, tidiness is psychologically 'chaotic', because it is impossible for them to imagine such a structure as being attainable. For the obsessional perfectionist, on the other hand, chaos lies in failing to achieve, or in not being always in order.

What I am calling 'chaos' is always personal and unique, though generalizations can also be made. The experience of it may be one of creativeness or dissolution, depending upon the moment, as well as the individual.

The abstract expressionist painter William de Kooning (1960) said:

Each new glimpse is determined by many,
Many glimpses before.
It's this glimpse which inspires you—like an occurrence
And I notice those are always my moments of having an idea
That maybe I could start a painting.

also:

Everything is already in art—like a big bowl of soup
Everything is in there already:
And you just stick your hand in, and find something for you.
But it was already there—like a stew.

and:

Y'know the real world, this so-called real world,
Is just something you put up with, like everybody else.
I'm in my element when I am a little bit out of this world:

then I'm in the real world—I'm on the beam.
Because when I'm falling, I'm doing all right;
when I'm slipping, I say, hey, this is interesting!
It's when I'm standing upright that bothers me:
I'm not doing so good; I'm stiff.
As a matter of fact, I'm really slipping, most of the time,
into that glimpse. I'm like a slipping glimpser.

[pp. 6, 7, 9]

But submission to the 'slipping glimpse' would not have been enough to produce a great artwork, without a craftsman's skills, in order first to survive the slip and then to express that glimpse.

Max Wall, the extraordinary comic genius who died recently, was quoted in his obituary (*The Guardian Newspaper*, 23 May 1990) as saying, 'Broadly speaking, I don't know what I'm doing on stage. I depend on myself. I make bricks without straw. I'm not asking for medals—I'm just telling you.' But the obituarist emphasized throughout that the master-clown's ability to perform, ranging from his own bizarre vaudeville act to Shakespeare, Pinter, and Beckett, involved 'laying bare the mechanics of his craft'. This was possible only because Wall based it upon a lifetime of theatrical skills—voice, physical presence, gesture, exquisite timing—allied to a wealth of personal human experience, much of it tragic and painful.

In psychotherapy, Fritz Perls (1973) called this process 'withdrawing into the fertile void'. He said that if a person was capable of staying with the accompanying experience of confusion to the utmost, then perhaps 'a sudden solution will come forward, an insight that has not been there before, a blinding flash of realization or understanding' (p. 100).

Describing the need for such an ability from an alternative angle, the psychoanalyst Wilfred Bion (1970) has suggested that in entering a session, therapists should try to leave behind all memory of what has happened in previous sessions, lay aside all desire for results or cure, and even suspend their understanding of what has gone before.

These actions necessarily increase the therapist's anxiety at first, but if adhered to will allow, he says, for the experience of each single session as an event that is complete in itself. As Bion points out, in any session, it is only out of the darkness and formlessness that anything *can* evolve (pp. 41–54). By the deliberate introduction of what I might call chaos, the therapist makes creation possible.

> As an example of the fear of entering chaos, I remember Doris, who had suffered from Post-traumatic Shock Syndrome for two years, following a car accident in which she and her husband had literally stared death in the face. Now she could hardly be driven in a car at all without feeling that disaster was just round the next corner, or beside her in the fast lane. She would have loved to talk of nothing else but her terrifying feelings, yet she felt that no one would listen. The only peace of mind that she experienced was in the countryside, especially among trees. By dropping their leaves and growing them anew each spring, they reminded her of renewal, she told me. Nevertheless, for herself there seemed to be only the possibility of extinction. Obviously the accident had triggered off these emotions, but they were also feelings that had great significance to her present life. Doris came from a family who seldom shared their feelings— especially if they were negative ones. She had been brought up always to do what was expected of her, which was to care for others; and this she had done all her life, even becoming the family breadwinner when her husband retired early due to ill-health. Now close to her own retirement, she would have to face the fact that there would soon be nothing for her to do; and if her son married or her husband died first, she would have no one to look after. Bereft of the selfless activities with which she had buttressed herself, Doris might have to look after her own needs, that felt like the chaos of a car crash, and these she could not face.

People might be changed if they could only enter the chaos they fear, however difficult that might be to bring about. I remember a patient who lived in a world filled by delusion, and who entered a psychotic state, which was brought about by acute separation anxiety, for a period of about ten days. When she emerged into the daylight of consciousness again she was changed, and the fantasies, which had previously appeared to be factually true, could now be seen as being 'just my imagination' (Tatham, 1984, p. 120).

Nevertheless, chaos, or entry into it, should not be romanticized and over-valued as always possessing a positive aspect. Using the 'black hole' of astronomy as an image, Giles Clark has shown that submission to a destructive chaos can be a remorseless and irreversible process, despite any skill the therapist has to offer (Clark, 1983, pp. 67–80). A malignant regression, suicide, chronic psychosis, and fatal physical illness may all be seen as representing the experience of a chaos that overpowers any attempt to transform it or to extract insight from it.

However, there is another drawback to this notion of 'submitting to chaos'—one that is best understood with reference to what has been said previously about new techniques leading to unimagined possibilities. Today it is not just a matter of chance that new ideas are generated. There now exist 'think-tanks' and 'brain-storming sessions', and people 'think laterally'—all these are methods of putting into operation, in a mechanical way, the techniques of problem-solving. Minos-type commissions would be child's play to a twelve-year-old computer hacker of this century. Unlimited imagination (which is not true imagination) working hand in hand with technical ability becomes a monster out of control, like a Minotaur eating up the flower of Athenian youth. Valuable techniques become just pyrotechnics, or they can be debased into mere technicism and techno-worship. It becomes a blind repetitive loop between Icarus pushing out the boundaries to extremes and Daedalus just providing what he is asked for.

It keeps the armaments factories busy and fills the gift and craft shops with gaudy gew-gaws for people who have everything but get nothing. The bastardy of the Minotaur can be viewed in this light.

My diagram is therefore incomplete without some limiting morality. Neutrality in this respect has been important until now, so as not to judge the material too harshly at too early a stage—a necessary craftsman's skill. Nevertheless, having invoked the name of the goddess often enough, it is to Themis that I now turn.

Themis

After introducing *ṛta* as ordering principle, Bennveniste (1973) takes it further. If something works, or is useful, then it is repeated. What is repeated becomes a habit ('that which is held'—*OED*) and a custom; and it is a short step from custom for a practice to be regulated by law. The Vedic word for the law that governed *ṛta* is *dharma,* meaning that which is established in usage and therefore takes on reality (p. 381). It is held fast to.

Dharma, in Buddhist practice, is the law that governs the universe as well as the way in which individuals ought to order their lives. From *dharma* descend such words as 'doom', which originally meant a statute of law but now refers to a fearful judgement, as well as the Greek *'themis'.* *Themis,* says Bennveniste (1973), originally covered only family law. Though of heavenly origin, it represented a code of unwritten laws in the conscience of the head of the family, telling him how to proceed whenever order was at stake. Its usage was often expressed in the phrase *'he themis estin',* translated as 'what is meet and right'. *Themis* is, in other words, a proper way of behaving (p. 382).

Whether the custom came first and the goddess later or vice versa is immaterial, since both will be true; but Themis herself was known to be the first wife of Zeus. On

Olympus, it was she who brought the assemblies together, ranging the whole world to call the Olympians home. She also arranged their seating at the table. She governed what was fit and proper for humans, as well as for deities, to do. For instance, it would have been offensive to Themis for women to walk around nude; and it was the goddess's own daughters who clothed Aphrodite when she emerged, naked, from the ocean. Jane Harrison describes Themis as a by-name for Gaia, the earth goddess, and in this guise she is over and above all other gods and goddesses (Harrison, 1963a). As a property of behaviour, *themis* stood for the conventions that bound humans together: the things that had become hallowed by custom rather than by direct intervention of the gods: a kind of collective conscience. Its presence or absence is obvious in *daidalos*. It was lack of *themis* that led Daedalus to spill blood upon the Acropolis, as it was *themis* for him to carry away a snake. Minos's appropriation of the Poseidon bull showed lack of *themis*, as did his wife's copulation with it. It was lack of *themis* to fly, or for Icarus to fly so high, but *themis* for Daedalus to lay up his wings. And over and through all, it was a strict accordance with the *themis* of their culture that saved the lives of metalworkers who dared to work upon the body of the mother, Gaia/Themis herself.

In *themis* we can view the human quality of habit-formation elevated to a cosmic, archetypal quality—or, if you prefer, an archetype of right-mindedness, keeping to allotted bounds, behaving as one should, which then expresses itself upon earth as habituation. Yet too much *themis* or too slavish acceptance of it becomes in itself one-sided and so in need of overthrow.

For the Greeks, the pair to this quality was *hubris*, which describes actions that were insolent and contemptuous, ignoring custom. This is personified in our field also, by Orion. At the festival of the *Hubristika* women wore men's clothing and vice versa, as a deliberate flouting of *themis* (Harrison, 1963a, pp. 505–507). In making a festival such as Saturnalia or Carnival of *hubris*, it becomes

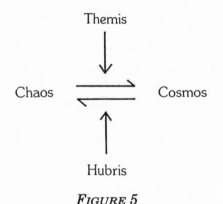

FIGURE 5

institutionalized and so controllable. But *hubris* itself, as a human quality, would have none of that, for that which is hubristic despises control: it is unconventional, embracing change and rejecting habit.

Themis and *hubris* can also now be placed into the diagram (see FIGURE 5). This pairing governs what is allowed or disallowed in the connection between chaos and cosmos. In my inner world it is now up to me to decide whether to do what is meet and right or whether to kick over the traces. It *is* possible for me to say, 'I was only obeying orders' (though I may be hanged for it); but there is no excuse for burying a talent in the ground just because something 'isn't done'.

The opposites are also true. Moderation may win through, but mediocrity takes no prizes. Going for broke, the winner takes all—or is perhaps bankrupted. And which course to settle for is a case of timing and personal style—but more of that later.

If gods and goddesses represent archetypal qualities, then Themis is that which acts within each of us to gather our part-personalities, complexes, or archetypal images together. Where there was emptiness, the goddess brings about a meeting. Clearly, she prevents a no-thing from occurring, because it is just that sort of occurrence that calls her into being; while her involvement brings about relationship and the healing of splits. Some-thing must result, and it is easy to see this as cosmos (FIGURE 6). It is just as obvious how *hubris* destroys, to bring about disorder (FIGURE 7). However, it is more difficult to accept that the same outrageous principle of overdoing things and going too far can also be a source of order or, similarly, that right-mindedness is an attitude that can usher in 'chaos' (FIGURES 8 and 9). It is just that their order and confusion are of a different type. Pasiphaë's passion for the

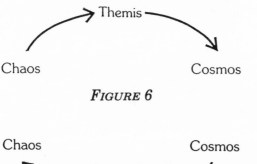

Chaos   Cosmos

FIGURE 6

Chaos   Cosmos

FIGURE 7

Chaos   Cosmos

FIGURE 8

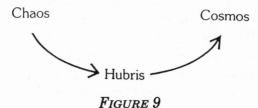

Chaos   Cosmos

FIGURE 9

bull (*hubris*) results in Asterion, a dispersed kind of order. Cocalus inviting a guest ashore to dinner (*themis*) results in the guest's death (*hubris*) and a falling apart of the order that was Minos and his troops (a chaos). In re-drawing the diagram (FIGURE 10) I have been more true to the nature of the psyche as system in that the relationships now run both ways, between all the elements shown. It is not just oppositional, a duality, nor binomial, but a field. As such, it is more in keeping with present-day concern with self-organizing systems, with co-evolution, with groups, and especially with networking.

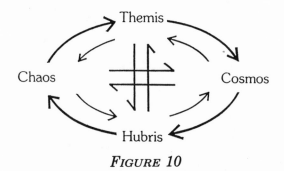

FIGURE 10

What's in a net?

The story has contained various happenings linked by time, and I have also described the same events as belonging to the field of *daidalos*. Taking a historical, synthetic approach, the myth-ego is seen as tracing a path that brings Daedalus to new and further qualities, which then adhere to his person. But it can also be insisted upon that all of these other characters or events should not be lost by inclusion in some mythical image of wholeness as unity. Instead, they can be seen as standing alone, complete in themselves, connected only by the passing of the thread that is Daedalus. Once he has moved on, they still exist, just as they were, and outside any history. This approach is one that is diachronic but also includes synchrony: elapsed and circular time. Jung himself never denied a polycentric nature of the psyche, always emphasizing its inherent tendency to fall apart. In his later, alchemical books, especially *Mysterium Conjunctionis (CW 14)*, he deals, as has been seen, with the possibilities of the *scintillae* possessing individual consciousness. Some post-Jungian writers have also taken the same direction. Making this plain, Samuels (1985a) writes of the similarity between so-called developmental and archetypal 'schools' of post-Jungian thought:

> Fordham and Hillman are each proposing a situationist, relativised, pluralistic self in which clusters of experiences carry the feeling of being 'myself', rather than that of being or feeling 'whole'. *If the part-self or psychic fragment is lived out fully, then wholeness will take care of itself.* It should not be forgotten that the feeling of being oneself is often extremely uncomfortable. . . . [p. 110, my emphasis]

Redfearn agrees that there is little difficulty nowadays in the idea of possessing many 'sub-personalities', his preferred term. He agrees that the notion of an 'I', or of behaviour, moving about from one to another of these part-personalities is more difficult to accommodate, perhaps because this requires us to take an objective view of ourselves. He goes on (Redfearn, 1985):

> It is the outside observer who can see this more easily than the subject whose "I" usually feels of a piece, continuous with the past and embodied in one's body and so on. [p. 129]

In other words, because we feel all of a piece, we tend to assume that we are one. It cannot be by chance that these two schools (developmental and archetypal) seem to be saying the same sorts of things in their different ways. Hillman calls his approach 'polytheistic', contrasting it, as already seen, with the heroic, strong ego that becomes for him an ego stuck in but one style of operation and there-fore pathological. Fordham (1985) himself has stated that his model of the psyche is neutral, since the part-selves he speaks of are no less important than the whole self, but that this remains an abstraction (pp. 89–91).

Guggenbühl-Craig (1980) has also written of his diffi-culties with the self as an integrated whole, symbolically expressed as roundness and completion. He feels that we now need to pay more attention to incompleteness and invalidity as self-images.

Being oneself, having multiple styles of 'I', knowing one's own invalidity, experiencing sub-personalities can indeed be uncomfortable and very hard to hold on to. It may feel like chaos, which does not mean, however, that there is anything wrong with it, nor that the ego has been thrown away or weakened thereby. What is needed is the strength to hold it all together.

I have already suggested a different model for ego-strength, associated with the confrontation of Proteus, which might provide this. This style of ego is both a strong enough response to a particular situation and one that can hold a Protean nature together, as a beekeeper must be able to contain many bees in a single hive. For another who questioned the sea god, holding him until he answered, was Aristaius of Sardinia, who wanted to know why his bees had mysteriously died. In a similar fashion, Daedalus is the protean myth-ego who can build a suitably appropriate container for an Asterion: call it a maze if you will, or a honeycomb.

Daidalos is more than that, for it is itself a container of various styles of craft and creativeness, as well as styles of being, párt-selves, personifications, and possibilities to come. At times one of them will be to the fore, at others a different perspective rules the kaleidoscope. The contain-ment of *daidalos* is not like that of a flask, a box, or a bowl; it is, rather, a network of connections and relationships that, united, form a whole that is greater than the sum of the parts: a system. I am describing a single style of psychic functioning, but one that is itself not unitary, for it includes its own image as one of the parts that make it up. Its unity is not monolithic, or even that of a honeycomb, but lies in the strength that holds all of its parts together. Another word for this system would be 'a network'.

What is *a net?*

A net is a reticulated structure, usually made of knotted string (the word is cognate with strong), whose filaments and nodal points enclose a lot of no-thing-ness, while being related directly and indirectly to one another. Von Franz in her book *Number and Time* (1974) has described the idea of field-like arrangements of archetypes, each surrounded by a web of overlapping and interconnecting amplifications, or nodal points in the field of psychic energy (p. 140ff), which is the same kind of image.

The Old English '*wyrd*', usually translated as 'fate', has been shown by Brian Bates (1983) to correspond to a belief that an invisible network of fibres, like a three-dimensional spider's web, pervaded the created world. All things were connected by this network running through them; and it follows that any action at one spot would affect all others, since they were always in contact by means of *wyrd*. For the Anglo-Saxons, what an individual did or did not do would materially affect all other parts of the network, and thus the universe. Bates compares it with the Chinese concept of the Dao (p. 9ff).

Looked at another way, the image of a net or network also approaches what was said about the notion of 'matriarchal consciousness', which functions as a total realization of the whole, but in which the ego focusses on a particular part at any one time. It is also, with a slightly different emphasis, similar to the imaginal ego, which, in Hillman's (1972) original description,

... is more discontinuous, now this, now that, guided as much by the synchronistic present as by the casual past, moving on a uroboric course which is the circulation of light and the darkness. It includes the downwards turns, the depressions, the falling away from awareness. Pathology has its place: is necessary. Does that not accord with experience? The movement of the imaginal ego should be conceived less as a development than as a circular pattern. [p. 184]

I will take it further. Jung's work has, from the first, shown us the value of the symbolic and its powers of transcension, which unite and synthesize the human psyche with its in-built tendency to dissociate. A symbolic approach is a throwing together [Greek: *symballein*] of two separated objects, which then stick together to re-form an original whole. This activity is itself a cure for dualism, which is dia-bolic, in the sense of its having been thrown into two parts [Greek: *diaballein*]. It is a diathetic process.

The style of functioning that I believe expresses itself through the network could be called amphibolic or amphibolous [Greek: *amphiballein*], meaning something that is thrown in both directions. It contains diabolic as well as symbolic activity. It is, in fact, the style of Jung, exalting ambiguity and equivocation at the same time as unison. But, on the other hand, to amphibolize is not to draw things together nor to synthesize. It also avoids the accusation of 'throwing away the ego' and the babel of voices that is evoked for some people by the term 'polytheism'. They may be missing the point, however, for polytheism is by nature *henotheistic* in that it values many gods, though only one at a time (Miller, 1971). And in any case for the Greeks it was the greatest *hubris* of all to accept only one god. Hillman's (1983) work has itself, in fact, also been described as amphibolous, in the publisher's foreword to his book, *Healing Fictions* (p. xii).

The amphibolic denies neither unity nor multiplicity, though it may attract the criticism of sitting on fences, eating a cake while having it too, or taking both sides of an argument. But in Greek *amphibole* means a casting net, which those who use it throw in such a way (in both directions) that by the time it falls upon the water it has opened to its fullest extent. The net is one, as is the fisherman skilled in his craft. The knots in the string, the interstices, and the fish it catches (hopefully) are many. Its image encapsulates ambiguity, which word itself stems from the Latin 'ambo', 'agere', meaning 'to drive both ways'.

Samuels (1989) has extended his above-mentioned ideas by considering pluralism further, regarding it as a model both for the relationship between psychological schools and for the actual mosaic that is the psyche. He sees pluralism as a way of overcoming dualism that is neither holistic nor heading for unity. It is not just a theory but 'a tool or instrument to make sure that diversity need not be a basis for schismatic conflict' (p. 1). Pluralism reconciles the conflicting demands of the one and the many, providing 'a place for ultimate reality *and* for a plethora of phenomena' (p. 4). He accepts that depth psychology, just like present-day views of particle physics, 'is less about "things" than about the relations between things and, ultimately, about the relations between sets of relations' (p. 9). I have already discussed the wider meanings of the word 'thing', showing that in fact a thing itself may *also* be seen as a set of 'relationships between things' and even 'relationships between relations'.

Pluralism is anti-hierarchical, each component claiming equal status with every other and being linked with all others, though those linkages may shift and change over time. Samuels points out that a pluralistic perspective does not deny the possibility of single elements taking over, so that the individual feels 'all of a piece'; and he quotes with approval López Pedraza's (1971) statement that 'the many contains the unity of the one without losing the possibilities of the many' (p. 214).

It is a short step to describe this view as one of networking. Indeed, Samuels (1989) himself suggests the notion of an 'imaginal network', in which content takes priority over any containing structure. As he points out, such a structure can, in any case, never be experienced *without content*.

If the content changes, then so does the structure. All events and experiences may therefore be looked at as being rooted not in psychic structures, but in a network of images themselves, which possess, like all images, a capacity to make other images, 'thus crafting experience without direct contact with external stimuli'. Samuels quotes Lipnack and Stamps (1985) to point out that a network is many-headed, does not collapse when one element is removed, has a high degree of shared values—yet disagreements also—among its components, and possesses indistinct boundaries (pp. 5–8). It is also hard to define the membership, or extent of influence, of a network (Samuels, 1989, pp. 39–47).

There is a great deal in all that which resonates with what has been said of *daidalos*: the separate elements, connected intermittently by Daedalus, or myth-ego, as he moves among them; their non-hierarchical status; the repetitive nature of the mythic elements, which share similarities as well as differing; their imaginal quality; the fact that they are without structure and yet have a determining power; and that they possess boundaries that shade off into unknowing.

An important point that Samuels (1989) makes concerning a pluralistic attitude is that it is not easy to hold on to 'without seeking to impose more than co-existence upon the separate and conflicting parts' (p. 6). It is hard, he says, to be passionate about tolerance (p. 6), because 'if all views are considered to be equally valid, what is to become of the freedom to feel a special value attaching to one's own view?' (p. 227). It is this that leads us back to craft and the craftsman, for it is Daedalus himself who displays, thoughout the story, an ability to stay with, move between, contain, and suffer the various contradictory pulls of the imaginal network that is *daidalos*.

CHAPTER TWELVE

The two genders

That man again

I t is necessary to look at Daedalus once more in the light of all that has gone before, and especially with regard to the statement in chapter eleven that it is his nature that holds everything in the field together. What has been identified which might make him able to perform this role?

Whatever the trade followed, every craftworker has many different tools with varying qualities that are specific for differing tasks or circumstances. Some of these will be for more general use, while others have a specialized purpose. Only one is likely to be used at any one time. Tools may share a basic action but differ in quality—for example, axes and adzes both cut wood, but there are things I can do more easily with my adze than with my axe, like the hollowing out of a canoe from a tree trunk, for instance. A gouge is more sophisticated than an adze, and its cut is more subtle; a chisel cuts straight across, instead

of the curved strokes of the gouge or the adze. Chisels come in varying widths, making cuts of different sizes. In other words, the more varied the tools that craftworkers possess, the better able are they to do their work. The wider the range of tools and the more skilful they are in the using of them, the more confident craftworkers can be of coping with any unexpected problems. Some tools may be seldom used, but even when hanging on the workshop wall to gather dust, they instil confidence—like the single tranquillizer tablet in the bathroom cupboard. Possession, as well as knowing the way about—including all previous relevant experience—leads to freedom from anxiety. Having the tools also means that the craftworker can, at any time, choose one and use it for the job it does well, before putting it back into the toolbox. So the skilled artisan can relax and allow things to happen at their own pace, going wherever the way leads, to explore the unknown, and experience 'chaos', fairly certain of having the ability to get out of any trouble. The alternative is to grasp at straws or only to go down known pathways, not letting anything get out of hand. The craftsperson does not always hold skills in hand but does know where to find and use them—if and when needed.

Craftworkers cannot attempt those things for which they do not have the skills; and, indeed, in a sense, without the necessary skills, such 'things' do not even exist. They are unimaginable. Conversely, the more such people know, the more they can do—and the less they find it necessary to interfere with the process, being sure in the knowledge of having the skills to intervene only as, or if, it starts to run away from them.

This is the way of the first-class midwife who tries to facilitate the birth process in taking its own natural course. And it is similar to the 'wu wei' of the Chinese philosopher, Lao Tzu. These words, usually translated as 'not doing', are claimed by A. Cooper to be more correctly represented by the phrase 'without-making-to-be'. Thus:

That is why the sage deals with affairs without-making-to-be and conducts a not-telling form of teaching. [Lao Tzu, Dao De Jing, translated by A. Cooper, unpublished]

Not-making-to-be does not mean sitting idly by, but rather being able to go with the nature of the material and its processes, merely nudging it, when needed, in the direction it *wishes* to take. It is also the way of the skilled psychotherapist. Earlier, it has been seen that the yawning void of chaos was a state where things had not yet been made to be, because 'un-met'. To exist as one who does not make-to-be requires a trust of, and a belief in, nature—that it will perform its natural functions adequately. This is held to be so even if the outcome is necessarily uncertain, as when pouring metal into the recesses of a mould that cannot be inspected to see whether it has 'taken' the image, or when awaiting the birth of an infant. In one sense, it is always a fearful risk, chancing all, and also a nail-biting suspense filled with doubt. Additionally, there is the helpless, hopeless suffering of not being able to do more than wait for an unknown future. But for the master craftsman there is also a certain calm awareness that he has done the best that he could, used all his skills, and also that he has acted in his own style, one with which he feels happy. He has his own personal mix of *themis* and *hubris,* chaos as well as order, long experience as well as a beginner's eye, all of which is unique to him. Finally, he can be content with knowing that he was not perfect, but good-enough. He may fail, as all do at times, but that does not make him a failure.

To all of these attributes Daedalus has access as he passes through the field that is his story, lighting up each individual element in passing, when appropriate. And how does he know which *is* appropriate? Well, that is his craft and his cunning.

It will be obvious that some of the qualities mentioned above belong to the women of the story and thus to femaleness, which seems to have crept in, when I said that it would be kept out. I have hardly commented on this, until now; but here is the moment to explore its presence and its nature.

What about the women?

I have said that this book was about males only, but I have taken a good deal of time discussing goddesses or the females who do enter *daidalos,* and the qualities they bring to it, for use by the myth-ego. What do they represent, if not the feminine principle?

Certainly a standard psychological interpretation, as already stated, would accuse Daedalus of lacking a relationship to the feminine, by both starting and finishing his story uncoupled. But I do not feel content with that, for I wish to study the man on his own as a model for maleness, while at the same time being true to his story just as it is. If *daidalos* is to be my image of maleness, what can it mean that such maleness includes females, and in the way that it does?

Once again, the standard answer would be that they represent the 'anima' or soul; and once more that answer is not enough. This leaves no option but to try to re-imagine what 'female' means, as an image, in the context of *daidalos,* which may lead in turn to a re-imagining of maleness also. One hint has already been given in the suggestion that the 'absent feminine' also has an archetypal basis in the image of the darkened moon.

Boy children have different bodies from girl children, and they are aware of this from an early age. They are also treated differently by their two parents in obvious ways. But in addition there are subtle and unconscious differences in the way in which parents handle and respond to children of the two genders.

I remember exactly the time, the place, and the shock of my *conscious* discovery that my sister did not have a penis, although I would often have seen her naked before then. I was around six years old. Since my parents did not hide their nakedness to their children, I already knew, by then, that there were physical differences between male and female. I also knew well the different ways in which my mother or father treated or handled me, and what they expected of me. In an instant, however, I suddenly became aware of the difference between me and my sister. At first I thought she had some clever way of holding her penis between her legs so that it did not show. I could not do this, and I was envious. Slowly I had to accept the amazing fact that she was not like me. We were different; and my emphasis here is upon things that differ, rather than that I was masculine and she was feminine, or that I had what she did not, or that she could do something I could not.

The word 'differ' means to 'carry things apart' and so to make unlike or distinct (*OED*). People, bits of them, or their qualities, which are felt as 'different' from me, are placed by this process of differing into variant groups. To this whole process belongs psychological splitting, as does differentiation also. These are all universal processes that occur in the same fashion and belong naturally to a child of either sex. The *way* they operate is indifferent to gender; and exactly *who* is 'different' will depend on whether it is a boy or girl child who observes. What or who is different from me is now felt to be *other* (not this, not the same, *OED*). An 'other' person is someone who is different from me, and one style of that difference can be gender. What is different from the boy-me is imaged as girl. What is different from me in terms of generation will be either parental or babyish. What is live but other in terms of reflexive consciousness is imaged as animal; and what is different as well as lifeless appears an inanimate matter. The girl, the parent, the baby, the stone are all metaphors for different kinds of otherness. However, though they are different from me, yet there is a relationship between us.

The words 'male' and 'female' are descriptions both of physical types of people and the roles we put upon them or expect of them in our society. What they represent, as images within the human psyche, is suggestive of difference and otherness; they will therefore be treated there as things that are 'other' generally get treated; that is to say, these psychic images of otherness will carry with them any mixture of curiosity, excitement, adoration, or worship, as well as bemusement, fear, antagonism, rejection, destructive feelings, etc.

The anthropologist Mary Douglas (1966), concerned with the ways in which societies treat difference and ambiguity, says in general of those qualities (self and other) that, first, one category is made important or true and the other baseless. Secondly, what is other can be physically controlled. Thirdly, the anomalous can be avoided as unclean. Fourthly, it may be labelled as dangerous; while lastly and paradoxically, it may be elevated to a higher level to 'enrich meaning or call attention to other levels of existence' (pp. 39–40). The object of all these processes, of course, is that the self should be able to control those things that are other and therefore to be feared.

The male-oriented society of the Western world and individual men behave towards femaleness in all of these ways. In addition, so does the human psyche treat what is experienced within it as 'other' as a similar anomaly. What is anomalous to the male psyche may be imaged as female, therefore to be both denigrated and adored. If men treat women as 'other' and wish to keep them so, it is because then they can control them; but, of course, they still wish to worship them, thus confirming Douglas's hypothesis.

From the female point of view, Simone De Beauvoir (1960) said of this situation more than thirty years ago:

> Women have no grasp on the world of men because their experience does not teach them to use logic and technique; inversely masculine apparatus loses its power at the frontiers of the feminine realm. There is a whole region of human experience which the male deliberately chooses to ignore because he fails to *think* it: this experience woman *lives*. [p. 310]

And she goes on:

> It is understandable, in this perspective, that woman
> takes exception to masculine logic. Not only is it inap-
> plicable to her experience, but in his hands, as she
> knows, masculine reasoning becomes an underhand
> form of force; men's undebatable pronouncements are
> intended to confuse her. The intention is to put her in a
> dilemma: either you agree or you do not. [p. 310]

According to De Beauvoir, therefore, women are expected
by society to behave not as their selves, but as other (i.e.
male), although this may have changed somewhat since
the times in which she wrote.

The age-old definition of the two genders has been that
males are active and outgoing while femaleness refers to
in-dwelling and passivity. In recent times, such biological
descriptions have been discredited and seen as largely representing the gender roles expected of the two groups of
people in our civilization for many thousands of years.
Nevertheless, they represent a tandem of qualities that are
very present in the field of *daidalos,* the latter being
mainly, though not exclusively, carried by the women. I
shall examine this further.

The word passive comes to English from the Latin
'*patio*', meaning 'I suffer', and does not so much imply a
sense of inertness but an earlier notion of 'suffering something from without to happen' (*OED*). Other words that
share the same root are patient (noun as well as adjective)
and both patience, and passion. From the Greek equivalent
[*páthos*] comes 'pathos', 'pathetic', 'pathological', as well as
all words ending in '-pathy', including 'sympathy', and
'empathy'.

The English word 'suffer' originally meant 'to allow
something to happen': to put up with, or to bear it; and
these qualities have also been traditionally associated with
femaleness, though that fact does not necessarily make the
feminine principle into a psychic fact.

Nevertheless, in *daidalos* the two categories male and female are often imaged as possessing different qualities from each other. What is male tends to be transitive, going beyond itself, passing from one state to another, as when modulating from skill to skill appropriately or moving on from place to place. That which is female seems to represent immanence: 'an act which is performed entirely within the mind of the subject and produces no external evidence' (*OED*). It is indwelling, inherent, abiding. As a positive experience it means to be used as an object, without objection: to allow, to bide one's time. Negatively, it represents resistance to change, inertia, and a blockage of potency (in this respect, see Lambert, 1981, p. 52).

Now it is clear that in real life both men and women possess each of these qualities (transition and immanence), though in our society there are often 'blind spots' towards qualities that transgress the expected categories. As an example of this, it is a fact that women who are convicted of white-collar crime are dealt with more leniently than men, but those who commit 'grievous bodily harm' (a supposedly more male activity) are dealt with over-severely. The categories are, of course, made by *themis*.

In this story, note that Talus is a man, yet his name means sufferer. Cocalus bides his time, while his daughters act aggressively. In another sphere altogether, the uncertain waiting period of a woman's pregnancy ends with the powerful thrust that is birth. Using the notion of the *Dao*, this expulsive or 'exertive' ability of the womb has been taken as an example of so-called 'Yang-femininity' (Pauli Haddon, 1987, pp. 133–141).

Equally, there would seem to be no more feminine activity than breast-feeding, and the breast itself is a powerful female symbol. Yet a similar blind spot obscures the fact that it is not the breast that is put into the baby's mouth but the nipple, as Bradley (1973) has pointed out. The word 'nipple' is derived from 'neb' or 'nib', meaning a bird's beak (the Latin for vulture is *Nibbio*) or, alternatively, as a diminutive of the verb to 'nip'. Neither of these images is especially nurturing. Bradley has also pointed out that the nipple protrudes, is made up of erectile tissue, and is inserted into a cavity. In addition, a nursing mother can describe the exquisite moment when, presenting the breast to her baby, she knows that she cannot prevent the milk from expressing itself, just like the male orgasm. Breast-feeding might therefore be just as well called a male phallic activity but is better seen, in part, as another example of 'Yang-femininity'.

Yin and Yang are often loosely thought of as representing female and male qualities, respectively, but in a 'knee-jerk' kind of way that equates the female only with being receptive, nurturing, gestating. These are, indeed, the nature of Yin: 'receiving, encompassing, enclosing, global, wholistic [sic], welcoming, sustaining, protecting, nourishing, conserving, embracing, swallowing, entombing, containing, centripetal, stable, holding together, inclusive' (Pauli Haddon, 1987, p. 133); and the list could probably be extended indefinitely.

The *I Ching,* on the other hand, describes Yang as having the basic meaning of 'banners waving in the wind' and Yin as 'overcast'. From these two are derived Yang as the sunny side of a mountain or river, with Yin as its northern, shady side (*The I Ching,* Wilhelm, 1950, p. lvi). *It is vitally important to realize that all other meanings are secondarily derived from these, and that this includes the gender with which they are so frequently labelled.*

Cooper (personal communication) has shown that the earliest drawing for Yang is of an upright staff, while that for Yin is something liquid which flows. By these means, he suggests, the Chinese recognized, and stated thereby, a major difference between things that stand (stay still) and others that are fluid (or move). There are things that will not change and others that will. A staff will be still unless moved, while that which is fluid flows until stopped. Liquid adapts itself to the shape of any different container, while a staff will not.

He went on to point out to me that in the *I Ching* the two are also, for numerological reasons, associated with the numbers nine (Yang) and six (Yin). Nine is drawn by a 'bearing hand', an arm crossed with a line, which Cooper recognizes as a convention for drawing attention to its action. Six is drawn as a simple house (FIGURE 11), in which the walls can be seen as 'bearing' the roof. The two, therefore, demonstrate active and passive bearing, says Cooper. I would add that they represent something that can bear an object, or be borne in motion (i.e. lifting or carrying: lifted or being carried), which is Yang; and, secondly, an object that bears and is borne without moving. The walls carry the roof, or it is borne by them, and this image suggests Yin.

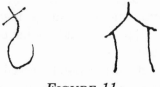

FIGURE 11

Neither of these qualities need be restricted to the roles that men and women play in the world. Indeed, Yang and Yin have many correspondences that have nothing at all to do with being male or female.

YANG	*YIN*
Light	Darkness
Sun	Moon
Brightness	Shade
Heaven	Earth
Round	Square
Time	Space
East	West
South	North
Left	Right

Yang and Yin are not different as men and women are different, nor as masculine is from feminine. *It is in fact precisely the other way around.* Female and male differ from each other *in an exactly similar kind of way to that in which Yin differs from Yang.* This still does not mean that female equates with Yin, or male with Yang, for what the two kinds of qualities share is difference as well as relatedness.

One difficulty lies in the fact that since 'female' and 'male' suggest an actual biological difference, they then are taken as concrete psychic facts, rather than as metaphorical qualities inherently available to people of either gender. Because a man is male, it is assumed that male images within the psyche refer to men. Instead, for a man, a male image represents self, while 'female' is a metaphor for otherness. The reverse is also obviously true.

The Dao presents these qualities as real ones and lasting (Yang), but which are at the same time capable of endless flux and permutation (Yin) within people, their behaviour and activities, as well as events in the world, or in concepts themselves. Things change and do not change.

What is clear also is that there is no unbridgeable difference between the two images. They change into each other, the one increasing as the other decreases, though the total 'amount' remains the same. Yin can never exist without Yang: it is only the relative proportions between the two that alter; and it is the differing proportions of the two in anything that provide it with its own peculiar nature. Even so, it is still permissible to examine the nature of 'Yang-ness' without complaining that it contains too little or too much 'Yin-ness'.

It is this experience of, and relationship to, otherness that the women bring to *daidalos,* not merely their so-called 'feminine' patience, passiveness, passion, sufferance, all borne in the suffering silence to which I originally condemned them. In fact, at Camicus, a total reversal is found, as already mentioned several times, when Cocalus is invaded by Minos. It is he who suffers it, retreating passively while, within his realm, it is the daughters who scheme, act, kill. To them belong the power and violent aggressiveness that are more usually equated with maleness. But what they represent is difference from the behaviour of their suffering father.

However, one way in which Yang and Yin as asexual, cosmic functions express themselves within an individual is by images that are correspondingly male or female. So the female image in a male field is one of Yin-ness, and not the absent feminine putting in a minor appearance. This may feel as if I am splitting hairs, but it is important to remember that as Yin (and not femininity) it was never absent, because 'more Yang than Yin' is, on occasion, a natural state of affairs, merely expressing an artificially fixed moment of the endless flux of the Dao. The reverse is equally true of Yang within a predominantly Yin field. Thus 'what about the feminine?' is a meaningless demand, for as Yin she was always present sufficiently for that moment.

Yet there is more, for, as De Beauvoir (1960) has pointed out, women can know themselves as subjects, just as men do, while always being made forcibly aware, because of society, of their existence as objects, or what she calls their 'alterity'. They know this moreover in a way of which men have been, and largely still are, unaware (p. 357). Female lives have for many centuries enshrined ambiguity as something they have had to learn to live with—and this has nothing to do with whether it should be so or not. What I am claiming for femaleness, as known today, is that it possesses more of an ability to exist, painfully, with otherness as well as with its own identity. Males are at present less able to do this, in a similar way—because, historically, they have never had to do it. They therefore find it difficult, impossible, or frankly unnatural; and it is this ability that the women also bring to *daidalos,* this which Daedalus takes on. He learns to suffer his own otherness.

In one sense he has always had it, his prototype being born from only a mother, working upon the mother's body, bringing his good things back to her. But from another angle he remakes and develops this quality of ambiguity, until it is interchangeable and its actual gender has meaning no longer, as in the role-reversal of Cocalus and his daughters. Things change, but at the same time stay the same.

Confucius, standing beside a river, said: 'Everything flows on and on like this river, without pause, day and night', expressing the idea of that inevitable process of change (Wilhelm, 1951, p. lv). Heraclitus, living at around the same time (500 B.C.), said, 'As they step into the same rivers other and still other waters flow upon them' (D. 12, Kahn, 1979, p. 166). He thus extended the Confucian image to account not only for the changing water within the river, but the sameness of the river as well as of those who step in it. It is 'The preservation of structure within a process of flux, where a unitary form is maintained, while its material embodiment or "filling" is constantly lost or replaced' (Kahn, 1979, p. 168). But this need not always be so, as we can see now, for if you stop the flow of water, then the river is a dried-up bed and the stepper-in can no longer be a wader or a swimmer. The structure is therefore dependent upon its content.

There is one image that recurs within *daidalos* which is closely related to the women. It is that of disappearing and of reappearing later in a changed form. Together with my amplifications, these would include the festival of Daedalia to tempt the absent Hera back into the open; Pasiphaë lying in the cow-frame; the dark nights of the moon; and all that happened at Camicus when the Minos-nature was renewed as a group of colonizing sailors and the monolithic became the multiform. Those crafts that are said to have been traditionally associated with women—planting, brewing, baking, pottery—are of a similar nature and are all modelled on pregnancy. The hero performs a similar kind of task in rescuing 'the treasure hard to attain', but more often than not he does it in another way and in another light: publicly and in the open.

In a recent paper, Coline Covington (1989) examined the differences between hero and heroine, reaching similar conclusions. The hero's moment of glory, she says, 'that moment which turns a man into a hero—is . . . constituted by an action which derives its powers from being entirely visible'. By contrast she describes the heroine's act of heroism as taking place out of sight, that is to say, unconsciously. The hero's act is one of separation from the mother, while the heroine's implies an internalization of matter—mater, mother (p. 251). Covington notes the exceptions to this association of hero with independence and heroine with dependency—he with deintegration, she with reintegration—and asks that her readers accept that heroes can be heroines and vice versa. In considering separation from the mother and the gender of the child who would separate, she says:

> . . . while the relationship to mother is inevitably different for boys and girls, because of their sexual identity, both share a basic need to separate and must achieve this by exploring how they differ and how they are similar—through opposition and identification [p. 252]

These images are clearly present in the women of our tale, and through them Daedalus himself is transformed, being able to retire within but produce something never known before, *from within*. But his nature is more than just that, and the method of lost wax casting together with its product is the pinnacle of that nature. It is the creation of something real from imagination as well as, psychologically, a metaphor for deintegration, reintegration, and the 'unpacking' of the Self. To Daedalus belongs the wax model, the mantle, the skill in heating, the making of the metal, the pouring, the cooling, the forging, the chasing, and the burnishing. It is the image of the craftsman who makes the container and holds the anxiety of what is unknown, as well as producing the finished piece in all its detail. In this he acts as both heroine and hero, Yin as well as Yang: his story is filled with female images, although he himself is all male. I shall return to this later.

PART FOUR

THE SPACES IN-BETWEEN

CHAPTER THIRTEEN

Male, made

Dadilos [sic]

A creative typing error produced the title for this
section—in order, I suppose to make me realize
that the loss or absence of the father and, indeed,
the father complex itself must be considered as part of
daidalos, whether I liked it or not.

The father has received a lot of attention recently in
depth psychology, as what he represents, in reality as well
as an image, is rediscovered; I am referring here both to
the facilitating father and to his critical and abusive
aspects, as well as to his total absence (e.g. Pirani, 1989,
Samuels, 1985b). This re-awakening means not only that
conscious interest is being directed his way, but also that
what he represents is becoming more active in the human
psyche. So I am not really surprised to find myself forced
by the word-processor to consider 'daddy-loss'—but which
daddy? Does this mean looking for the father who is either
not there (that of Talus) or inadequate (a dead loss,

Cocalus)? Or is it a demand that the interfering daddy (Minos) should *get* lost? Moreover, in relation to what directly concerns me here, rather than just considering family reality, I find myself asking just what kind of daddy it is that must get lost from the image which is *daidalos,* or what kind of father it might be that is already missing.

Here is the kind of fathering that does appear. The father of Talus seems not to exist. Zeus sees to it that Athene passes on his words, deeds, or thoughts, intact and unchanged. His own beloved son Minos is an ashamed and confining father to the illegitimate Asterion. Daedalus is long-suffering of Icarus and his playfulness, but in the end a loving, caring, and grieving parent as well. Cocalus shows an indulgent side towards his daughters before handing over to them the executive role; and this action could be looked at in two ways: as his own ineffectiveness, or by showing him as able to liberate them.

The 'absent father', whether he is physically or emotionally missing, needs to be made present; and this, as has been noted, is where Daedalus, as the mother's brother, steps in to direct Talus's gaze outwards. It is the role of the father as 'awakener from sleep'. Although much has been made of this 'absent' father as a cause of later psychological illness, such a type of fathering can, nonetheless, also be looked at from a positive aspect, in that his absence allows the son full access to the mother, as a creative ground. Alone, she brings forth the craftsman son; and, as already noted, without a father he is allowed to monkey around with her: daddy-loss can here be seen as a creative withdrawal.

The kind of fathering practised by Zeus towards Athene is coercive, demanding from the child a faithfulness of action so as to gain approval. Many women have known that father well. Either they do as he wishes, unable to disobey, which will find them failing to be themselves, but pleasing him—as well as pleasing the father image that they carry along within themselves. Or else, in rebellion, though still unable, because of the father's introjected power, to be themselves, they may exhibit such illnesses as anorexia, agoraphobia, or depression.

But Zeus is a father who can also love, favour, and reward his children. He does so with Minos, favourite of all his mortal children, over whose death he is said to have grieved the most. Minos has the advantage, however, of being male and is therefore a reflection of Zeus himself. As I have pointed out before, it seems to be sons who are expected (and therefore allowed) to expand and extend the work of the father, not daughters, who merely pass it on.

Minos himself, on the other hand, ashamed of Asterion's attributes, denied him a free existence. But the Minotaur was handicapped in being a pleasure to his father by being different from him: he was a mother's child and therefore monstrous. And yet, such an attitude is not always negative.

A child (in this case the son) needs a father who is sure enough of his own views to provide boundaries, even to the extent perhaps of scorning the boy's own growing identity. In this way, provided the process is not overly castrating, the son can come into his own creativity, as does Asterion when transmuted into Daedalus-plus-Icarus.

The craftsman, now acknowledged for the first time as a father, is a steadfast one: a creative father in his own right, a demonstrative father whose skills could be copied, a patient and accepting father, a moderating father with good advice to give, and as such a polar opposite to the absent, or coercive father. He is, in addition, a father who has to learn that his son may possibly take in none of this. The father may be totally ignored, and that is a very painful parental discovery to accept without hitting back.

As has been seen, Cocalus transforms the father/daughters role by being on their side; he also transforms the capacity for standing firm by, paradoxically, drawing in. Then, and only then, can he hand over power to them. I have already mentioned the notion of an appropriate 'erotic playback' by which a father can help his daughters to break out of the equation 'woman = mother', thereby to fulfil their individual possibilities and to take on other roles (Samuels, 1989, p. 82). It is somewhere within this area that Cocalus acts, as described above, while the presence at Camicus of Daedalus as a surrogate, enabling father is also undoubtedly significant.

All of this could be taken merely to confirm that a good-enough father—neither too harsh nor too indulgent, neither too powerful nor too weak, emotionally present and focussed upon his child, but able to be separate and ignore it too—is necessary for healthy growing up. Yet in all of these descriptions the father is seen as only secondary to and following on from the mother: the Great Mother archetype, which stands before and beyond everything as origins, container, wholeness (see Neumann, 1955). If she is primary, then the role of fathering can only be in leading outwards from her.

I would like to challenge this view; for *that* is the kind of daddy I wish to lose, the daddy-loss I believe in. I wish we could lose for ever the notion that the father can be only a secondary figure. Instead, I would like to see the father properly acknowledged as an image of a primary source of maleness as well, adding what Marion Woodman (1985) has called a 'patrix' to the matrix that is so well known and described (p. 39). Let me explain.

From Uroboros out

Chaos, the first goddess, has a male ending to her name, as already noted. The Elohim who created the world of Genesis are plural, in Hebrew, and of both genders. In translation, their name is written as 'God' but that is only because we, who think of God as male and singular, *must* therefore translate the word that way.

In fact, our word 'God' comes from the Indo-European root, 'ghu-', meaning to invoke. So God is 'the one invoked' without any question of gender entering into it (*ODEE*). Cooper found the same image in the early

Chinese script (FIGURE 12), while the Vedic god, Indra, is known as 'the much invoked'. God does not therefore imply any particular gender and is not necessarily singular or plural. In fact, the earliest gods were both, just like Chaos. They are described as 'uroboric'.

Neumann (1949) describes the earliest symbols of original perfection as the circle, the sphere, the egg, the Dao, and the *rotundum* of alchemy (p. 8). They are expressed also, he says, in 'the primal dragon of the beginning, which bites its own tail, the self-begetting Uroboros'. It is claimed for this ancient symbol that 'it slays, weds and impregnates itself'; and that 'It is man and woman, begetting and conceiving, devouring and giving birth, active and passive, above and below, at once' (p. 10). In our field, we can recognize uroboric aspects in the first snake-man, Erichthonios, as well as in the self-conceptual abilities of the darkened moon, imagined as Asterion.

Neumann (1949), however, having established that this primal symbol possesses both genders, immediately goes on to consider what he calls 'the maternal uroboros' as a source for all future development as Great Mother, of whom Chaos then becomes an example—having lost its male side. He agrees, though, that the two cannot really be separated, and that:

> [the] initial movement, the procreative thrust, naturally
> has an affinity with the paternal side of the uroboros
> and with the beginning of evolution in time, and is far
> harder to visualise than the maternal side. [p. 18]

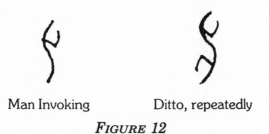

Man Invoking   Ditto, repeatedly

FIGURE 12

This is a familiar-sounding difficulty, for the inherence of one image in another is something wrestled with throughout this book. As for the psychological model now, it is the male that inheres within the female to the extent that maleness has become subservient to the Great Mother in Neumann's account of the origins of consciousness. And he goes that way, despite quoting an Egyptian text of male creation, from Heliopolis, thus (Neumann, 1949):

> I copulated in my hand, I joined myself to my shadow and spurted out of my own mouth. I spewed forth as Shu and spat forth as Tefnut. [p. 19]

The 'I' of this quotation is Atum, image of the setting sun as well as the sun before dawn, i.e. the darkening or darkened sun—itself an archetype, perhaps, for an absenting father. Atum was the origin of all gods and all people, able to divide and reproduce himself. Shu, the first male, holds up the sky and is the god of emptiness and the life principle, while his sister-wife, Tefnut, goddess of dew and rain, aids him by establishing world order (Larousse, 1959, p. 7). These two are children of Atum and represent two gendered aspects of the masculine uroboros. The female has been born from the male.

Following Neumann's failure to look at the ability of males to give birth, the cry could become, with some justification, 'What about the masculine?' For it seems as if the paternal origin of things, a World Father who is generative, stands invisibly behind the bulk of the Great Mother, while maleness, which is transformative, becomes just an appendage to the female. Certainly this picture of the male who is only allowed second place has been emphasized in mythology, where he is often seen as the son of his mother first, and later as lover. But this does not mean that it necessarily *must be so*: Neumann (1949) expressly states that 'the initial movement . . . naturally has an affinity with the paternal side' (p. 15); and just because, or even if, it is 'harder to visualize', this should not mean that it can be ignored with impunity or its possibilities denied. Depth psychology has again developed, it seems to me, a scotoma in this respect. I shall allow myself to question these assumptions, to explore the suppressed, and so, hopefully, to recover another viewpoint.

Atum, it is clear, demonstrates the possibility of a maleness that conceives and gives birth. A later myth from Memphis sees Atum as nothing but an expression of the will of an obscure earth god Tatanen (later known as Ptah), who created everything by and from within himself (Larousse, 1959, p. 11). Ptah, sometimes seen as dwarfed and crippled, has already been recognized as similar to the Greek Hephaestus, and therefore to Daedalus himself.

In Norse mythology, where the ice from the north and the sparks and embers to the south of Ginnungagap met, there the giant Ymir formed. As he lay there, he began to sweat, and from his armpits were born a man and a woman, while his two feet copulated together, giving birth to all of the frost giants. Ymir's name has been related to the Sanskrit word *yama*, meaning hybrid or hermaphrodite, and once again there is contained within his person the image of the creative powers of the male uroboros. Later, the god Odin, with his two brothers, Vili and Vé tore Ymir's body to pieces to make the world (Ellis Davidson, 1964, pp. 188–189). Yama, as a divine entity, has been described, it should be noted, as the god of *ṛta* (von Franz, 1974, p. 255).

However this may have been historically, there seems to be no doubt that only myths that confirm the maternal origins have been selected, and that these have been interpreted only from a viewpoint that confirms expectations or current prejudices. And this is not just a modern phenomenon but reflects the psychology of the myth-makers themselves. Let us take a Greek cosmogony as example.

Hesiod tells us that Chaos first of all produced Gaia, the earth as fundament, from within herself. Gaia then bore Uranus, as son and husband, in order that he should father on her the Titans. But his habit, as sky god, of lying nightly upon the earth prevented their children from having an independent existence. Kronos, the youngest son, was encouraged to cut off his father's genitals with a sickle provided by his mother. From then on, the sky lay no more upon the earth to procreate, and their children, already born, could inhabit the earth in the space thus formed.

The two world parents, sky and earth, were then replaced by two of their children: Kronos the reaper, and his sister Rhea, the fertile earth. Kronos, however, repeated the father's trick of preventing his children from living in freedom, this time by eating them up as soon as they were born. Enraged and in grief, their mother Rhea asked for help from her parents. It was mostly Gaia, her mother, who assisted at the secret birth of Zeus, also his father's youngest child, by giving Kronos a stone to eat instead. When Zeus was adult, he asked advice of the Titaness Metis in consultation with Rhea and so became cupbearer to his father: he gave him a potion, obtained from Metis, which caused Kronos to vomit up the swallowed children. There followed the war of the gods against their father and his fellow Titans, that led to the founding of Olympus as the home of the new order. Later Zeus, now married to Metis, was warned that any son she bore would depose him. He therefore swallowed his pregnant wife (Hesiod, transl. Wender, 1973, p. 27; Kérenyi, 1951a, pp. 18–24 & 118).

Fathers do not come too well out of that story. They are all, at first, sons prevented from living free who must then kill off their father. In turn, they become autocratic and repressive figures themselves. On the other hand, all of that meaning depends upon how the story is told, and it could be told differently, without the patriarchal slant of those who wrote down the oral myths.

The innate bisexualism of Chaos has already been pointed out: both genders possess an equal image. Hesiod elevates the female aspect as that which gives birth, and then only to another female, who must make her own son/lover, although the Egyptian texts presented above showed a different kind of possibility. Clearly, some part of the uroboros has to produce, but that does not give the procreative, parthenogenetic piece any superiority, except an assumed one. Uranus, says Graves (1955),

> . . . gazing down fondly at Gaia as she slept showered fertile rain upon her secret clefts and she bore grass, flowers, and trees with the beasts and birds proper to each. This same rain made the rivers flow and filled the hollow places with water, so that lakes and seas came into being. [p. 31]

What a charming scene it evokes. This was Uranus, in a loving, fertilizing role, who lay nightly upon Gaia, helping her to bear children as well as all the fruits of the earth. These were, first of all, unruly giants and Cyclops in semi-human form, whom Uranus very sensibly confined, for they could have done a lot of damage. Enraged by this containment of her destructive powers, Gaia sought revenge through her Titan children. These are said also to have been kept shut away—this time within her vagina—by the nightly copulation upon which Uranus insisted, 'enflamed with lust'. But the sky god, it is said, lay with her only at night. What was to prevent the children escaping by day? Not Uranus, certainly, for he was not there. Instead, Gaia can be imagined feeding them tales of what this terrible father would do if they dared to put their noses outside. It was not the vengeful father who prevented their freedom, but the all-embracing mother. And so Kronos, knowing no other story (just like present-day children who must believe the 'family myth' they are presented with), attacked the only aspect of the father that he was allowed to see or feel: father as phallus; and this he cut off, flinging it behind him into repressive unconsciousness. Since his mother put him up to it and gave him the sickle, and since Uranus is also her son, this is a castration of the father by the mother, just as the keeping of her children always inside her is also a 'castration' of their possibilities. She will not allow them any generativity that is not of her. Is it any wonder that fathers fear castration by their sons and wives, and will do anything to prevent it?

In his turn, Kronos also fertilized the earth, now imaged as the bountiful Rhea [Greek: *flowing*]. Knowing what mothers get up to with their children, and the old wives' tales fed to them when confined within her, Kronos took his own children safely into himself for their protection, until they should be mature. Rhea was furious that her birthgiving activities had been taken over and her plans thwarted. She plotted revenge and sought advice where it could best be obtained—from Gaia herself. These two mothers now share the family falsehood concerning the destructiveness of the male and consequent female vengefulness. Again they use the unwitting youngest son as their tool, even involving in their plots the woman he will marry.

When Zeus is king in his turn, knowing all too well what wives and mothers get up to, he ingests the pregnant Metis to safeguard himself as well as his unborn children from female destructiveness. Metis was, as already seen, a shape-shifter, a female Proteus, and since she was the very first of his wives, it follows that all of the children fathered by Zeus are, in fact, products of Zeus in combination with the internalized Metis. By this creative act of swallowing, the sky god put male and female back together. Joined, though different, they produce all of the earthly possibilities that are represented by the Olympian gods, their wives, the nymphs, heroes, and all of the children of the various gods and goddesses.

But of course this imaginative reconstruction of the story has no basis in mythology, so how can it be justified?

The archaeologist Marija Gimbutas has examined Palaeolithic cult images found at sites in 'Old Europe'—which covers the area now known as 'the Balkans', the north of Greece and southern Italy. She has drawn conclusions from these figurines concerning a mythical imagery, which she sees as demonstrating 'a dominance of woman in society and worship of a goddess incarnating the creative principle as Source and Giver of All'. The male element she saw only as representing spontaneous life-stimulating powers. This was borne out by the number of female figurines, with large breasts or buttocks, often possessing 'inarticulate legs' and long, slender 'phallic necks'. The conclusions she draws as to the wide presence of this goddess are no doubt true. What she fails to notice or to comment upon, it seems to me, is the presence of an ambivalence of image among the figurines, so that the neck and breasts (or buttocks) could just as well represent an erect penis with its twin testicles. Indeed, some of these 'phallic necks' are pierced by a narrow passageway as if it were the urethra. I believe this ambiguity to be intentional. Gimbutas called her book *The Gods and Goddesses of Old Europe,* when it was first published in 1972. In 1984, she revised and retitled it as *The Goddesses and Gods of Old Europe.*

I remember being shown, in 1958, on the island of Hydra, a pottery 'wedding cup' from Northern Greece. It was in the shape of a standing penis, pierced at the top, while possessing at its base two testes that were made to look like breasts as well and were pierced at the nipples. It was apparently required of the bridal pair that they should each, in turn, drink from this loving cup: it being necessary for them to stop up the holes in the breasts/testes with two thumbs in order to avoid being sprayed with wine while drinking—or maybe being sprayed by the testicular breasts was the point of the libation.

Lévi-Strauss (1979), in an article concerning the uses to which 'beans' are put as a symbol in both the Old and the New Worlds, has shown that in many quite unconnected cultures, the bean, growing within its pod, is seen as representing the nubile breasts of young girls as well as the swelling testicles of adolescent boys. Thus, he says, the bean mediates between the two sexes by denoting an activity (swelling) that both genders undergo. Swelling is also presented by the erection of the penis and the enlarging pregnant abdomen, and one Greek verb, meaning 'to swell', is *phallein*.

There is also psychological evidence to turn to.

Phallos

Eugene Monick, in his book *Phallos* (1988), describes how we have been led up a certain path by the founders of depth psychology: one that demotes the masculine origins of the psyche in favour of a universal matrix. Femininity is taken as absolutely basic and given, while maleness is a mere reaction, an outgrowth, a response. He recalls that Freud insisted that repudiation of the feminine was the bedrock of psychoanalysis and that possession of a male genital—whether in fact, or as envied—represented the goal to be striven for (p. 43). This has to do with the fact that the mother is the biological source of life, as well as the source of the well-being that came from the original blissful closeness to her. Those experiences then gave rise to the tendency to identify with her psychologically, as alone capable of being that source or providing that bliss.

Jung, on the other hand, insisted that ego activity was symbolically masculine, while the unconscious was the maternal dragon from which consciousness could only break free and stay free by superhuman (i.e. heroic) effort. Yes, the unconcious could be a 'good mother', but mother nonetheless. Monick points out that in neither Jung's nor Freud's case is any primal value given to the father or paternal origins of the psyche.

The reason for this, the author suggests, lies in the fact that both Freud and Jung were born into and lived within 'a culture where patriarchal supremacy was an unquestioned assumption' (Monick, 1988, p. 43ff). Certainly Switzerland, a country where women have only fairly recently been given the vote, has been described by Jung himself in his memoirs as being almost medieval in out-look at the time of his childhood (Jung, 1952).

As unconscious compensation for this conscious collec-tive attitude, says Monick (1988), both men elevated the importance of the mother and the maternal, thus devalu-ing paternity. They then found themselves faced with the need to salvage maleness as a force to be reckoned with. For Freud this took the form of 'penis envy' and 'castration anxiety', while Jung put forward the heroic as a way out of the impasse. Is it any wonder, Monick asks, that if both men unconsciously agreed as to the problem, they would later disagree in putting forward totally different answers to it?

> Whether Freud was leery of mystery and Jung was leery of physicality, the fact remains that neither did signifi-cant direct research work on phallos, and little has been done by their followers. This has resulted in a funda-mental disservice to the importance of the archetypal masculine, a theoretical imbalance that cries out to be redressed. [p. 56]

For Monick, the notion that everything flows from the matrix does not work, because it pushes analytic theory into all sorts of distortions regarding the nature of gender and its differences. Therapists have had to take in these 'facts' with the milk of their mother–analysts. They must believe in them implicitly too (the family myth), for not to do so would be regarded as defensive or a resistance to be analysed away.

Monick's own answer is to put forward *phallos* as a mas-culine archetype in its own right, which can be linked back to a *patrix*, using Woodman's term. It gives us an origin, as shown above, that is alternative to the mother, and this possibility is confirmed by the hieroglyphic text mentioned above, as well as the story of Ymir. Monick is also trying to prevent the idea of masculinity from being caught in 'the fashionable disease of patriarchy'. I would add that it is now possible to take such revolutionary views only because the times are culturally ready to question and to deny such patriarchal assumptions, which were necessary in their time, in order to overthrow the power the matrix had assumed.

If the mother has all possibilities held within her, one response could certainly be the way of the hero. Another, different, and more fundamental course of action would be to reinstate father as an alternative origin and to lose the daddy who is only secondary. The two parental roles would then become of equal importance.

Hillman (1973) has also struck out against the domination the maternal has been allowed to exercise over psychology to the exclusion of all other rulers. He points out how often the child archetype becomes muddled up with both hero and *puer*; and that they are then all subsumed under the mother. But although hero rightly belongs with mother, *puer* is more correctly paired to *senex,* and the child descends from father as well as mother (p. 75ff).

I am, myself, a male child of both my parents. They made me; and yet I am not entirely made of either, physically or psychologically. For the purposes of this book, it was the male within each of them, the patrix, that engendered me.

CHAPTER FOURTEEN

Self-made

Archetype and archetypal

Monick's view of phallos has been to see it as an archetype of the deep unconscious, capable of being expressed imaginally within the personal unconscious of individuals and therefore in their external lives. He is *not* talking about a phallic maleness of rampant sexuality and disconnectedness. Instead, he is describing 'chthonic *phallos*' as the uroboric *patrix,* compared with 'solar *phallos*', whose job is to escape from the chthonic matrix, or Great Mother. In this he follows Jung's view of archetypes as 'inherited, universal, psychosomatic, structural elements within the human psyche, which can only express themselves by means of image' (Samuels, Shorter, & Plaut, 1986, pp. 26–28). By 'deep unconscious', I mean Jung's concept of the *psychoid* realm, which is, by definition, completely inaccessible to conscious awareness. The psychoid has properties in common with the organic world but is neutral in character, being neither physical nor psychological (Samuels et al., 1986, p. 122). Archetypes, which reside in the psychoid realm, possess 'transgressivity': that is to say, they tend to pass over into either state. The physical is at the same time spiritual and vice versa. In the depths, says Monick, lower and higher phallos are one.

Since archetypal images, as discussed previously, tend to fade off and merge into one another, they must be reflecting what is even more true of any 'archetypes per se' within the psychoid realm. Inter-archetypal transgressivity can therefore be presumed to exist also (Samuels et al., 1986, p. 122), which means that, in the psychoid, matrix will be identical to, but different from, patrix.

This experience of the psychoid is also referred to by Jung as '*unus mundus*', or the one world, in which, as in particle physics, the emphasis is on relations between things and even relations between relations. The term *unus mundus* as used by Jung is, in essence, a ground plan for the whole psyche. It is the unifying field that makes sense of everything, for all experienced fragments are but a part of it (Samuels et al., 1986, p. 157).

These views of archetypes, the psychoid and *unus mundus*, are useful ones. They have been used as if they were scientific hypotheses to make predictive statements that were subsequently shown to be clinically true. But *do* archetypes actually exist? Are they really there? Or are they problem-solving devices 'put there to do a job' (L. Stein, quoted in Samuels, 1989, p. 26)? This job would be an explanatory, theoretical one. Certainly Jung said of the Self, the central archetype of order, that it was a 'working hypothesis' (*CW 6*, para. 791). Those who came later have sometimes tended to make a real thing of this concept.

There are, however, other ways of looking at the psyche and its archetypes, as this book has tried to make clear; and these stem from the archetypal psychology of James Hillman. Hillman (1975b) argues that archetypes are indefinable; thus, instead of grounding the psyche on their presumptive existence, psychologists would be better employed in looking at the world archetypally—that is to say, in any way that gives it significance. For Hillman, the archetypes are no longer actual entities, but have instead become metaphors for looking at things (p. 138ff).

Samuels (1989), whose avowed aim is 'to marry Fordham's technique with Hillman's vision' (p. 173), puts it another way. He suggests that when we look through a filter, 'there is a sense in which the filter *is* the experience, or in which the experience would be dead without the filter. *The filter is what we term archetypal*' (Samuels, 1989, p. 26). As example, he suggests that 'the archetypal father is not in the father at all, but in the child's perception of the father' (p. 27). And, I would add, in its perception of the maleness of other people whom the child experiences parentally, whether men or women. In other words, Samuels sees the archetypal as existing in the eye of the beholder and not what is beheld. He defines his idea as an 'archetypal state of mind', to each of which pertains its own psychology or psychologies, potentially separate, but probably in interaction: which may sometimes be unavoidably conflictual (p. 26).

Taking this view, the *scintillae* are not just the almost conscious intimations of a psychoid realm but express the real possibility of multiple archetypal states of mind. Neither is *unus mundus* only an objective psychic area to which access is possible for each, and within each, person, but also a conscious condition of mind in which pluralism can exist. This would be a way of looking at the world and its events that allows for many 'true' descriptions and even accepts the *necessity* for each of them. Different constellations of *scintillae* (relations between things) become permissible, as do plural interpretations of those constellations (relations between relations). The grouping of stars in the sky we call the plough is also the bear, the dipper, Odin's wain, and seven wise men, too. The stars themselves do not decide upon which interpretation is used, nor do they move their position in order to accommodate a different vision. Instead, it is the observing eye that, by means of imagination, adds a whole structure to the bare bones of what is constellated; and the constellation is but the container for that imaginative process, as the comb contains the honey.

Structure and content

Daidalos, which I have called a field, is just such an archetypal state of mind. It contains many different images, each of which can be said to possess its own psychology: the mother, the nurse, the hero, the king, *puer, senex,* the captive, flight, suffering, intercourse, death—and so on and so on. The list is interminable. But *daidalos* is not just an archetype from deep within my experience of the 'psychoid' realm—or anyone else's, for that matter. It is a unique, individual 'filter' through which each person may view their own world.

As a state of mind, '*daidalos*' is also a network of elements which holds its constituent parts together at the same time as it allows a freedom of movement around that which is thereby contained. Yet as a network it is not a given, unvarying structure remaining in the future as it is now and was in the past. The mix of what it contains, the relationships of one to another, are ever-changing (shapeshifting)—or at least that is how they will appear to the observing eye, which is itself responsible for that shiftiness. I can make a statement about things today that I will repudiate tomorrow, or even in an hour's time, because everything, including me, has moved on. It is deeply disquieting—piratical—to a Minos nature, or heroic consciousness: but not to such as Menelaus or to his protean consciousness.

A network, with its nodes and connections, is never an expression of some ultimately unknowable absolute. Instead, the contents by their very nature suggest and determine the unique structure of *daidalos,* which will differ for each person who reads this book.

An actual fish-net never changes its shape or nature. Not so a human network made up of people, for network members both come and go, so that, at any given time, there will be uncertainty as to the exact number and nature of its membership as well as all their other interests and the overlap between them. In addition, unlike any actual net, each member of a network can be in direct communication with every other, at will. It has become a 'wyrd' kind of a net. And here the analogy with a kaleidoscope breaks down, for it is as if the contained elements could change of themselves, so that the apparatus becomes able to generate new images from within itself. The changing elements multiply the possibilities, seemingly without the intervention of the operator, so that there is a sense in which the structure—that is to say the image produced within the walls of the apparatus—is determined by its contents and not by the movements of the operator. However, since the contents also change indeterminately, we can only remark upon the structure seen and not upon the nature of the bits and pieces that made it up.

A more fluid model for what I have tried to describe, which does not rely upon such concrete things as nets, knots, strings, and strength, or even kaleidoscopes, is provided in particle physics by what is called 'relational holism'. This term, put forward by Paul Teller and quoted by Danah Zohar in her book, *The Quantum Self* (1990), refers to the behaviour of electrons confined, as it were, in a box. If such particles were to be seen as a number of billiard balls just lying there, as in Newtonian physics, each would be discrete and related only externally to its neighbours, while the boxful would be the whole. But in quantum mechanics the situation cannot be described in this way, since electrons must be both waves and particles at the same time. The wave aspects of each electron within the box will inevitably be the subject of interference from every other, so that as a consequence they overlap and merge, with the result that their qualities as particles are also brought into relationship. The position, mass, charge, and spin of the particles will accordingly become indistinguishable from their inter-relationship, and they cease to be separate entities, becoming parts of a whole. This whole will itself then possess spin, mass, and so on. But, as Zohar points out, 'it is no longer meaningful to talk of the constituent electrons' individual properties, as they continually chop and change to meet the requirements of the whole' (p. 81).

There has been a synthesis of the elements in the box, in the sense of a 'placing together' in which they have lost their individual nature to the greater whole, but this is combined with a sense of diathesis—meaning that each is disposed to exist in its own individual ways under certain particular circumstances (*OED*). The resulting whole has a nature made up of its parts, but just what that make-up consists of cannot be stated. At the same time, the parts can be examined as separate entities.

I have mentioned diathesis before. As an example of diathesis from the medical field, some families are said to possess an 'allergic diathesis', that is to say, a tendency to suffer from allergic phenomena. This diathesis may express itself in various family members over the generations by such illnesses as asthma, eczema, hay fever, or urticaria.

Neither synthesis nor diathesis can on its own satisfactorily decribe the situation, any more than symbolic or diabolic activity was alone sufficient. It seems as if conscious reality, when viewed as quantum mechanical on the one hand or as psychologically amphibolous on the the other, looks remarkably similar. Nevertheless, as a psychologist, I believe that Zohar pushes her case too far when she claims that the nature of the particle/wave duality *is* the physical basis of human consciousness, and that consciousness is therefore ultimately physical.

Relational holism, amphibolism, or the self-generating kaleidoscope can clearly give us another way of approaching the problem of the one and the many, or the 'I' and my sub-personalities, which has been carried in this book by the relationship between Daedalus and *daidalos*.

Perhaps it can be well approached in an everyday manner, outside quantum mechanical terms, by means of a word coined by Bill Mollison, inventor of Permaculture. He talks of '*work-netting*' (*Guardian Newspaper,* October 1989). I understand this to mean that whatever 'the work' needs or requires, it must and will net for itself as and where it finds it. The individual natures of the ingredients, or of the nodes of the network, or of the part personalities have been lost, since they chop and change to meet the need of the work that is at present in progress. Going further with the analogy, some of the people contacted by the work-netter would be helpful, while others would not. Some might respond with appreciation, others with indifference or anger, and yet others remain silent or unobtainable. Nothing could be predicted in advance.

The work-netter would accumulate the resource required, just as craftworkers acquire their sets of tools or skills. Interestingly, Charles Handy (1989), a professor of Business Studies, has described the nature of the successful operator in the coming 'age of unreason' as a 'portfolio person'. Over the passage of time such people would deliberately assemble the portfolios of different skills and contacts that they felt would assist them in their working life. Handy expands the notion of work to include wage work, fee work, home work, gift work, and study work. All will include relationships with others (even if through their books, as in study), for which the portfolio person has also learnt the relevant skills. Not all of the items in the portfolio would be needed at any one time, but they would still be there as and when required.

Just as any particular vision of the quantum world depends upon an observer, so, too, does the human psyche. In psychological terms this would be the 'I' or ego, which has been imaged here as the kaleidoscope operator, as the work-netter, as the portfolio person, and as Daedalus.

Breaking the rules

Daidalos is ruled by Daedalus. He, the myth-ego, is an observer-operator who scans the field. He is also an element within it and as such, therefore, only a nodal point in the total network. This contradiction, that he is an observer as well as a part of what is observed, need not dismay. It has always been a stated fact that the ego is a part of psychic wholeness but, at the same time, the organ of consciousness, and executive of the larger Self. The one, ego, is part of the many, and yet controls them also—to adapt the axiom.

If Daedalus controls, then he is *contra-rotulus* (Latin), which means he is 'against rolling': he therefore restrains. But to permit *bricolage* is to allow for the fact that the horse may suddenly shy, despite the restraint of harness, and yet will survive that unexpected alteration. Daedalus allows and incorporates a breaking of his own rule *and at the same time he is changed thereby*. He can cope with the sudden unsuspected alteration, which is related to chaos and to alterity, and he is able to do this, I suggest, because he possesses well-craftedness.

Craftiness

Craftworkers make things that are useful as well as beautiful. Theirs is not art for art's sake, but, in an important sense, utilitarian. Artists, however, must be well-crafted in their chosen medium, or else be unable to express their vision. On the other hand, a craftworker who has no contact with that 'vision' will be nothing but a competent manufacturer. A musician may be perfect in technique and yet be lacking soul and intelligence in playing. So technique is therefore clearly connected with the expression of that inner impulse. Conversely, of course, a genius with soul but a bad playing technique will get no concert bookings.

But more than just a connection between craftworkers and their inner idea, the well-crafted act is a three-way relationship between maker, material, and the tool or instrument. By these means contemplation and action are linked, with the product as outcome, which will then evoke a response within the eye of the beholder. Too often nowadays craft is regarded as a hobby, for evening classes; yet behind it lies an attempt, however dimly understood, for the hobbyists to get in touch with a part of themselves. They are trying to put themselves in an archetypal state of mind and to give a significance to their lives.

For example, in her late sixties my mother went to a course on 'creative writing', the first piece she produced being a nostalgic story of childhood and the old nurse who had cared for her when she was young. This tale was brushed aside by the teacher, probably correctly, as 'unmarketable'. Yet of all the things she wrote (and she did eventually get something published), the unsaleable piece was the only one she kept, to be found, carefully filed among her papers, after her death. It represented a part of herself she was trying to contact through the craft of authorship; but it was one that was pushed aside in the course by the emphasis on 'getting yourself published'. For today the emphasis is much more upon the production of objects and their possible value than upon any effect the process might have on the artisan. This is, in part, the effect of secularizing the sacred, as mentioned previously. According to D. M. Dooley (1986), it is not considered today

that the material can or should modify the craftsman, only vice versa; or least of all that the user of the crafted object—the 'consumer'—has in his way of using it the smallest responsibility to a whole possible process of creation. [p. ix]

It would be a 'consumer revolution' indeed to recover such a notion. Yet it is exactly what Daedalus demands, for in his own nature he is maker as well as user in that deeper sense of craft which is the paradigm of man's total activity—a making, a doing, and an act of contemplation—as it refers to man the maker, man the user, man the tool, man the receiver and transmitter of forces of creation much greater than himself. [p. i]

And to these I would add: man the audience and observer. All of these roles, quoting Coomaraswamy's words, can be 'invented'—that is, 'found' and 'entertained' in what I have called *daidalos*—and are therefore available to Daedalus himself, who, 'coming upon' (inventing, finding) them can both 'hold' and 'keep among' them (quoted in Dooley, 1986, p. x).

The craftsman must first allow himself to be a conduit for an in-spiration or possession by a god (Greek: *en-thou-siasmos*), which has been previously described as an *Einfall*. His skill, then, is to be at the service of this divine breath in such a way that it may be expressed and re-born not as it was, but altered. It is, once again, the image of the darkened moon. As Dooley points out, the process of alteration works upon the artisan also, his material modifying the maker in proportion to his openness to the exchange that is taking place (Dooley, 1986, p. x). This openness, too, is an element of his technical skill.

Skill

The word 'skill' actually meant, originally, 'reason as a faculty of mind (*OED*), referring to the power of discrimination or ability to distinguish that which is reasonable, proper, right, or just for any given time or circumstance. Its meaning as practical knowledge came later. A skilful worker will have discerned the right or proper way of doing things, by which I mean the appropriate fashion. It is Themis again.

The word 'technical', on the other hand, comes from the root '*tek*', to shape or construct, from which also descends the Greek '*tekne*', an art or craft. Technique is 'the manner of artistic execution in relation to formal details' (*OED*), which, as stated before, is wooden without inspiration or soul. Each is necessary, and neither alone is enough. And that is just where skill comes in, for its nature implies exactly that power which discerns how to or when to use any particular technique, as well as suggesting the actual possession of technical ability. To skill—a verb now obsolete—meant 'to know how', and, by implication, a process of knowing how, as well as if, or when and for what duration. For us today it has been nominalized so that there is no more skilling, just skills that are nothing but *the* know-how.

Mechanic or midwife?

The word 'technique' can have a very negative ring to it, suggesting that what is done, whatever its field, is nothing but a mechanical process that lacks the true inspiration of the craftsman. Techniques are regarded as wooden, standardized actions or automatic responses, which deny the individuality of the moment, or the person. In psychotherapy, for example, there are some who see any technique as being a kind of Procrustean bed upon which patients are either stretched or fit or cut down to meet the size and shape of a particular theory, regardless of the needs of their own souls. Therapists (Greek: '*theraps*', an attendant), who believe this to be so would put intuitive behaviour in the place of technique. Instead of the technician, they prefer an image of the midwife, whom they see as a person who stands beside the wife, attending, encouraging, and awaiting the arrival of a child. She is with (*med*) the wife.

If the image that this brings to mind is of someone who stays beside the labouring mother, boiling large quantities of water, getting her to push, and otherwise doing nothing much more than wait to smack the baby on the buttocks, then it is clear that such people have never delivered a baby themselves or watched a midwife at work. They have certainly never tried telling her that she uses no techniques, or they might get a blow on the buttocks themselves.

Midwives are craftworkers who have learnt their trade theoretically, practically, and under supervision (just as therapists do). They have learnt the necessary techniques and skills, which they now apply with skill. If they are good midwives, they may do so unobtrusively and seemingly by intuition; but in reality they are responding to all of the signs that they see or elicit, albeit subliminally, from the mother-to-be. The phrase used of their correct behaviour is 'masterly inactivity', which is to say that they have learnt that nature can be trusted and that 'fiddling' is one of the greatest crimes. If they do nothing, it is because nothing needs to be done. They do not behave mechanically, just because they are technically accomplished. Their apparent inactivity masks the fact that they are continually assessing the situation and doing what is required of them at that moment. Any apparent passivity is related to the mastery of their craft and therefore to a lack of anxiety. They are birth attendants who do not stand around doing nothing unless the situation demands it. They are not passive, but patient.

It is also a skill of the midwife to recognize when the process of nature needs her aid or her interference. At such a time the emphasis passes over from the person who is 'with the wife' to one who is obstetrix, which is to say 'stands over against', being the Latin name for midwife. Operative intervention, whether by caesarean section, forceps delivery, stitching, or an intensive care for the baby, is still the activity of the midwife, but she is acting in an interventionist mode and using the skills appropriate to the situation that now obtains. It is only our culture that has medicalized that process, giving these skills away to the doctors (most often male), who then usurp the title of obstetrician. By doing this, part of the image of midwife/obstetrix has been amputated, and the midwife aspect becomes denigrated, or over-praised, as being non-technical; the midwife's skills are ignored. The two roles belong together, with their Yin and Yang components.

Mastery

In a discussion of the psychotherapist as craftsman, Deryck Dyne bases his understanding of craft upon the work of the philosopher Michael Polanyi (Polyani, 1958, quoted in Dyne, 1985, p. 104). Polanyi claims that all knowledge is personal, being made up of what has been done before as well as the present skills of the practitioner. He relates the achievement of those skills to the use of tools.

At first, with a new tool, I have to discover, haltingly, how to use it. It is external to me, and I am 'focally aware' of *it* rather than its *use*. As I become more adept with it, so does my awareness of the tool become 'subsidiary' to the way I actually use it. I do not have to think any more about how to use it: I just do so. Consider the act of learning to ride a bicycle: at first, the child must be supported as it wobbles along. It has no balance, cannot turn corners, avoid trees, or stop without falling. But gradually, it learns these abilities: they just seem to happen, until the child is cycling freely and with confidence. It cannot tell you how it manages to do so, for the skills have become inherent—or subsidiary. What is more, if it comes back to the bicycle after an absence of days, months, or even years, it will still possess those automatic skills. Indeed, it may be impossible to forget those skills. For instance, as Polanyi points out, people who have learnt the skill of swimming cannot allow themselves to sink when placed into the water.

This need not always be so: he cites the example of stage fright, when actors may become so distracted that they suddenly forget their lines; the same is true of the person who suddenly panics.

For example, Dennis had a lowly job in a firm that sold expensive limousines, but he longed to be promoted to the sales department. A few weeks after being told that he had been selected to go on a course for trainee sales-man, he had to be hospitalized with a crippling attack of panic, which made him totally unable to function at all. On discharge he started in therapy, supported by his firm, who also held the traineeship open. Some months later, when walking through the showroom, he was asked for information by a potential customer and started to try to sell her a car without any second thoughts. Five minutes later it was as if another voice had begun speaking inside his head: 'You can't do this', it said, 'You're not a salesman. You don't know how to do it.' Stammering and shaking, he made his excuses and went to fetch a proper salesman, though the satis-fied customer repeatedly asked him to stay. For Dennis, the skill lost its subsidiary nature, just like the child who can ride very well until it realizes that the parent is no longer holding onto the saddle, at which point it promptly falls off.

The more a skill is practised instrumentally, says Pol-anyi, the more a subsidiary awareness of it is committed to the unconscious, which leads to a gain on the operational level. The skills, the tools, have become, as it were, exten-sions of those who operate them, giving them thereby a freedom to concern themselves with other things. Too often this kind of mastery of craft is described as though it were some kind of unconsciously derived intuitive response, when in reality it is one that has been carefully and laboriously achieved before being committed to unaware-ness—thus to *appear* as an intuitive leap.

For example, metalworkers who have mastered their trade can take a flat sheet of silver and, by repeated hammer blows over a curved anvil, shape it into a bowl, moving the metal from the bottom towards the rim by repeated, glancing strokes of the tool. They know from past experience how to proceed, and this will tell them where to strike next, when to change the angle of blow, and whether to use another hammer or to select a different shaped anvil. They will know when the hammering has caused the metal to lose its resilience so that it must be 'tempered' by heating to red heat and plunging it into cold water (shades of Icarus). If it is struck too hard or for too long in one place, then the metal will become over-thin; so, being aware of that possibility, the master craftworker will, as if 'instinctively', move on to strike elsewhere or risk destroying the piece. All of this they know, almost without knowing it. It is their craft and their cunning, working through their feeling hands, their ears, eyes, and other senses that give them the clues that, like the midwife, they are hardly aware of having perceived. Certainly they would find it difficult to give a blow-by-blow description of what they are doing and why.

Knowing what to do and when or how to respond appropriately through skill frees them to concentrate upon, for example, the shape and beauty of the bowl. Equally, possession of those skills provides a space to fill with other, more sophisticated ones. For no craftworker can ever know enough. It is these clues of the craftsman that Daedalus gives, in the story, to the hero. It is this with which he enriches that type of maleness.

But technical skill can also have a downside. An accomplishment that is subsidiary and has become second nature carries with it the danger of becoming habitual and being used unconsciously, whether or not it is appropriate to the moment. Yet it is not the simple possession of a technique that makes it become mechanical, but the way I may absentmindedly use it. The *senex* within me can make me fly on automatic pilot. Then I find only what I expect to find, and the familiar can deaden my craft into a set of procedures designed as if to insulate me from the shock and fear of the unknown, of otherness. Technique can indeed slide into technicism and mere technicalities: the 'knee-jerk response'. It is mastery, on the other hand, that overflies these dangers.

CHAPTER FIFTEEN

Made–male

A self made male

In a previous chapter I discussed the ways in which a self that is male could be understood as having its roots in an unconscious archetypal patrix, by which and from which it is therefore made. Now I shall reverse the process, examining the way that maleness can be seen as making itself from above. But first I shall consider auto-poiesis—that is to say, self-making.

Self-making

I make something. They made me. God created the world. Objects seem to be made by others and our language enshrines this in its grammar, every sentence being made up of subject, verb, object. It is difficult to speak or write otherwise. But because that it how it is, or seems to be in the outside world, it is assumed, by extension, to be the case for inner psychic worlds. This need not necessarily be true.

It was Jung who suggested the existence of in-born, unconscious patterns within the psyche, the archetypes, which were reponsible for the growth of an individual's conscious mind, as well as for the internalization of relevant outer objects that 'fitted' those in-dwelling patterns. And since then, the nature of the human psyche as a self-organizing, self-regulating, and self-transcending system has been recognized. What I shall be trying to do here is to draw attention away from such inherited possibilities towards the actual self-making process of the conscious ego as practised by craft.

Our language has, indeed, a sequential grammar, moving from left to right, subject to object, but this need not necessarily be inevitable. Written Arabic, Chinese, or Hebrew, for example, are all different. Chinese, for instance, starts at the top right-hand corner of the page and is read downwards in columns and to the left. Secondly, each character is complete in itself, while its relationships to those that come before or that follow on are not immediately clear to Westerners. Thirdly, there are also no tenses for verbs, so that the characters therefore present an ambiguity of meaning. Lastly, in poetry use of a particular character may suggest another well-known piece that used that same character, depending on how educated the reader is. The language copies the tendency of Chinese thought to be concerned with things that happen together, as well as why they do so.

For example, a literal transposition of the first two verses of a poem by Liang Wu-Ti (c. 500 A.D.) would be written as follows:

Still	River
Grieving	Mid
Ten	The
Three	Water
Able	Towards
Weave	East
Fine silk	Flow
Ten	Lo-
Four	-Yang
Pick	Maid-
Mulberry leaves	-en
South	Name
Row	Still
Top	Grieving

Arthur Cooper's own deceptively simple translation follows:

> The waters in the rivers
>   All Eastward flow,
> At Loyang was a maiden
>   named Don't-cry-so:
>
> Don't-cry when she was thirteen
>   could weave and sew,
> At fourteen pick mulberry leaves
>   South on the row.

And so on (Cooper, 1973, p. 69ff). The images, apparently disconnected to Western eyes, can be translated into a grammar that is known and familiar. They have been given a different structure, though the meaning is shared in both. It reminds me of the trick inscription on a Staffordshire pottery mug that I once owned. It looked like this:

down	and	you	if
and	you	love	you
up	shall	I	love
Read	see	that	me.

The meaning is totally contained by the muddled words, whose understanding depends upon discovering and following the (unstated) rules.

Returning to the field that concerns me and putting it another way, I know the ego not only as that thing, structure, organ of consciousness with which I am familiar as a bit of me and which has been so well described by psychologists, but I see it also as an unceasing process of making, by interaction with its surroundings, both conscious and unconscious. It processes all of these pieces of information to make itself, as well as leaving them as they were—separate but related, like the Chinese characters. And like them it could have expressed itself differently. It makes, by its attitude to its own world, as well as with the various filters it uses as tools to describe what it sees, and by its attention and response. Yes, it unfolds, unpacks, expresses what comes from within; but at the same time these actions result in a 'rearrangement of the flow of energy' that is unique and a direct expression of its skills. And in addition neither description (i.e. ego made from below, or ego self-made) is more 'correct' or 'true' than the other.

Daedalus is certainly one of the components of *daidalos*, since this is the field that makes him exactly what he is and nothing else. At the same time, amphibolously, he makes the whole thing up as he goes along. I am saying that a mythic-style of ego is not just one that is seen as story, nor is it merely consciousness as seen from the perspective of story. It is, in addition, an ego that tells its own tale. According to this view, the ego becomes the representative of the fictive process itself—the means by which any imaginal network forms, and the maker of its own state of mind. The well-crafted ego is a fictive one: precisely that and only that. In one sense it is formed by outer and inner influences. In another, more revolutionary sense it makes *them* too, as it makes itself.

Notions of the processes of self-organization and self-actualization have come a long way since the beginning of this century. With the passage of time and increased understanding, less interest is now shown in the *structures* so formed as in the mechanics by which those structures come about. The study of such systems has become more process-oriented and information-centred.

Since the 1960s Ilya Prigogine, with his Theory of Dissipative Structures, for which he won the Nobel Prize in 1977, has shown that systems can exist far away from equilibrium, holding themselves together despite fluctuations. It is as though they wobble along, although never quite collapsing. At the same time, while appearing to be structures, they exist only because of the constant movement of energy through them, rather as a whirlpool would vanish if you shut off the flow of water. Prigogine decribes such structures as 'meta-stabilities'.

There will always come a time, he says, when the fluctuations amplify to such an extent that they become too great to be dampened down, and breakdown seems imminent. But instead of any destruction of the system occurring, as would be expected, its components will 'unhook' themselves, in order to reform as a meta-stability of more sophisticated complexity, which can then withstand the very perturbances that the 'old' system previously could not. At the moment of crisis it is impossible to predict in which of several possible ways such a system will evolve. Indeterminacy rules, but following that, the system reverts to its old pattern of resisting fluctuations. Innovation will be followed by confirmation.

Such systems naturally defend themselves from change and resist the fluctuations, however certain their evolution will be in the end. Interestingly, the higher the resistance to change and the more powerful the fluctuations that result, the richer and more varied will be the unfolding. The process is one in which innovatory moments occur, to be followed by periods of confirmation, and it is one of increasing order, punctuated by passage through chaos (Prigogine & Stengers, 1984). In this case, a 'higher' order is not built directly upon previous ordered states, for the new order is derived directly from the chaos that preceded it.

All living systems can be described as dissipative structures, because they are open systems that grow and do not 'run down' owing to the increase of entropy. Entropy is the name given to the tendency of systems to become increasingly random until change can no longer occur. Thus the molecules of a blue fluid poured into a red one would slowly disperse until all the molecules of the two colours were evenly dispersed in the mixture and nothing more could happen. A dissipative structure is named thus, because it dissipates entropy into the environment at the moment of crisis.

Erich Jantsch (1980) used the theory to describe the universe we live in as one that has always been self-organizing, making itself as it goes along. 'With the abandonment of permanent structural stability, evolution becomes open and unlimited. No end is in sight, no permanency, no telos' (p. 255). And Prigogine and Stengers add: 'We can no longer speak of the end of history, only of the end of stories' (quoted in Jantsch, 1980, p. 255). To which Jantsch comments that it is predictable that there will be many such stories.

I have written elsewhere (Tatham, 1987, 1988, 1989) of the relevance of this model for analytical psychology and of its likeness to Jung's individuation process, as well as of its use in understanding physical illness. It can also, I believe, be used to resolve differences between Analytic and Systemic models for the psyche.

Its similarities with the images of *daidalos,* as already described, will also be obvious. A process-fictive-ego likewise fits into the patterns described by Prigogine and Jantsch. It makes itself and regulates itself as well as plotting its own end, when it will exchange a known present for an unknown and unpredictable future. There is no way forward for it except by chaos, danger, suffering, and destruction. This is the death-in-life that was previously associated with images of *puer* and Dionysus, *koré* as Arihagne and the lost wax method, as well as with the darkened moon. That there will be resurrection or rebirth, and even the nature of that which will emerge therefrom, cannot, at the time, be predicted. For when you are right in it, it feels like breakdown: it *is* hell. On Good Friday neither Jesus Christ nor his disciples could believe in the possibility of his resurrection, as later Christians living with Easter can do.

What follows any such seeming catastrophe, though, is life-in-death shining out for all to see as the waxing crescent and imaged in Asterion, *kore* as Aridela, and *da-pu-ri-to-jo* as the turning towards the light.

And after that? Well, the facts will differ, but the process that comes into play is always that of Minos: it includes organizing, confirming, ruling, judging, smoothing the turbulence, and always working within fixed boundaries, however far he pushes his empire out.

As for Daedalus, he partakes in all of it, performing a vital role; his image is similar to that of a midwife, which encompasses all in the birth room: the father, the wife in labour, the child to be, and the obstetrix as conductor. She brings to her task a calmness that defies anxiety, strength for all, patience, and a total commitment to the needs of the moment. It is her craft that makes her able to bear it. Of this kind of being, Jantsch writes (1980):

> to live (like this) means to engage with full ambition and without any reserve in the structure of the present, and yet to let go and flow into a new structure when the time has come. [p. 255]

So the craftsman cannot live for the future or even predict it. He stays only in his present, practising a 'without-making-to-be' and a 'not-telling form of teaching' that may be non-attachment but is never dis-engaged. An educator described it to me once as the art of being 'a quiet presence'.

And, as all therapists know, the fear of an imminent breakdown is always, in fact, a memory of the breakdown that has already happened. In Prigogine's model breakdown is, however, an inescapable part of any process, to be followed by build-up. Perhaps it is that which is to be remembered.

Bootstrapping the psyche

Baron von Münchhausen, in danger of drowning, saved himself by seizing his own hair in order to lift himself from the waters. Pulling yourself up by your own bootstraps is a similar impossibility, and yet 'bootstrapping' is the name given to a serious theory of particle physics developed by Geoffrey Chew.

The 'bootstrap approach' proposes that there are no fundamental building blocks of matter and indeed no fundamental laws, constants, or entities of any kind. The universe is seen as a web of inter-related events, and the nature of each part follows from that of the others. It is the overall consistency of the web that determines its structure. Subatomic particles are seen as 'interrelated energy patterns in an ongoing dynamic process' rather than as separate entities. Any existence outside the web would be meaningless; and, as interrelated patterns, each one 'contains' every other one, in any case (quoted in Capra, 1982, pp. 84–86).

This approach can, of course, be applied far beyond physics. Fritjof Capra (1982) says of it that it raises Western thought to the level of Buddhist or Daoist philosophy (p. 84). In psychology it demands of us that we cease to believe in the total correctness of any one school or its theories. Nor, in a single case, of the over-riding importance of any one of its concepts. For instance, the fundamental origin of all consciousness from an archetypal uroboric Self becomes but one of an interlocking pattern of possible ways to describe the human psyche. One alone is insufficient fully to describe its plural nature. Some will not yet even have been put forward as theories. By its nature, the dissipative structure behaves similarly to a bootstrapped model, says Jantsch (1980, pp. 31–32); and Prigogine has written:

> The world is far too rich to be expressed in a single language. Music does not exhaust itself in a sequence of styles. Equally, the essential aspects of our experience can never be condensed into a single description. We have to use many descriptions which are connected by precise rules of translations (technically called 'transformations'. [quoted in Jantsch, 1980, p. 303]

For Samuels, the notion of bootstrapping is what he calls pluralism (Samuels, 1989, p. 219). He quotes, with approval, Chew's statement that a person 'who is able to view any number of different, partially successful models without favouritism is automatically a bootstrapper' (Chew, quoted in Capra, 1975, p. 87).

Bootstrapping, like pluralism, is also itself a difficult model to be true to. It is not at all the same thing as being eclectic, for this means to choose such doctrines from every school, *which please* (*OED,* my emphasis). Bootstrapping, on the other hand, implies not only holding on to what pleases, but to all those bits of theories and models with which one heartily disagrees as well. To bootstrap demands the sort of hermeneutic tolerance that is hard to believe in or to cultivate without going too far and just accepting any view at all as being of equal value. Bootstrappers believe passionately in their own theories while accepting the right of others to hold as fervently to contradictory ideas. The differences of approach or opinion become of greater interest than the notions that are shared, because they may provide a bootstrapper with novel information and increase his skills. The person who can manage it successfully is, I suggest, well-crafted.

For instance, in Mario Jacoby's recent book, *Individuation and Narcissism* (1985), he compares the theories of Jung with those of the originator of 'self psychology', the psychoanalyst Heinz Kohut. Comparing the two men's theories and establishing their similarities in a convincing manner, Jacoby does not demand priority or absolute truth for either. Instead, he clearly states the value, for him personally, of Jung's notion of individuation in his work with narcissistically damaged patients while accepting the empathic approach to the therapeutic encounter that Kohut advocated as being of equal value. In his book he moves easily between the two without demanding a synthesis. His approach is a synoptic one, he says (one that takes a comprehensive view—*OED*), recognizing that this may not find favour either with the followers of Kohut or with those of Jung. Nevertheless, he feels that this kind of approach is required both by the complexity of the human psyche and by the meandering paths of the individual human soul (p. 247).

Making it male

If I accept that my ego makes itself, that it is a process as much as a processor or a product, and that to it belongs an ability to see the world through a large number of different, even contradictory filters as well as being able to modulate between them, then one of those modes or archetypal states of mind will be called 'male'. It is so for me, because I am a man. Male is a filter that makes the world look in a certain kind of way, which therefore structures the content of what it sees to a certain style. It makes the self-which-I-am a male one. Yet 'male' is at the same time only one of the modes that make up the overall web or network that is me. Male is me, yet it is also only one of my modes of being; but because it connects with all other crossings of the web, it contains and is contained by all those others. All of the different filters are stained by its colouring as it is tinted by theirs; and if it seems farfetched to adapt the bootstrap approach in this way, then recall the myth of Indra, as quoted by Gary Zukav (1979):

In the heaven of Indra, there is said to be a network of

pearls, so arranged that if you look at one you see all of the others reflected in it. In the same way, each object in the world is not merely itself but involves every other object and in fact *is* everything else. [p. 255]

And if that can be brushed aside as 'nothing but a myth', then no less a person than Ananda Coomaraswamy has stated categorically that 'myth embodies the nearest approach to absolute truth that can be stated in words' (quoted in Capra, 1982, p. 410).

Women again

The women in *daidalos* have been seen as bringing 'otherness' (alterity) to the image of well-craftedness that the field represents. Female within a male story contradicts, by its very difference. It refuses to allow the overall tint of maleness to get past without a clash of colours. It operates as disagreement, incongruity, discord, without which there could be no true, sweet, light harmony (Harmonia), for one of the parents of that goddess *is,* as has been noted, the god of war.

The coupling of female with male is also said to be an image of completion and of the union of opposites. Their wedding is seen as productive, for without it there can be no child. They were made for each other, they belong together. Yet I can re-frame that through the filter of the dissipative structure to say that without the oscillations, without the turbulence that the male/female difference represents, no evolution to a more complex state could ever come about. And this is the significance of the one to the other, that they should be joined yet separate. Together, they perturb and further the process: separate, they make things in their own likeness, keeping to order.

An image favoured by Samuels (1985a, 1989) is that of the-parents-in-bed. At first he sees their union as where they belong while each relates to the child in their different ways. With the parents in bed together as they should be, the child is freed to become truly itself. More recently Samuels has emphasized that aspect of the image which sees the parents as belonging together as well as being allowed their separate existence. By these means the psyche expresses its nature of diversity and unity.

Jung described this process as a '*syzygy*', meaning the relationship of two stars that can appear sometimes in conjunction, though in opposition at other moments. In the psyche, the syzygy is where 'the One is never separated from the Other, its antithesis' (*CW 5,* para 106), and it leads directly to the experience of individuation. Hillman talks of 'syzygy consciousness' as the experience of juxtaposition, citing *senex/puer* as an example.

Robert Hobson (1985), in writing of his 'conversational model' for psychotherapy, expresses the same image, with a greater clarity of language, as 'aloneness-togetherness', implying by this neither isolation and abandonment nor fusion and pseudo-mutuality. As a state of being, he says of it: 'I can only be alone in so far as I can be together with another. I can only be together in so far as I can stand alone' (p. 194). Conversation, he points out, means not just talking to another, but 'the action of living or having one's being in or among'. Yet, of course, any two who engage in conversation are also always separate from each other.

Guggenbühl-Craig, in his book *Marriage—Dead or Alive* (1977), points out that the saintly image of the Holy Family has ruled our minds for too long. Conflict in marriage is also, he says, a means of inviduation. As an image rather than a painful reality, this confirms the relevance of using Prigogine's model with regard to the human psyche—that is to say, it is not just by the *hieros gamos*, or sacred marriage, whose offspring is the child/hero, that the psychic system advances, but also by the disagreement and perturbance of parents in conflict. Fresh structure is not just made by building upon the old order, but by breaking it down and reforming it as something new. In any case, no marriage is complete, if seen just as an image of the happy pair at the wedding reception.

CHAPTER SIXTEEN

In concluding

Take-over?

The danger of working with mythic images is that they tend to take over. Their 'attractive' power is great, more and more connections to the story are made, so that, in time, it will appear that the chosen image is the only one to lie behind and beneath all psychic functioning. As a result of this process, a serious distortion of perspective will occur. It seems to me that Robert Graves's writing about the *White Goddess* (1952), Neumann's interest in the *Great Mother* (1955), and Joseph Campbell's *The Hero with a Thousand Faces* (1949) are all examples of books that have this quality. Doubtless those images were of great relevance to the individual author's own life and were then invested by him with too universal a significance—no matter how valuable the insights have proved for all readers. It might appear that the same accusation could be levelled at this book, as though I have worked on my own 'Daedalus-problem' through my writing and now present it to the world as another 'grand narrative', or as a

253

panacea for all problems. There is of course some truth to this, for in writing books of this nature one *is* writing about oneself. Only by doing so can one make a beginning. And yet any such image, because it is archetypal, *does* also have a transpersonal value and may therefore be making important statements about the nature of psychic functioning, which are worth making; it may therefore be of use to others, as well as being personal to the author.

There is a major difference, however, in the case of Daedalus, for even if he takes over consciousness, his is an image of plurality of styles which encourages and even demands a changeable nature. *Daidalos* is no solo star but a galaxy, which, by its nature, abolishes all attempts at sticking to the single image. It contains and allows for a way of being that is earthy, puerile, or heroic—and many more things besides. As a portfolio person, his shifting multiple vision, with no view more fundamental than any other, avoids the criticism of the one-eyed stance. In fact, it is his innate shiftiness, as well as an ability to tolerate the indeterminacy that such fluidity implies, that is fundamental.

And Daedale too

First I called Daedalus the myth-ego. Later I have described him as a process- or fictive-ego. From these names it would be easy to assume that I have fallen into another trap, namely that of assuming that the ego is naturally male, now and forever. I wish to rebut that criticism also. Daedalus is indeed male, but his story comes from a time when the patriarchal slant of the conscious human psyche was already fully evident. So the stories of that era are presented to today's readers as male-dominated ones, fixed and ever thus as if by nature, rather than because they come to us only in the style that was then current and which therefore expresses merely the vision of that time.

And, as I have already pointed out, Daedalus's gender is derived from the earlier notion of *daidalon* as the thing-well-made and *daidalia* as acts-well-performed. I have also drawn attention to one of the imagined mothers of Athene who was named Daedale, she-who-is-well-crafted. Thus a fictive ego *can be of either gender, or even none at all*. It can be imaged as a male or female person, a thing, or a deed, even singular or plural. Because the story, as we have it, belonged to Daedalus, I have chosen to have him strut about at the front of the stage. He is a male fictive-ego, to be found in men. Equally, there could be described a female well-crafted fictive-ego for women, who would be called Daedale. We do not have her story, yet all that has been said of Daedalus could, I believe, be said of her.

Let me give a clinical example that bears out this comparison.

Daphne was the daughter of parents who were intelligent but had not had the chance of a good education. They always felt inferior and ill at ease with people more used to living a life of the mind, nor were they comfortable with any expression of emotion. The mother spent much of her life feeling panicky and depressed, of which everybody around was made very much aware. The father was a woodworker, highly skilled at his trade, who dealt with his own anxieties by going for a walk and returning with them well under control. Wanting the best for their children—that which they had not had—they encouraged them in the idea that academic excellence was of the highest importance. Nevertheless, since Daphne soon outstripped their own capabilities, they were quite unable to deal with the inevitable difficulties she came up against at school. They also shied away from any emotional problems that these brought up for her. Daphne remembers panic and depression from her teenage years, especially before exams, which could only be dealt with by working harder to make sure that she was totally prepared for whatever might unexpectedly come her way. She indeed excelled at university, leaving with a first-class degree. She then got a good job, married, and had two children, all through whose childhood she continued to work freelance. Soon the family lived in just that kind of social and intellectual milieu in which her parents would have felt inferior. In her forties, Daphne herself began to panic that her work wasn't good enough, that her career wasn't progressing sufficiently, and—as if that was not enough—that she had failed as a good mother to her children. She developed recurrent bouts of depression, usually twice a year, which were at first treated with drugs with some success, but which finally led her into therapy.

During the five years we continued to meet, all of these themes presented themselves as inner problems as well. She strove, especially, to live up to her own perfectionist ideals, towards the reaching of which she could get no help—and, indeed, the task was impossible. No piece of completed work ever gave her any lasting satisfaction, no matter how well-received it might be by those whom she respected. She could only see her skills in terms of deficits—not doing something well enough. On one occasion, entering a bookshop in a university town, she was struck with the realization of 'all of the thousands of books I shall never write'. The fact that she had already had several published was somehow irrelevant. Small things were petty and meaningless, while doing nothing was a crime of idleness, and all of this was, of course, accompanied by feelings of shame and hopelessness, which often left me feeling as helpless and de-skilled as Daphne herself. Whenever she felt better, she would try to make the sessions less frequent or to stop the therapy altogether. I learned that there was no alternative but to insist on our continuing to meet three times weekly if things were to change.

Finally, after the deepest and lengthiest depression we had ever experienced together, she became herself again, but in a different way. She did not immediately take on too much to do, with too many deadlines to reach, nor did she try to decrease the sessions, which now had a more relaxed feel to them. Once, in passing, she told me that she had started to make paper models again: a hobby of which she had never spoken before. Serious model-making had begun for her in childhood, with kits of aeroplanes or boats that soon filled up her corner of the living-room, some hanging from the ceiling. It was a way of being like, though different from, her father. She had never liked working with wood, as he did, but it was always important to do things with her hands that involved fine manipulations and many different skills: cutting, fitting, gluing, stretching of paper, painting, and decorating. Other activities, which called for similar abilities, were also important when she was not depressed.

Making other types of models from kits started in adulthood and has been a winter occupation. She sees it as something that is easy to take up and put down, after only a short period of work. She does it for herself (free-lance), they are not built for others (no commission), there is no urgency to finish (no deadline), nor any need to be perfect (no expectation of perfection or judgement that she has failed). Skill is involved, more so because the models are all small ones, while it is noteworthy that the process of the making is as enjoyable and gratifying as the product. It is an activity that she shares with her husband as well. The significance of her starting this again (and in summertime, too) lay in its connection to her no longer being depressed or panicky. It was possible to see the craft that she performed with her hands as representing an internal well-craftedness that now suffused her being.

The improvement that she experienced could be explained in many different ways. For the purposes of this book, however, I will say that Daedale had been constellated, and this was evident externally not only by the model-making, but by her acceptance of two public-speaking engagements ('I couldn't have done that six months ago') and accepting a commission she would previously have rated as inferior. She also began painting her nails (clear varnish only), wishing to make them look nice, and she came to the sessions more often in a skirt or a dress rather than in a tracksuit or trousers. Nine months later she successfully applied for an important job with a large organization, taking the application and interview more or less in her stride. She also coped with the death of one of her parents and the near-fatal illness of the other, who then had to come and live close by.

None of this is to say that Daphne will never be taken over by panic again, nor that she is now free from depression. Nevertheless, it was a significant change of pattern.

Though her father had also worked with his hands, and while model aeroplane kits are usually bought by boys, she has never seen her hand-skills as a masculine activity, relating it directly to her love of putting little things together, and especially of sewing.

Embroidery, in our times, has been seen as a female occupation (though my father embroidered a set of chair covers and my uncle, a banker in the City of London, did needlepoint all his life). Roszika Parker (1984) has pointed out, in her book: *The Subversive Stitch,* subtitled 'Embroidery and the Making of the Feminine', that in medieval days women and men worked alongside each other, as equals, in the embroiderers' guild workshops. From the eighteenth century until today, however, such activity has generally been seen as being suitable only for women. Parker shows that despite the limitations of this notion women have always used embroidery to '. . . make mean-ings of their own in the very medium intended to inculcate self-effacement' (p. 215). It is an expression, through hand-work, of the well-crafted female ego, just as Daphne's model-making also was.

Daedale and Daedalus, each of them, are parts of the field I have called *daidalos,* as well as signifying the myth-ego that can pass through it. My image, the notion I am concerned with, is that of the craftsperson; somebody who is well-crafted and a person first and foremost, while being of one particular gender only secondarily. Each possibility entails the possession of a fictive-ego, a male or a female self. To each, their otherness will be imaged by a person of the opposite gender, while it is in relationship to, encoun-ter with, or opposition from that otherness that helps to bring about self-transcension, or growth.

That is what happens within an individual. For the rela-tionship between men and women it implies, as I have said before, that any oppositional stance is defused, not by understanding what the contest is about, but by changing the nature of the contestants.

Daedalus and daidalos

Nevertheless, because of his story, my image for *daidalos* has been the craftsman who is the makings of his own male-ness. He is a part of the net but also wields it. It is he who solidifies, yet melts, who will order an empire, yet feel at home in the wilderness that is chaos, who both judges and yet is piratical. It is he who can attack to destroy, but suf-fer and wait patiently as well, and who will die in order to live, for he lives only to die. He stays with his old, well-worn ways, yet he invites novelty; and, knowing certainty, he can also tolerate an unknown future. He is both one and many. He is continually changed by his material and by his work upon it, for the material is himself. He possesses the possibility of being not only a strong ego, not just an imaginal ego, but a skilled ego: skilled at being the many things that he can possibly be.

Daedalus represents a post-modern, ecological ego whose exploits both are and are not an exploitation of the world around it. His field, as well as being environment-friendly, is also, inevitably, a killing field. He is both author and authority, powerful and yet disempowered, just possessing expertise though also setting himself up as an expert. Finally, he possesses an extra-ordinary genius as well as being the epitome of ordinariness. Such a consciousness should not be a surprise, for the philosopher Edward Casey (1987) has already shown that Jung's psychology, with its 'polyformity' of images, was always 'post-modern'.

Daedalus is no stereotype, for his material is malleable, able to modulate through any shape into which he is moulded. He is waxen, which is just one of the paradoxical qualities of the alchemist's stone, able to take up any possible form that Daedalus himself sculpts for it. Robertson Davies, in his novel *The Lyre of Orpheus* (1989), has one of the characters say:

> It's been said since—well, at least since Ovid. He says somewhere—in the *Metamorphoses,* I think—that the great truths of life are the wax, and all we can do is to stamp it with different forms. But the wax is the same forever— [p. 130]

In this book, that notion is presented as the well-craftedness of Daedalus, as well as his *daidalos,* for he is the wax, the type, and its printer: both the teller and his tale. His is a self that is made male, amphibolous, and forever ravelling the maze that is himself, with increasing wisdom as well as ever-deepening ignorance. It seems to me that Dao Tzu speaks of someone like him when he says of the *sage* (*Dao De Jing,* chap. 2, translated by A. Cooper):

> The countless things that have been created, he rejects none of them;
> that have been born, he possesses none of them;
> that have been made-to-be, he depends on none of them.
> Success achieved, he never stays
> for only by never staying does he not depart.

APPENDIX

Greek mythological figures

reek mythology may seem like a daunting and confusing alien world to those without any previous knowledge. A deep understanding of the subject is not necessary to get the most from this book. However, since it is sometimes difficult to remember just who is who and who did what and where, I have included this Appendix of the most important characters that appear in the text.

Further information can be found in the many easily available books on the subject. For personal preference, I use those of Karl Kerényi (1951, 1959).

MISCELLANEOUS GODS AND GODDESSES

Chaos. In some cosmologies, the first goddess, though her name has a masculine ending (*-os*).

Gaia. Earth goddess, first-born of Chaos.

Uranus. A sky god, son of Chaos and husband to Gaia.

Kronos. A corn god and youngest son of Uranus and Gaia. He castrated his father to free himself and his siblings from imprisonment within their mother. When a father himself, he swallowed his own children.

Rhea. The fruitful earth, sister and wife to Kronos, mother of Zeus.

Aphrodite. The matchless goddess of passionate love, she was fathered on the ocean by the floating phallus of Uranus, after his castration. Eros was her son.

Poseidon. The god of the sea, one of the three sons of Kronos and Rhea.

Hades. Brother to Poseidon and Zeus, he was the god of the underworld, and famous for snatching Persephone away from her mother, to be his queen.

Demeter. Goddess of the bountiful earth. One of the three daughters of Rhea, she was mother to Persephone.

Zeus. Sky god, foremost of all the Olympian gods. He had several 'wives', by whom, as well as by his many liaisons, he fathered other gods, heroes, and humans, too.

Themis. Goddess of order. The first wife of Zeus, and also his aunt.

Metis. Another of the sky god's wives. Since it was foretold that a son of hers would replace Zeus, he swallowed the pregnant Metis. At term, the child Athene sprang, fully grown, from the father's head.

Hera. The acknowledged wife of Zeus and goddess of marriage. Envious of her husband's virtuosity, she had three attempts at virgin birth, producing Typhoeus, a monstrous dragon, Ares, the god of war, and Hephaestus, the craftsman god.

Ares. So huge and clumsy a god that he was always falling over. In liaison with Aphrodite, he fathered the goddess Harmonia.

Hephaestus. Misshapen and dwarved, though incredibly talented, this craftsman god waddled through the halls of Olympus, making everyone laugh. Improbably, he was married to Aphrodite.

Proteus. The 'old man of the sea', able to change his shape at will. His name means 'the first'.

Apollo. A sun god, who rode across the heavens in a chariot, he was the son of Zeus and another wife, the goddess Leto.

Artemis. The wild huntress, sister of Apollo.

Dionysus. Zeus's youngest son. His mother was either Persephone or Semele, a human princess. Semele, while pregnant, was burnt to a cinder for insisting on seeing the father of her child in all his majesty. Zeus rescued the unborn foetus and brought it to term in his own thigh. It was said of Dionysus that he would eventually replace Zeus.

Herakles. Sometimes known by his Roman name of Hercules, he was the epitome of the hero. Immensely strong, he was condemned to perform twelve labours by Hera, whose servant he was.

Prometheus. One of the giant Titans, born of Chaos, he was a wily creature, who continually played tricks upon the Olympian gods, always siding with humanity. Known as 'the forward-thinking', he could foresee the outcome of his actions, unlike Epimetheus, his 'after-thinking' brother.

AT ATHENS

Athene. The goddess of the city that bore her name. She had been born from her father Zeus's head, under the hammer blows of Hephaestus and Prometheus. The goddess of cities, of wisdom, of crafts, and also connected to heroes, she had a savage and underworldly side as well. Virginal, she fought off the advances of Poseidon and Hephaestus. She was, however, known to have children, each nursed in turn by the daughters of Kekrops.

Kekrops. One of several snake-man creatures associated with Athens, and its first king. On his death, he was put in the sky as the star Arcturus.

Erichthonios. Another snake-man, born of Athenian earth and the spilt semen of Hephaestus.

Erechtheus. King of Athens, descended from Erichthonios and an ancestor of Daedalus.

Eupalamos or **Metion.**   Supposed father of Daedalus.

Alcippe, Iphinöe, Merope.   Possible mothers for Daedalus.

Polycaste.   Also known as Perdix. The sister of Daedalus and mother of Talus.

Talus.   Called Perdix too, also Tantalus and Circinnus, he was apprenticed to his uncle, Daedalus.

ON CRETE

Europa.   A princess, whose name has affinities with the moon. Picking flowers on the sea-shore, she was ravished by Zeus, in the shape of a bull. She was the mother of Minos.

Minos.   A reputed king of Crete, who built up the sea-trading empire we call 'Minoan'. He rid the Mediterranean sea of piracy and was renowned as a wise judge. The most favoured of Zeus's human sons, he was sent, at death, to judge the souls of the recently dead.

Pasiphäe.   Wife of Minos, she was the child of a marriage between the sun and the moon.

Ariadne.   Daughter of Minos and Pasiphäe, she helped to kill the Minotaur and fled with Theseus. Another story tells that she was the wife of Dionysus, who killed her because of her infidelity.

Minotaur.   The bull-man, born to the queen after her impregnation by Poseidon's bull. Imprisoned within the labyrinth and killed there.

Theseus.   Prince of Athens who journeyed to Crete for the purpose of killing the Minotaur.

Naucrate.   A slave of Minos and the mother of Icarus.

Icarus.   Son of Daedalus and Naucrate. He died from flying too near the sun during the escape from the labyrinth.

Talus.   A bronze giant given to the people of Crete by the people of Sardinia, which walked daily around the island to frighten away invaders.

IN SICILY

Cocalus.   The king of Camicus, who sheltered Daedalus and at whose court Minos met his death at the hands of the royal daughters.

Eryx.   Mortal son of Aphrodite, who gave his name to the mountain upon which her temple stood.

SARDINIA

Those who joined Daedalus here were:

The Herculids.   Descendants of Herakles.

The Daedalids.   Children of Daedalus.

Iolaus.   Son of Iphicles, Herakles's mortal brother, he acted as the hero's charioteer.

Norax.   A minor god from Libya.

Aristaius.   A son of Apollo and the nymph Cyrene, he was an agricultural deity and the patron of beekeeping.

REFERENCES

Alexander, M. (translator) (1971). *Beowulf.* London: Penguin Books.

Ayrton, M. (1967). *The Maze-Maker.* London: Longmans Green.

———. (1971). *The Rudiments of Paradise.* London: Secker & Warburg.

———. (1972). *Fabrications.* London: Secker & Warburg.

Barley, N. (1986). *The Innocent Anthropologist.* London: Penguin Books.

Bates, B. (1983). *The Way of Wyrd.* London: Century Publishing Co.

Beauvoir, S. de (1960). *Second Sex.* London: Four Square Books. Paris: Librairie Gallimard, 1949.

Bennveniste, E. (1973). *Indo-European Language and Society.* London: Faber & Faber.

Beowulf. Translated by M. Alexander. London: Penguin Books, 1971. Translated by K. Crossley-Holland. London: Macmillan, 1969.

Bion, W. R. (1970). *Attention and Interpretation.* London: Tavistock Publications [reprinted London: Karnac Books, 1984].

Boardman, J. (1964). *Greek Art.* London: Thames & Hudson [revised edition 1973].

Bradford, A. (1972). *The Craftsman in Greek and Roman Society.* London: Thames & Hudson.

Bradley, N. (1973). 'Notes on theory-making, on scotoma of the nipples and the bee as nipple'. *International Journal of Psycho-Analysis 54*: 301.

Branston, B. (1955). *Gods of the North.* London: Thames & Hudson.

Brody, H. (1987). *The Living Arctic.* London: Faber & Faber.

Campbell, J. (1949). *The Hero with a Thousand Faces.* Princeton: Princeton University Press.

267

————— . (1974). *The Masks of the Gods*. New York: Souvenir Press.

Capra, F. (1975). *The Tao of Physics*. New York: Wildwood House.

————— . (1982). *The Turning Point*. New York: Simon & Schuster.

Casey, E. (1987). 'Jung and the Post-Modern Condition.' *Spring Magazine*.

Chilton Pierce, J. (1977). *Magical Child*. New York: Dutton. London: Paladin, 1979.

Cirlot, J. E. (1962). *Dictionary of Symbols*. London: Routledge & Kegan Paul.

Clark, G. (1983). 'A Black Hole in the Psyche.' *Harvest Magazine, 29*.

Cooper, A. (translator) (1975). *Li Po and Tu Fu: Selected Poetry*. London: Penguin Classics.

————— . (1989). 'Chinese evidence on the evolution of language.' In: R. Gregory (ed.), *The Oxford Companion to the Mind*. Oxford: Oxford University Press.

Covington, C. (1989). 'In search of the heroine.' *Journal of Analytical Psychology 34* (3): 243.

Crossley-Holland, K. (translator) (1969). *Beowulf*. London: Macmillan.

Davies, R. (1989). *The Lyre of Orpheus*. London: Penguin Books.

Dawkins, R. (1976). *The Selfish Gene*. Oxford: Oxford University Press.

Dooley, D. M. (1986). *A Way of Working*. New York: Parabola Books.

Douglas, M. (1966). *Purity and Danger*. London: Routledge & Kegan Paul.

Dyne, D. (1985). 'Questions of "Training"?' *Free Associations, 3* (b): 92.

Eliade, M. (1962). *The Forge and the Crucible*. Chicago: Chicago University Press.

————— . (1968). *Myths, Dreams and Mysteries*. London: Fontana.

Ellis Davidson, H. R. (1964). *Gods and Myths of Northern Europe*. London: Penguin Books.

Fordham, M. (1969). *Children as Individuals*. London: Hodder & Stoughton.

————— . (1985). *Explorations into the Self*. London: Academic Press.

Gennep, A. van (1960). *Rites of Passage*. Chicago: Chicago University Press.

Gimbutas, M. (1984). *The Goddesses and Gods of Old Europe*. London: Thames & Hudson.

Graves, R. (1952). *The White Goddess*. London: Faber & Faber.

———. (1955). *The Greek Myths*. London: Penguin Books.

Grigson, G. (1978). *The Goddess of Love*. London: Quartet.

Grzimek, B. (ed.) (1972). *Animal Life Encyclopedia*. Amsterdam: Van Nostrand.

Guggenbühl-Craig, A. (1971). *Power in the Helping Professions*. Dallas: Spring Publications.

———. (1977). *Marriage—Dead or Alive*. Dallas: Spring Publications.

———. (1980). *Eros on Crutches*. Dallas: Spring Publications.

Handy, C. (1989). *Age of Unreason*. London: Hutchinson.

Harrison, J. E. (1963a). *Themis*. London: Merlin Press [originally published 1911].

———. (1963b). *Mythology*. New York: Harbinger [New York: Longmans Green, 1924].

Henderson, J. L. (1967). *Thresholds of Initiation*. Middleton, CT: Wesleyan University Press.

Hesiod, *Theogony*: see Wender, 1973.

Hillman, J. (1972). *The Myth of Analysis*. Evanston, IL: Northwestern University Press [Harper Colophon edn., 1978].

———. (1973). 'The Great Mother, her Son, her Hero, her Puer.' In: P. Berry (ed.), *Fathers and Mothers*. Dallas: Spring Publications.

———. (1975a). *Re-Visioning Psychology*. New York: Harper & Row.

———. (1975b). *Loose Ends*. Dallas: Spring Publications.

———. (1977). 'An inquiry into Image'. *Spring Magazine*.

———. (1978). 'Further notes on Image.' *Spring Magazine*.

———. (1979a). *The Dream and the Underworld*. New York: Harper & Row.

———. (1979b). 'Image-Sense.' *Spring Magazine*.

———. (1983). *Healing Fiction*. Barrytown, N.Y.: Station Hill.

Hillman, J., et al. (1979). *Puer Papers*. Dallas: Spring Publications.

Hobson, R. F. (1985). *Forms of Feeling*. London: Tavistock.

Homer, *The Odyssey*: see Shewring, 1980.

Hubback, J. (1990). 'Tearing to pieces: Pentheus, the Bacchae and analytical psychology.' *Journal of Analytical Psychology 35* (1): 3.

Innes, M. (translator) (1955). Ovid, *Metamorphoses*. London: Penguin Books.

Jacoby, M. (1980). *Longing for Paradise*. Fellbach: Verlag Adolph Bonz. Boston, MA: Sigo Press, 1985.

————. (1985). *Individuation and Narcissism*. Munich: Verlag J. Pfeiffer. London: Routledge, 1990.

Jantsch, E. (1980). *The Self-Organising Universe*. Oxford: Pergamon.

Jung, C. G. References are to the *Collected Works* (*CW*) and by volume and paragraph number, except as below. Edited by H. Read, M. Fordham, G. Adler & W. McGuire, translated in the main by R. Hull. London: Routledge & Kegan Paul; Princeton, NJ: Princeton University Press.

————. (1963). *Memories, Dreams, Reflections*. London: Routledge & Kegan Paul.

————. (1976). *The Visions Seminars*. Dallas: Spring Publications.

Kahn, C. H. (1979). *The Art and Thought of Heraclitus*. Cambridge: Cambridge University Press.

Kerényi, K. (1951a). *The Gods of the Greeks*. London: Thames & Hudson.

————. (1951b). 'Koré.' In: C. G. Jung & K. Kerényi, *Introduction to a Science of Mythology*. London: Routledge and Kegan Paul.

————. (1959). *The Heroes of the Greeks*. London: Thames & Hudson.

————. (1975). *Zeus and Hera*. London: Routledge & Kegan Paul.

————. (1976). *Dionysos*. London: Routledge & Kegan Paul.

————. (1978). *Athene*. Dallas: Spring Publications.

Kirk, G. S. (1974). *The Nature of Greek Myths*. London: Penguin Books.

Klein, M. (1975). *Envy and Gratitude*. London: Hogarth Press.

Kooning, W. de (1960). From film script, *Sketchbook 1: Three Americans*. New York: Time Inc.

Lambert, K. (1981). *Analysis, Repair and Individuation*. London: Library of Analytical Psychology, Academic Press.

Larousse (1959). *Encyclopedia of Mythology*. London: Hamlyn.

Leach, M. (Ed.) (1949). *Standard Dictionary of Folklore*. New York: Funk & Wagnalls.

Lebeck, A. (1971). *The Oresteia: A Study in Language and Structure*. Washington, DC.

Leinhart, G. (1976). Quoted in: B. E. Ray (Ed.), *African Religions*. New York: Prentice Hall.

Lemprière, J. (1788). *A Classical Dictionary*. London: Routledge & Kegan Paul [various editions 1879–1972].

Lévi-Strauss, C. (1962). *The Savage Mind*. Paris: Librairie Plon; London: Weidenfeld & Nicholson, 1966.

———. (1979). 'Pythagoras in America.' In: R. H. Hook (Ed.), *Fantasy and Symbol*. London: Academic Press.

Lewis, C. Day (translator) (1986). Virgil, *The Aeneid*. Oxford: Oxford University Press.

Liedloff, J. (1975). *The Continuum Concept*. London: Penguin Books.

Lipnack, J., & Stamps, S. (1985). *The Networking Book: People Connecting with People*. London: Routledge & Kegan Paul.

López Pedraza, R. (1971). 'Comment on psychology: Monotheistic or polytheistic', by J. Hillman. *Spring Magazine*.

Maeterlinck, M. (1958). *The Life of the Bee*. London: Allen & Unwin.

Marshack, A. (1972). *The Roots of Civilisation*. London: Weidenfeld & Nicholson.

Miller, D. (1981). *The New Polytheism*. Dallas, TX: Spring Publications.

Mollison, W. (1989). 'Just let nature do all the work.' *The Guardian*, 7 October.

Monick, E. (1988). *Phallos*. Toronto: Inner City Books.

Moore, T., et al. (1979). *Puer Papers*. Dallas: Spring Publications.

Neumann, E. (1949). *The Origins and History of Consciousness*. Zürich: Rascher Verlag; Princeton: Princeton University Press, 1954.

———. (1955). *The Great Mother*. Princeton: Princeton University Press.

———. (1973). 'The moon and matriarchal consciousness.' In: P. Berry (ed.), *Fathers and Mothers*. Dallas, TX: Spring Publications [*Eranos-Jahrbuch XVIII*, 1950].

Onians, R. B. (1951). *The Origins of European Thought.* Cambridge: Cambridge University Press [reprinted New York: Arno Press, 1973].

Ovid, *Metamorphoses*: see Innes, 1955.

Parker, R. (1984). *The Subversive Stitch.* London: The Women's Press.

Pauli Haddon, G. (1987). 'Delivering Yang Femininity.' *Spring Magazine.*

Perls, F. (1973). *The Gestalt Approach and Eye Witness to Therapy.* London: Bantam Books.

Pirani, A. (1989). *Absent Father: Crisis and Creativity.* London: Arkana, Penguin Books.

Polanyi, M. (1955). *Total Knowledge.* London: Routledge & Kegan Paul.

Prigogine, I., & Stengers, I. (1984). *Order out of Chaos.* London: Heinemann.

Purce, J. (1974). *The Mystic Spiral.* London: Thames & Hudson.

Raglan, Lord (1936). *The Hero: A Study in Tradition, Myth and Drama.* Facsimile edn., London: Greenwood Press, 1976.

Redfearn, J. W. (1985). *My Self, My Many Selves.* London: Library of Analytical Psychology, Academic Press.

Room, A. (1983). *Room's Classical Dictionary.* London: Routledge and Kegan Paul.

Samuels, A. (1985a). *Jung and the Post-Jungians.* London: Routledge & Kegan Paul.

———. (Ed.) (1985b). *The Father.* London: Free Association Books.

———. (1989). *The Plural Psyche.* London: Routledge.

Samuels A., Shorter, B., & Plaut, A. (1986). *A Critical Dictionary of Jungian Analysis.* London: Routledge & Kegan Paul.

Segal, H. (1978). *An Introduction to the Work of Melanie Klein.* London: Hogarth.

Segal, L. (1990). *Slow Motion.* London: Virago.

Shewring, W. (translator) (1980). Homer, *The Odyssey.* Oxford: Oxford University Press.

———. (1984). *Artist and Tradesman.* Marlborough, Wilts: Paulinus Press.

Stein, L. (1958). 'Analytical psychology: A modern science.' In: M. Fordham et al. (Eds.), *Analytical Psychology: A Modern Science.* London: Heinemann, 1973.

————. (1962). 'An entity named ego.' *Journal of Analytical Psychology* 7 (1).

Stevens, A. (1982). *Archetype*. London: Routledge & Kegan Paul.

Tatham, P. H. (1978). *Renewal of the Old King Archetype*. Unpublished diploma thesis, C. G. Jung Institute, Zürich.

————. (1979). '*Beowulf*, and the renewal of the old king.' *Harvest Magazine, 25*.

————. (1984). 'A black hole in the psyche: One personal reaction.' *Harvest Magazine, 30*.

————. (1987). 'Order in chaos.' *Harvest Magazine, 33*.

————. (1988). 'Item and motion.' In: M. Kidel & S. Rowe-Leete (eds.), *The Meaning of Illness*. London: Routledge & Kegan Paul.

————. (1989). 'Analytical psychology: A systems view and vice versa.' Unpublished lecture.

Thom, A. (1967). *Megalithic Sites in Britain*. Oxford: Oxford University Press.

Turner, V. (1967). *A Forest of Symbols*. Ithaca, NY: Cornell University Press.

Virgil, *The Aeneid*: see Lewis, 1986.

Von Franz M.-L. (1971). *Puer Aeternus*. Dallas: Spring Publications.

————. (1974). *Number and Time*. London: Rider.

————. (1980). *Alchemy*. Toronto: Inner City Books.

Wender, D. (translator). (1973). Hesiod, *Theogeny*. London: Penguin Books.

Whitmont, E. C. (1969). *The Symbolic Quest*. London: Barrie & Rockliff.

Wilhelm, R. (translator) (1968). *The I Ching*. London: Routledge & Kegan Paul [English version translated by C. F. Baynes, 1951].

Winnicott, D. W. (1971). *Playing and Reality*. London: Tavistock [Penguin Books, 1980].

Woodman, M. (1985). *The Pregnant Virgin: A Process of Psychological Transformation*. Toronto: Inner City Books.

Zukav, G. (1979). *The Dancing Wu Li Masters*. London: Rider.

Zohar, D. (1990). *The Quantum Self*. London: Bloomsbury.

INDEX

274